Kind for

Heart of a Man

This anthology should be required reading not only for girls and women but for boys and men. ... Very moving, hopeful and mind-opening on so many social issues.

PEGGY SEEGER, OXFORD, U.K.

It's wonderful. What great writing. You've got a hit on your hands. It's got it all. I laughed, I cried and was amazed at the honesty.

BONITA COLE, SONOMA, CA

This anthology is needed now more than ever. I found it enlightening.

AMA BOLTON, WELLS, U.K.

Thank you for posting these glimpses into men's hearts.

BETSY F., OCEAN ISLE BEACH, N.C.

I was blown away by your anthology. Not since my foray into John McPhee and his books have I felt such a strong connection to the authors and their subjects.

You have my heartfelt thanks for the work you are doing.

HERB FRANK, MIDDLETOWN, DE

Thank you for this. It is a gift.

MARCY G., PHILADELPHIA, PA.

HEART OF A MAN

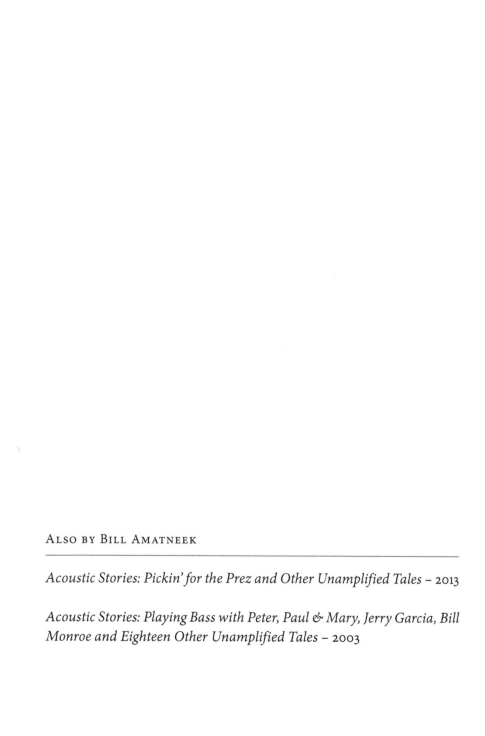

ALSO BY BILL AMATNEEK

Acoustic Stories: Pickin' for the Prez and Other Unamplified Tales – 2013

Acoustic Stories: Playing Bass with Peter, Paul & Mary, Jerry Garcia, Bill Monroe and Eighteen Other Unamplified Tales – 2003

HEART OF A MAN

Men's Stories for Women

EDITED BY BILL AMATNEEK

ILLUSTRATIONS BY EUGENE KARLIN

Vineyards
Press
Sebastopol

Uncorrected Pre-publication Proof
Publication date: 2020 subject to change
– For Review Purposes Only –
Not for Resale or Distribution
V60P23 7/18/20

Vineyards Press
P.O. Box 716
Sebastopol, CA 95473
web: heartofaman.net
Heart of a Man/Bill Amatneek, ed. – First Edition, First Printing
ISBN 978-1-928578-24-6 (pbk.)
Library of Congress Control Number:2019907464

to
Lenona
Ethel & Karl
Evelyn & Gene

Preface

This anthology's story began in May 2000, when the National Storytelling Network (NSN) published *Red Hot and Cool Cool Mamas,* an issue of their bi-monthly publication, *Storytelling Magazine.* Guest-edited by Carol Birch, it featured stories by and about women of the storytelling revival community.

But what about guys? I wondered. *Don't we get an edition?*

I phoned the NSN and asked if anyone had volunteered to guest-edit an issue by men.

The voice on the line sounded surprised: "What a concept!"

I called it *The Men's Issue.*

It began with a call for submissions to the men of the storytelling revival movement, asking each to send me a true story about something that had happened to him, could only have happened to a man, and that showed who men are. I received 75 submissions and culled 11 for the issue, cover-dated March, 2001. The NSN printed 4,000 copies and mailed them to the association's 3,500 members.

The remaining 500 copies sold out in eight weeks. They had to order another thousand to keep up with continuing demand.

Who was buying these copies? Who wanted to know who men are?

Women ... women who'd learned about guys from *The Mens' Issue* and wanted to share what they'd read with their women *and* men friends.

One called with an order saying, "I couldn't put the issue down; my heart was beating so." Another phoned to say, "I had to put the issue down after each story. My heart was racing." A mother of two called to order ten copies: "Four for my nephews, three for my brothers, two for my sons, and one ... for my lover."

As *The Men's Issue* came together, I knew that if women embraced it, I'd expand the issue into an anthology of men's stories.

Heart of a Man is that embrace returned. Work on it began in 2014, when I sent calls for submissions to a number of writers' services websites and magazines, netting 500 stories, poems, essays, lyrics, rants, and cartoons from around the world. Reading them was a water slide of surprise. When I found a piece that was guy-insightful, I asked my wife to read it. If it was meaningful to her as well, it went into the "Maybe Yes" pile, one that was sifted many times.

I also placed a call to complete the phrase, "A man is" in one sentence. A hundred came in, the first from Ethiopian doctor, Elias Gebru. His entry is on the epigraph page, one leaf over. There's another, by Haley Zilberberg, further on, and other quotations by both men and women throughout in the book. Some are germane to the chapter they accompany, some to the drawing or quotation they share the page with, and all to the book at large.

The submissions I accepted suggested eight sections. The sections and a few chapters needed introductions, and the book itself, a preface and Q&A ... or so I convinced myself. The unattributed passages and quotations you find here are likely mine.

Women friends volunteered to beta-read the anthology – to review the manuscript, red pen in hand. And I read many of the book's evolving introductions and chapters to a writers' workshop I attend, one of some two dozen women and six men.

The women's feedback showed me how differently women and men perceived the same story. My beta-readers had diverse – in some cases changing – takes on individual chapters. Their input was invaluable.

The men's feedback included coaching, razzing, and loudly calling me off base when they felt I deserved it. That is, they were typically supportive guys. I learned from folks of both sexes and a few genders.

And on that subject, learning, this anthology's story turns a page as with a mouse tap it slips into the cloud and on to the printer.

B.A.

Sebastopol

June 21, 2020

A man is
brave lion,
crazy lover,
sensitive believer

an
incredible
player.

Dr. Elias Gebru[1]

CONTENTS

1. Boy to Man

Boy-to-man starts with physical changes: the youngster's upper body strength quadruples and his lower body strength nearly triples;[2] his voice breaks in public one afternoon, embarrassing him; he may experience a growth spurt that makes him uncoordinated for a while; his beard starts growing. But beyond the physical changes that arrive imperceptibly, a boy's road to manhood will see a lifetime of passages, tests, competitions, and perhaps, initiations and battles.

The journey turns hazardous while he's a boy, an out-of-control period in most men's lives. My friends and I put ourselves in jeopardy every day with risky behavior. From the time we were seven years old, we led physical, out-on-the-streets lives: playing stickball in vacant lots, roller hockey on busy streets, football with older, bigger, merciless guys – games that sent us home limping, bruised, and beat up; tearing around the neighborhood on bicycles, dodging traffic; climbing to the tops of decrepit, abandoned buildings, picking up dirty lumber, linoleum, nails, and tiles, cutting our hands, getting stitches and tetanus shots; running, leaping, falling down hard; staging snowball fights between gangs of kids, twenty-five to a side; busting things up not meaning to – sometimes meaning to; playing hockey on a thinly iced pond miles out of town with no one else around; getting chased by a pissed-off trucker after we'd pelted his rig with snowballs – "Hey mister, we're only kids," we yelled back at him as we ran; breaking up pumpkins on Halloween and getting caught by the cops; bicycling to the train yard, jumping inside the tracks and bumping over the cross ties, dodging a freight train as it rolled in, whistle blaring – talk about stupid! – jumping back out, calling up to the engineer to throw us down a fusee,[3] lighting that fusee, running like hell.

We sustained injuries in some of these adventures, and others could have killed us, though I'm sure our lives were low risk compared to those of many other boys. Testing of strength and endurance, taking risks, running your body ragged – these are the boy's life. The masculinity

that starts at this young age has evolved over millions of years, and is imprinted in our genes, muscles, psyches and minds. I feel it.

INITIATIONS
As a male navigates manhood, he faces passages and perhaps, initiations. An initiation is a life-threatening trial the boy must pass to be welcomed into adulthood by his people. Traditionally, it has three parts. First, he is separated from the tribe, especially from women, and taken to a sacred place where one or more elder men guide him through a potentially lethal trial.[4] If he passes, he experiences a spiritual death and birth: a boy dies; a man is born. Finally, this new soul is reintegrated with the group and allowed to take a wife.

America has a few of these life-threatening initiations, some taking place in the country, as we're about to read. In "Bully Battle," we'll see David L. Walker's left jab-right cross combination launch him into manhood, and witness his acknowledgment by the tribe at large and a woman in particular.

In Scott T. Hutchison's "Farm Baptism," we'll see a boy's trial by steel, his removal to a men's sacred place, a second trial, this one by water, and finally, his integration into two tribes.

For his manhood initiation, Joe Armstrong leaps into a pen of potential death holding only a sticking knife, in a story he calls "Hog Killing."

PASSAGES
We can think of passages as turnstiles of relationships and experiences that mark the man as he passes through them: his father, who he chooses for friends, his first competitive sport, first fight, first dance, first girl, first intimacy, young love, marriage (and maybe divorce or divorces), his woman's first pregnancy, fatherhood, job, military service. Stories of passages blanket this anthology.

In this section, Don Doyle's "Am I A Man Yet?" tells of a father's

planned passage for his son that misfires. As both a boy, when the action takes place, and in later life, Doyle shows insight into his father, a man different from himself.

In "Being a Boy," Julius Lester recalls his painful passage as a bookish youngster running a gauntlet of agonies and beatings.

It's not scarring initiations that are missed; boy can become man without having to survive a life-threatening trial. It's in negotiating tricky passages, some arriving suddenly, that a boy needs help. Elder guides are not always around when the "Help!" moment arrives. I imagine most guys have missed needed male guidance at points in their lives.

The journey through manhood never ends. Every day of a guy's life sees tests of his skills and strengths. Every day his manhood evolves.

These are stories of boy as he passes to man
... rough
& tumbled.

Masculinity is aggressive, unstable, combustible.
It is also the most creative cultural force in history.

<div align="right">CAMILLE PAGLIA[5]</div>

Paglia is a reassuring author for a man to read.

<div align="right">JOHN UPDIKE[6]</div>

A man is strong.

OLD SAYING

DAVID L. WALKER

Bully Battle

A gang of thugs waited for me after school. They'd picked on me through junior high, and though I'd fought their ringleader in a wrestling match, the bullying continued. It was never clear why I was their target. Was it competition over Mary Alice, the answer to a teenage prayer? Was it because I was the son of a dentist, a terrible terror who could drill or pull the teeth out of a kid's head?

Dad knew about the bullying and finally bought some boxing gloves. I'd heard stories of his younger days; he was handy with his fists. We listened to fights on the radio and now he would be my trainer.

"Lead with your left, protect your face, bob and weave, look for openings," Dad said. "Keep your mouth closed and your teeth together; you're too young for dentures. Breathe through your nose. Save your strength so you'll have it when you need it."

We practiced every night after school. He taught me the proper punches and jabs. "No haymakers. Keep your guard up and protect yourself." The more I learned the more my confidence grew. At night I dreamed boxing, taking on the gang leader and winning. I was Floyd Patterson, Ingemar Johansson, the K.O. Kid.

It was my freshman year. The gang were sophomores. One day on the bus things came to a head. Gruber was a tall and lean country kid. We were in the aisle when he decided to throw his weight around. "Outta the way, rinky-dink. When you see an upperclassman coming, get outta the aisle." He pushed me toward a seat.

"I'm finding a seat. Back off." I pushed him hard.

He leaned into my face. "You wanna make somethin' of it, rinky-dink?"

"Yeah."

"Meet me after school," he snarled through chaw-stained teeth.

I put on my meanest face, puffing up like an alley cat facing a junk-yard dog. "I'll be there. Lemme know where you wanna get whipped." I paused. "By the way, you should do something about that barn breath if you want to get the girls."

My comment slowly hit home. "I oughta kick yer smart ass right now. You'd like me to get throwed out for fightin' on school grounds but I ain't so damn dumb to fall for that."

"A bath every couple weeks wouldn't hurt either."

"See you after school," Gruber hissed, marching back to his seat.

News of the fight spread through our little town faster than a hopped-up Chevy at the local drag strip. It would not be wrestling. It was understood the fight would be fisticuffs, no gloves, no quarter, just John L. Sullivan bare-knuckle.

A gang sympathizer drove me to the stockyards in his Corvair; he wanted to make sure I didn't chicken out. There was no talk on the ride past the Cedarview Cemetery to the cattle-shipping yard. I was pumped up but felt calm. This was my chance to end the tortuous tyranny and mental misery. It was showtime and the scrappy kid in me was confident.

When we arrived, it looked like half the town was there, hanging on the corral fence. A whiskey bottle passed among cowboy hats: some of those sauce-saturated saps would lose their wages today.

My adversary grinned like a fool as I crawled through the fence. Gruber was swaggering around, rolling up his sleeves, spitting in his hands, pushing his red hair behind his ears. There was no small talk. We squared off. The crowd was cheering and shouting, "Kick his ass."

I knew I was considered the underdog. What did some dentist's kid know about fighting?

No one knew I was ready. It was my moment, a long time coming. Tough Guy was going to take a fall. The gang's days were done.

We moved toward each other. I licked dry lips. The crowd roared; they wanted blood. I was at Madison Square Garden, people at home crouching by their radios. There would be no Marquess of Queensberry Rules here.

I did a few air jabs, danced to my left, bobbing and weaving, fists up to protect my face, elbows tight to my sides. I led with my left, looked for openings, a package ready to explode. It became clear that Gruber had not been trained in the fine art of boxing. His stance was as loose as his big mouth. I felt sorry for him but it didn't last long as I remembered his abuse and my mission – to walk tall out of this stockyard arena, leaving Gruber lying in the cow pies.

He threw a right, a left, a hook, another left. I blocked his punches. He tossed a couple of wild haymakers as I feinted and held back, saving myself, letting him wear down and drop his guard. I threw a punch now and again to remind him I was there, test his counters. He connected on some and I connected on others. It was back and forth: we both had long arms. My face burned. I tasted blood. Two steps backward, out of reach, I took big gulps of air, shook it out, then moved back, teeth clenched.

My arms were tired but my will was stronger than a buckin' bronc's. I looked for an opening. Who was in better shape? Who would weaken first, drop his guard? I saw Gruber's face was more open and moved in, working left. My plan was a combination, as soon as his right dropped enough.

I faked right so he would counter to his left and open his right, and there it was, the unguarded opening on the right side of his face. I took a quick step in and slammed a hard left to his jaw. Red hair flew one way as his head snapped the other. He dropped his guard. His face was exposed and I threw my upper body weight into a right cross, straight to his nose. He went down. The left jab-right cross combo had done its job.

"Get up Gruber, I got more for ya. Get up."

He did not get up. It was over. He'd had it.

I crawled back through the corral fence. The spectators looked at me, eyes wide. They seemed shocked. I smirked at their long faces, wondering who had lost money. Town had just kicked Country's ass.

It was quiet in the Corvair as the gang groupie took me home. Was he rethinking his loyalties?

My mother saw me coming up the driveway. "Oh my God, David! Your face!"

Dad was driving in. He rolled down the window and smiled. "Who won?"

"I did." I beamed, my open mouth full of intact teeth.

His smile widened.

At school the next day, I felt reborn. In spite of my puffy face and the looks from students and teachers, I was happy as a kid with his first car.

Gruber's wrist was in a cast. He'd broken it on my head.

That was the end of my problem with bullying and the beginning of another, more pleasant challenge: Mary Alice. She'd heard I'd won, her girlfriend told me, and said she thought I was cute.

Bullyism will, in the end, call for force.
 TIM O'BRIEN[8]

Women, it's true, make human beings,
but only men can make men.
 MARGARET MEAD[7]

A man is what he does.

JULIAN FELLOWES[9]

SCOTT T. HUTCHISON

Farm Baptism

At thirteen, something inside you already knew not to cry in the company of grown men. First time you helped unload a trailer of hundred pound sacks of horse feed packed in scratch-ass burlap, all other farm work was suspended. Everyone was pulled in to make a human conveyor from truck to feed room where Wesley was last-man-stacking. Big Nelson, Shelby, Captain Cooper Carter, Pee Wee, Angel, Bill, and Ned stood in line while Tank hefted each bag down off the truck. Clockwork left-right body swings fed the next man, and you, the new kid, hired for grass cutting, placed in the middle, with expectation to equally share what was coming down the line.

You learned the hard way, beyond the burlap sand-papering all exposed skin: if you bobble, if you can't handle the weight getting medicine-ball-times-ten slammed into your chest, then expect no mercy from men. The bags continued getting tossed your way, while everyone waiting created new names for you – "Mama's Boy," "Wussy" – the ones still active in the line smirking and silently jeering as they keep 'em coming, bag after bag burying you long after you're down. They only stop when they become too consumed with laughter at your buried predicament and your pitiful idea of what cussing back amounts to.

Kind of like the anvil now. Everybody saying they'd love for you to graduate from push mowers and the numbing buzz of weed eaters along the miles of fence line, and become a real horseman. But they got rules. If you can't pick up that black iron anvil sitting on the round-cut of hardwood out in front of the barn, then no, you can't test yourself against

a thousand pounds of fiery beast ready to kick-stomp-bite your insides out of you.

Two hundred and fifty-pound anvil – that's your man test.

You want to become a horseman, be part of a barn crew. Inside are the smells of rich sweet feed, cured hay, the dusty liveliness of horses, oiled leather from halters and lead shanks, and the ever-present bluster of men. The steady sounds of hooves scuffing, the tines of steel pitchforks ringing, a banging of buckets, and man-laughter.

You catch whiffs and glimpses when you take breaks to enter the barn's tack room where saddles and medicines are kept, poking your head under the faucet in the sink for the rescue of water. Letting it run over your head, face and neck, trying to calm the steady broil from cutting grass in the heat of the day.

The grass, at least, has no agenda other than steady growing. Sometimes when you find yourself out by the training track and you're trimming the grass around each and every fence post to keep the farm looking sharp to passersby, you pause while they're working out the horses being groomed and aimed at big purse races in Kentucky, Maryland and New York. You hold your breath at the majesty flying past you, the power and heart.

You tried the anvil at day's end one Friday, before taking off for the weekend. Everyone gathered. You felt the cords in your neck flaring like fish gills out of water, you asked the muscles in your biceps and forearms to obey, but you could not inch that piece of iron into the air, and the men sniggered and sniggered, awarded you new names – "Candy Ass" and "Girlfriend" – before taking off in dented trucks and on loud motorcycles with their payday checks, everyone intent on raising hell. Your mother picked you up in her Buick Roadmaster Estate Wagon.

The men allowed you in for unloading hay. A tractor trailer load of timothy and alfalfa shipping in from Pennsylvania. What you learned this time: bales are easy to toss from the top of a truck across and into the barn loft. But as layer after layer is removed, and as you grow more tired, you must toss the hay bales higher and higher. And if you miss

the loft, if an errant bale falls to the floor of the barn, then you become christened with new names. Ugly names. Names you don't want to own or live under. But you do, each day, as you roll your mower past the horsemen around the barns, heading to the outskirts of the farm.

Midsummer comes, and the Boss is unhappy with you. His cigarette-burned throat gravels at you, harsh edge to his praise.

"You're a damn fine grass cutter, but I need more help with the horses on weekends. The men work twelve-and-a-half days on, then a day-and-a-half off every other weekend. The horses don't care about man-needs. Water, clean stall, hay and feed, plus time to stretch legs in a grassy paddock – those are their every-day-gotta-happens. If it was Christmas Day they wouldn't care, their needs are their needs, and the men of this farm are entrusted to take care of those basic things. I want you here on weekends to help get the job done. It would be your first step into becoming a horseman." Some of the men shuffle along the poorly-lit edges of the barn's main aisle, eyeing you when the boss turns and walks into the office.

Your parents are devoutly worried about you. "Aged thirteen, and you have not yet accepted The Lord as your savior. We're not about to let you work weekends until you've gotten straight with God." They haul you to the First Baptist Church of Ashland every Sunday, hoping you will be converted, redeemed. But that light simply hasn't shone on you, that calling hasn't tugged away at your insides and made you whole just yet. Saturday nights your parents push conversation over fried chicken, tomatoes, and sweet corn on the cob, prepping you for the big decision you must make in front of the congregation in your suit and tie.

Nobody appears to be close-around one day when work ends, and you're once again waiting for your mom to pick you up. Horses snort softly, contentedly in the barns, the now-familiar aromas of cut grass, bush-hogged fields and manure, plus the rackety buzz of cicadas all fill you with confidence. Orange daylilies bloom around the barn front, a decorative aesthetic circling the anvil.

No one is watching, no one around to call you names. You put your arms beneath the mismatched points of the anvil, you assume that

bent-knee stance you've learned from hoisting feed bags and hay, and you lift. The anvil rises an inch. You drop it back in place and sit down with your back against it waiting for your mom.

A day later the Boss pulls up alongside the road you're mowing, rolls down the window and starts barking: "Forget the damn mower, get in the truck, the boys need you – just get the hell in, Snot!"

You obey. He has given you this job, and he has expectations you must fulfill to measure up. You forgive him inside yourself for calling you "Snot," because somewhere in the future you want a name like "Big" or "Captain" in front of what they all call you. You know: he pays you money for living your days in the open air, wages for this fight against the heat and the weight. And you realize you've never been more willing in your entire scratch-ass life.

Sliding to a halt, the truck throws gravel and doors bang open as if there's an emergency close by. He yells "Follow me and try to keep up!" The two of you go through a gate, into a pasture that tapers down to the Newfound River, a trickle that maybe shouldn't be called a river though such things get misnamed all the time. Still, there's a strong current, and there are fine pools that silver fish dart through. You're puzzled: the men are all gathered there, each and every one of them knee-deep in the flow, holding hands.

The Boss grabs you by the hair and wrenches you backward into the water. He begins to drown you. Correction: he commences baptizing you. Even under water you somehow grasp his words.

"Oh Lord, we are gathered here today to redeem the soul of this lame wussy-assed sinner. He who was a boy must now enter into the kingdom of heaven and work, the province of sweat and manure, blood and muscle."

Boss Man is holding you under a little too long.

"He was blind, but now he sees, he was weak, but now he's ready to kick some serious butt."

Bubbles begin fighting for sunlight.

"We are all witnesses – we who hitched back in barn shadow, we who stood on the hillside in the far-pasture, we who leaned on the railing in the barn loft – we who knew in the instant that your anvil of faith had

been lifted. Please Lord, bless this sinner so that he might work on Saturdays and Sundays, attending the Church of God-Given Hard Work. Let him emerge a new man, a man who can labor on weekends and learn about horses. In Your name we pray, amen."

Praise The Lord: you are lifted up, allowed to catch a deep and righteous breath of air. Tears all around, laughter, smiling, brotherhood.

Praise Him for enlightening your mother and father when later you get home all soaked and happy, recounting just the pertinent parts of the story for their appraisal. Heads nod in affirmation, their hallelujah arms raise high, and they wave you off to the blessed path of horse and God, farm and men.

For some men bravery probably comes naturally. But for most of us bravery is a habit that we acquire – if we acquire it at all – by practice.

<div align="right">JONATHAN GOTTSCHALL[10]</div>

JOE ARMSTRONG

Hog Killing

Dad awakened me long before the light showed on this cold winter morning. A norther had arrived during the night; by morning it was cold and clear, ideal weather for hog killing. The men in the neighborhood had concluded the approaching storm was suitable to provide the three cold days needed for the vital curing process.

We were town people, in our view distinct from farm or country folk, yet the population of 214 made the distinction fuzzy at best. Dad, the town's Methodist preacher, was provided a parsonage, which consisted of a house, a small barn, a pasture, a vegetable garden, pig pens, milk cows, and chickens.

Along with deciding if this particular weather front was a "killing front," the men of our neighborhood also decided what family would kill and ensure that everyone had help enough.

Knowing that hog killing time was approaching precipitated standard preparations: scalding barrels to sterilize them, collecting firewood, cleaning cutting tables, checking the heavy gauge wire loop for the block-and-tackle, and other chores. With the decision that hog killing was to be the next day, an air of excitement prevailed. I had tended both the hogs to be killed, and went to their pen for a final feeding and a sad goodbye. Of course, I knew all along this was to be their fate, and never questioned it. On farms, there is a gentleness and a genuine caring for all the animals, yet the necessity for sacrifice of meat animals is accepted as part of the reality of life. Then I went to bed early, for hog killing begins early indeed.

Dad came into my room and gently shook me. "Time to get up, son." I pulled on my shoes by the wood stove Dad had stoked. Jackets and caps were welcome, for cold weather was part and parcel of hog killing. While Mom fixed a hearty breakfast, I went out in the dark and lit the wood fire under the big barrel. With two hogs to be killed, sausage made, and the lard rendered, an early start was necessary. After getting the fire going under the water drum, likely with ice on top, and once again checking everything for readiness, I went back inside to Mom's breakfast of hot biscuits, sausage, eggs, and gravy. It was just daylight when Dad and I finished breakfast, put on coat, hat and gloves, and went out to continue getting ready. Neighborhood men would arrive soon.

The cold bit into my unprotected skin as we stepped out into the clear night of an early January morning in Arkansas. Just as we came out of the house, Dad, without a word or having previously mentioned anything about it, tapped my arm with the handle of the "sticking knife" and motioned for me to take it.

I had not given a thought to being chief of hog killing today, though I fully expected, as did all my friends, to be selected eventually. I had no time to be nervous and that was doubtless Dad's intention. With so much needing to be done, there was little time for the reality that I was "in charge" to settle in.

The owner of the block-and-tackle arrived, and went inside to get coffee while we bustled about, stoked the fire, honed the cutting knives again, prepared the killing pen, and checked the gun. One after another the helping friends quietly slid into what was a well-understood procedure. As each arrived, he would stand for a moment to observe and then ask, so it could be heard by all, "Who has the knife?"

One of the men present would give a slight nod in my direction – both had probably known of my selection from the previous day's meeting – and the person who asked would say something to acknowledge my position.

"Looks like you've got things well in order. Two good hogs this year, biggest will go 225–250 pounds, I reckon. If you like, I'll set the scalding barrel a bit deeper, Joe?"

My only response would be an affirmative nod. For me to give instructions to these far more experienced men would be rash and foolish, and that I would disagree or countermand something they suggested was unthinkable.

When the water was near boiling, the first hog, enticed with food, was brought from the pen. It was led to a sturdy makeshift pen near the killing area. Finally the reality of having the knife settled in. My mind had dwelled on the forthcoming ritual since my dad's tap on my arm two hours previously.

Someone handed me the gun, a 22-caliber, single-shot rifle, with the caution that the safety latch was on. The hog was positioned so I could put the gun through the wire fencing for a proper shot. The placement of the shot was critical, exactly between the eyes and slightly above a line connecting them. It must be accurate to within a quarter of an inch for a clean kill. All talking and movement stopped, a shushed expectancy prevailed. I well knew this was my test. Over previous years, I had been shown why the shot had been successful or missed the vital mark. If an old-timer missed the mark, there was lots of good-natured kidding. Not so with first-timers though. Then the comments were supportive. "Tough luck, she moved just as you shot." Or, "Good shot, sometimes it doesn't work, even when you hit right on."

So it wasn't fear of ridicule that haunted me at this time, but the reality that the man with the knife was required by custom to climb into the pen alone with the still thrashing hog and "stick" the hog in the jugular vein so the blood drained quickly. The urgency for a clean kill was real and pressing, for it was no light matter to struggle alone with a 225-pound hog to reach that vital point with the knife.

Though my first shot appeared to be well placed, I knew instantly it was a fraction too low. I turned and handed the gun to a bystander, took the knife in return, and climbed without hesitation into the pen with the squealing and thrashing hog, struggling to avoid those sharp hooves.

Tradition prevented any help whatsoever from the bystanders; they remained attentive but completely silent. Unbeknown to me, Mom and my sisters were watching apprehensively from a window inside the house; she felt that her youngest son, me, thirteen years old, was far too young for

this dubious honor. I'm uncertain whether Dad had talked the decision over with Mom; likely he had kept if from her as he had kept it from me.

Somehow I managed to get the knife inserted, although I had been roughed up considerably. Once the successful jab had been made and I backed away, a cheer-like response, expressed as grunts and ahs, arose from the men who had watched so intently. I somehow sensed this was out of respect for the life we were required to take for our food supply. It was clearly a solemn occasion. Then several men jumped into the pen and took over.

After taking a few minutes to get my breath, I was back in action. The hog was dragged to the scalding pot, cuts made just above the ankles exposing the tough tendons, hooks inserted and the animal hoisted up and maneuvered into the tilted scalding barrel. Boiling water was poured and sloshed around to loosen the hair; the hide was scraped until it was completely hairless. The hoist was once again affixed, the hog lifted and washed thoroughly.

Once the carcass was cleared, it too was washed thoroughly with warm water. Then men in front and back, with arms interlaced to form a sling, moved it to the cutting-up table.

The patriarch of the killing family then took charge, directing the cutting according to the traditions and preferences of his family. "Having the knife" does not extend to this part of the process; that comes only when the elder of the family turns this task over to a successor, likely the oldest son at home at the time.

It is traditional in Arkansas hog killing that fresh pork loin, the choicest cut of meat, is served to the workers in the late afternoon meal. I never saw or heard of that tradition being challenged.

During the critical few days during which the curing process happened, there was an anxious tension in the air. Weather reports on the radio were listened to with regularity and if a warming trend emerged, the concern became intense.

The next day at school, I casually mentioned, "Yesterday was hog killing and I had the knife for the first time." I think my friends had heard I'd done all right.

Don Doyle

Am I a Man Yet?

It was time. It was time to become a man, my father said.

One of the traditional fall outings for our family in Iowa was to go into the country armed with gunnysacks in search of black walnuts. Sometimes the nuts, encased in thick green and black hulls, could be found under trees beside country roads. But more often, after getting the farmer's permission, we would go through gate after gate to the area where the walnut trees lived. The ground would be covered with the tennis ball-sized nuts. It was not unlike hunting for Easter eggs, except there would be much work to do before eating any of the riches.

We took the walnuts home, spread them out on the garage floor, and ran them over several times with the car to crack open the hulls. After they'd dried out for two weeks, my dad, grandfather and I would put on old work gloves to keep the black stain from our hands, and sit on the garage floor where, one by one, we peeled off and separated the dried hulls from the shells. As we did this, we shared memories of past outings, of rich Lazy Daisy Cakes with brown sugar, coconut, black walnuts, and raisin frosting, and of the black walnut taffy, fudge and penuche that would be made at holiday time. The buckets of hulled walnuts were then taken to the furnace room in the basement to dry out further before cracking, and being used in cookies, cakes, and candy all year long.

It was on such an anticipated journey that, unknown to me, I would be tested to see if I was a man yet. My dad always brought his shotgun along in case monster rabbits, squirrels, tigers, or bears attacked us.

I must interject here that the reason my grandmother had such a

difficult time in childbirth was because my dad may have been born with a BB gun in his hands. He was born hunting. Every hunting season was on his calendar. He hunted pheasant, quail, duck, rabbit, squirrel, deer, elk, and even raccoons with coonhounds. Since he had grown up hunting, he was disappointed and confused when I didn't jump with joy to go with him to see animals destroyed. We did try to eat everything he killed if it wasn't too full of buckshot or too badly blown away. If he ever bagged a deer, however, he gave it to another "big-time game hunter" to eat. My mother never cooked or ate venison. We did not eat raccoons. They were usually torn apart by the hounds anyway.

It was my dad's nature to hunt. I can't condemn him for that, but somehow I was born wearing an actor's costume and asking for a little more stage light. Killing animals and birds was not and is not my nature.

On that day, my gunnysack was getting heavy to pull along the ground as I found new sources of treasures. Then I heard my dad say, "Well, looky there, way up in the top of that tree – there's a big squirrel's nest. I'll just go to the car and get my gun. We'll see if you're a man today, Donnie."

I knew what he meant. I guess I wanted to be a man, but I was afraid to shoot the gun, and I sure didn't want to kill any squirrels. I fed them nuts from my hand on our back porch!

When Dad returned with the shotgun he placed it in my arms. "I'll show you how to hold it and help you aim. Be careful now," he said, "it's loaded." Dad crouched behind me, helping hold up the heavy gun. "We're going to aim right at that big nest and see if there's anything in it."

I didn't want to cry. I wanted to be a man, but the tears were running down my cheeks. "I don't want to do it," I said. "I don't want to kill squirrels."

"Oh, come on, Donnie," he said, "you can do it. Be a man today."

Then my mother said, "Don't make him do it, Phil."

"He needs to," my dad shouted. "Now come on, Donnie, point the end of the barrel right on that nest. That's it, and when you're ready, pull

the trigger slowly. Now, it's going to kick a bit, but I've got you."

"Kick a bit." Never heard that before. There's another reason not to pull the trigger, I thought. "I don't want it to kick," I said.

"Well, it won't hurt you if you hold it tight against your shoulder."

I felt terrible. I wanted to be a man in my father's eyes, but I didn't want to shoot that gun. Is that what you had to do to be a man? I cocked my head to the right so I could see the tip on the end of the barrel in the middle of the sight, and with my dad's help holding up the gun, I resigned myself to the task of becoming a man.

I pulled the trigger. Bam! Kick it did. Knocked me back into my dad's chest and we both fell backwards. It really hurt. Tears were coming. I couldn't do anything about it.

My dad said, "Good job, look what you did."

Most of the nest was blown out of the tree and there were two squealing, squirming squirrels on the ground. I was crying hard by that time. I didn't care if I was a man or not.

My dad took my hand and we walked over to look at the bloody squirrels on the ground. "Now you need to finish them off, son," he said. "Put them out of their misery."

I knew they would never have been in any misery if I hadn't pulled that trigger. Through my tears I shouted, "I don't want to do it. I won't do it."

"Come on now," my dad said, "take the gun and be a man."

My mother was there with us by that time, also crying, "Phil, stop it for pity's sake. He's only six years old."

I broke away and ran back to the car, jumped onto the back seat and covered my ears with my hands. I heard it anyway. Bam! I knew those little squirrels were blown to pieces, and it was all my fault. If only I hadn't pulled that trigger!

With the sacks of walnuts and the gun secured in the trunk, we began the long, excruciatingly uncomfortable ride home. No one said a word. Everyone was thinking.

My dad's thoughts probably were: "Is my only son ever going to be a man and want to go hunting with me?"

My mother's thoughts probably were: "Why did I let that go so far? He's too young to kill."

Don Doyle

And me – well, I had many thoughts and questions: "I want to run away and never see my dad again. Do I have to kill to be a man? Are guns what make us men?"

I hated my dad with a six-year-old vengeance. However, with the passage of time and a somewhat more "grownup" point of view, I began to understand his passion for the hunt and his need to initiate me into his world, for his own sake, as well as for his image with his friends.

That was the last time I remember gathering black walnuts with my parents. Many years later when I was teaching at a university in Illinois I took my own family hunting … for black walnuts.

Now in the autumn of my own life, I have a loving wife, four sons, two daughters-in-law, two beautiful grandchildren, a gratifying, successful career in theater, education, and storytelling, and many loving friends whom I treasure greatly.

Sometimes when I feel especially happy with my life, I want to say to my dad, who may be looking down on me, "Am I … in your eyes, Dad, am I a man yet?"

Julius Lester

Being a Boy

As boys go, I wasn't much. I mean, I tried to be a boy and spent many childhood hours pummeling my hardly formed ego with failure at Cowboys and Indians, baseball, football, lying, and sneaking out of the house. When our neighborhood gang raided a neighbor's pear tree, I was the only one who got sick from the purloined fruit. I also failed at setting fire to our garage, an art at which any 5-year-old boy could be adept. I was, however, the neighborhood champion at getting beat up. "That Julius can take it, man," the boys used to say, almost in admiration, after I emerged from another battle, tears brimming in my eyes but refusing to fall.

My efforts at being a boy earned me a pair of scarred knees that are a record of a childhood spent falling from bicycles, trees, the tops of fences, and porch steps; of tripping as I ran (generally from a fight), walked, or simply tried to remain upright on windy days.

I tried to believe my parents when they told me I was a boy, but I could find no objective proof for such an assertion. Each morning during the summer, as I cuddled up in the quiet of a corner with a book, my mother would push me out the back door and into the yard. And throughout the day as my blood was let as if I were a patient of 17th-century medicine, I thought of the girls sitting in the shade of porches, playing with their dolls, toy refrigerators and stoves.

There was the life, I thought! No constant pressure to prove oneself. No necessity always to be competing. While I humiliated myself on football and baseball fields, the girls stood on the sidelines laughing at me, because they didn't have to do anything except be girls. The rising of each sun brought me to the starting line of yet another day's Olympic

decathlon, with no hope of even winning a bronze medal.

Through no fault of my own I reached adolescence. While the pressure to prove myself on the athletic field lessened, the overall situation got worse – because now I had to prove myself with girls. Just how I was supposed to go about doing this was beyond me, especially because at the age of 14, I was four foot nine and weighed 78 pounds. (I think there may have been one 10-year-old girl in the neighborhood smaller than I.) Nonetheless, duty called, and with my ninth-grade gym class jockstrap flapping between my legs, off I went.

To get a girlfriend, though, a boy had to have some asset beyond the fact that he was alive. I wasn't handsome like Bill McCord, who had girls after him like a cop-killer has policemen. I wasn't ugly like Romeo Jones, but at least the girls noticed him: "That ol' ugly boy better stay 'way from me!" I was just there, like a vase your grandmother gives you at Christmas that you don't like or dislike, can't get rid of, and don't know what to do with. More than ever I wished I were a girl. Boys were the ones who had to take the initiative and all the responsibility. (I hate responsibility so much that if my heart didn't beat of itself, I would now be a dim memory.)

It was the boy who had to ask the girl for a date, a frightening enough prospect until it occurred to me that she might say no! That meant risking my ego, which was about as substantial as a toilet paper raincoat in the African rainy season. But I had to thrust that ego forward to be judged, accepted, or rejected by some girl. It wasn't fair! Who was she to sit back like a queen with the power to create joy by her consent or destruction by her denial? It wasn't fair – but that's the way it was.

But, if (God forbid!) she should say "Yes," then my problem would begin in earnest, because I was the one who said where we would go (and waited in terror for her approval of my choice). I was the one who picked her up at her house where I was inspected by her parents as if I were a possible carrier of syphilis (which I didn't think one could get from masturbating, but then again, Jesus was born of a virgin, so what did I know?). Once we were on our way, it was I who had to pay the bus fare, the price of the movie tickets and whatever she decided to stuff her stomach with afterward. (And the smallest girls were all stomach.) Finally, the girl was taken home where once again I was inspected (the

father looking covertly at my fly and the mother examining the girl's hair). The evening was over and the girl had done nothing except honor me with her presence. All the work had been mine.

Imagining this procedure over and over was more than enough: I was a sophomore in college before I had my first date.

I wasn't a total failure in high school, though, for occasionally I would go to a party, determined to salvage my self-esteem. The parties usually took place in somebody's darkened basement. There was generally a surreptitious wine bottle or two being passed furtively among the boys, and a record player with an insatiable appetite for Johnny Mathis records. Boys gathered on one side of the room and girls on the other. There were always a few boys and girls who'd come to the party for the sole purpose of grinding away their sexual frustrations to Johnny Mathis's falsetto, and they would begin dancing to their own music before the record player was plugged in. It took a little longer for others to get started, but no one matched my talent for standing by the punch bowl. For starters, I would try to make my legs do what they had been doing without effort since I was nine months old, but for some reason they would show all the symptoms of paralysis on those evenings.

Although several hours of wondering whether I was going to die ("Julius Lester, a 16-year-old, died at a party last night, a half-eaten Ritz cracker in one hand and a potato chip dipped in pimiento-cheese spread in the other. Cause of death: failure to be a boy."), I would push my way to the other side of the room where the girls sat like a hanging jury. I would pass by the girl I wanted to dance with. If I was going to be refused, let it be by someone I didn't particularly like. Unfortunately, there weren't many in that category. I had more crushes than I had pimples.

Finally, through what surely could only have been the direct interventions of the Almighty, I would find myself on the dance floor with a girl. And none of my prior agony could compare to the thought of actually dancing. But there I was and I had to dance with her. Social custom decreed that I was supposed to lead, because I was the boy. Why? Let her lead. Girls were better dancers anyway. It didn't matter. She stood there waiting for me to take charge. She wouldn't have been worse off if she'd waited for me to turn white.

But, reciting "Invictus"[11] to myself, I placed my arms around her,

being careful to keep my armpits closed because, somehow, I had managed to overwhelm a half jar of deodorant and a good-size bottle of cologne. With sweaty armpits, "Invictus," and legs afflicted again with polio, I took her in my arms, careful not to hold her so far away that she would think I didn't like her, but equally careful not to hold her so close she could feel the catastrophe which had befallen me the instant I touched her hand. My penis, totally disobeying the lecture I'd given it before we left home, was rigid as Governor Wallace's jaw would be if I asked for his daughter's hand in marriage.

God, how I envied girls at that moment. Wherever it was on them, it didn't dangle between their legs like an elephant's trunk. No wonder boys talked about nothing but sex. That thing was always there. Every time we went to the john, there it was twitching around like a fat little worm on a fishing hook. When we took baths, it floated in the water like a lazy fish and God I wished I could keep it tucked between my legs, as if it were a tail that had been mistakenly attached to the wrong end. But I was helpless. It was there, with a life and mind of its own, having no other function than to embarrass me.

Fortunately, the girls I danced with were discreet and pretended they felt nothing unusual rubbing against them as we danced But I was always convinced that the next day they were all calling up their friends to exclaim: "Guess what, girl? Julius Lester got one! I ain't lyin'!"

Now, of course, I know it was as difficult being a girl as it was a boy, if not more so. While I stood paralyzed at one end of the dance floor trying to find the courage to ask a girl for a dance, most of the girls waited in terror at the other, afraid no one, not even I, would ask them. And while I resented having to ask a girl for a date, wasn't it also horrible to be the one who waited for the phone to ring? And how many of those girls who laughed at me making a fool of myself on the baseball diamond would have gladly given up their places on the sidelines for mine on the field?

No, it wasn't easy for any of us, girls and boys, as we forced our beautiful, free-flowing child-selves into those narrow constricting cubicles labeled female and male. I tried, but I wasn't good at being a boy. Now I'm glad, knowing a man is nothing but the figment of a penis's imagination, and any man should want to be something more than that.

Manliness is a human invention. ... Each culture constructs its own version of what men and women are – and ought to be.

E. ANTHONY ROTUNDO[12]

Masculinity is not a cultural invention. ... It is a real thing that has evolved over millions of years as a response to the built-in competitive realities of male life.

JONATHAN GOTTSCHALL[13]

Masculinity does not exist; there are more masculinities, multiple ways to be a man.

KEITH THOMPSON[14]

2. A Wonderment of Women

A boy's passage to manhood usually includes making love with a woman. His first confrontation with her nudity is slack-jawed, breathtaking wonderment. Ron Jones's tale, "Cool," finds him trying to deal with this first intimate encounter, one all men feverishly wish to get right, but rarely do.

Like Jones, American boys are often lost in their first intimacy with a woman, because unlike a girl, whose mother has more likely given her "the talk" by then, guys don't always hear it from Dad or any man. Some of what my generation of boys thought we knew about sex was locker-room jive. But even a well conceived talk (or talks) might not prepare a boy for the astonishment of being with a girl for the first time.

Other stories here find young men struggling to understand and ne-gotiate women's behaviors. In Marc Wilder's "Planned Parenthood," we see a teenage boy trying to do right by his girl and become a better man for her.

Jordan Legg's "Sharpie Stones" pivots on a teen pregnancy and how the young parents deal with this life dislocation.

John Biesecker's "April 3rd" finds an abandoned husband with a sick infant. It was the most read story I posted on the HeartOfAMan.net website. Both women and men had deep reactions to Biesecker's piece.

Michael Morgan's "A Premeditated Starving" shows men trying to understand and care for a woman in need. "Men grow quiet when we sense problems peculiar to women," Morgan writes.

In "It's Always About the Girl," Michael Estabrook pursues his sweet-heart and acts to protect his interest in her. Some of his actions, taken correctly (and I imagine most of them were), may have gone unnoticed by his inamorata.

These stories are rich with guys' honest efforts to understand what Jack London termed "the eternal mystery of woman."[15] By watching men watching women, I hope you see us more clearly.

But sweeter still than this,
 than these,
 than all,

Is first and passionate love.

 It stands alone,
 like
 Adam's
 recollection
 of
 his
 fall.

The tree of knowledge
has been pluck'd

 – all 's known –

 And life
 yields nothing
 further
 to
 recall.

LORD BYRON
DON JUAN, CANTO I

The pride of the peacock
 is the glory of God.

The lust of the goat
 is the bounty of God.

The wrath of the lion
 is the wisdom of God.

The nakedness of woman
is the work of God.

WILLIAM BLAKE[16]

Ron Jones

Cool

I was twelve years old growing up in San Francisco's Sunset District. It was the '50s, and everything was changing. I turned the radio dial and heard, "Shrimp boats are coming, their sails are in sight." I turned that dial a little farther and "Sh-boom!" And at the end of the dial "I found my thrill on Blueberry Hill." Everything was changing.

The street conversations went from talking about the San Francisco Seals to hard-ons and heat-ons, though I wasn't sure what a hard-on or a heat-on was.

Hair was a big problem for a twelve-year-old. Hair had to be just right because hair was connected with doing IT. The big IT! I wasn't quite sure what IT was, but knew IT had to do with hair and girls. And hair in the '50s had to kind of like swirl from the back of your head and then dangle right up in front with a little curl right there like the Big Bopper. You know, the Big Bopper[17] on TV, that's who I'm talking about.

I always had concoctions to save me. Of course I had to explain them to Bobby Ensign, my best friend. A mixed drink of pineapple juice, a little vanilla extract and lots of mint jam. And for tanning, Ron's Real Zorch Suntan Oil: baby oil – now this is a secret, mind you – iodine and mint jam. Yes, you mix it up, Bobby. Yeah, I know, we look a little bit green lying out in the sun, Bobby, but no one will notice us here, I think.

IT. IT. Yeah, doing IT. My first experience with doing IT was at Ben Lomond, California.

My family had a little summer place. Every family had a little summer place with a cute name. Ours was "Ronnie's Dug Out." Ronnie, that's me. My brother is Doug. My dad named the place. If you were a working-class family in the '50s in San Francisco, you went to the

Russian River, and if you were a wealthy family you went to the lake, Lake Tahoe. All the in-betweens went to Ben Lomond to lie next to the dam and look at the girls and comb your hair. That's where I met Kay Casselli.

My, my, my, my, my. Actually, she met me at this dance at the dam.

She walks right up to me and says, "Can you do the dirty bop?"

Feet don't fail me now; think of something. My feet are doing the Charleston, my hands are doing the hokey-pokey, and I'm doing the dirty bop with Kay Casselli, looking so cool.

She likes me; she thinks I'm cute, cuddly. We like the same things. It's a match made in heaven. She likes Juicy Fruit gum with Milk Duds; she likes to play Canasta; she likes Coke splashed with chocolate syrup, lemon on the side, and mint jam. We are a match and she likes to slow dance. Dancing with Kay Casselli, doing a slow dance. Of course that leads to feel-ups, oh yeah, and that of course would lead to doing IT, I'm sure of that.

I know her sister, Marge Casselli, had done IT. She was going with Jerry Granelli. You remember Jerry Granelli, the drummer, went to Balboa High School. He always had these drumsticks in his pocket. Well, he stole this Nash Rambler, drove Marge up to the dump, and when they came back she was smiling, he was smiling, and he had his drumsticks out. He was pounding everything in sight with a bop doodly dum dum, de dum de bop, yeah, yeah, yeah. He had done IT for sure.

Now it's my turn. Got to have a plan, got to be cool, got to solve the hair problem.

What I'll do is pin Kay Casselli, say we're going steady. Steady will lead to lots of, you know, feel-ups that lead directly to IT, I think, and then cool – got to be cool. No problem. I'll simply roll up my sleeves – that looks good, yeah – pop my zits, peg my pants, put them under the mattress and sleep on them for about three months. That gives them a much better crease than using mom's steam iron. Yeah, now I'm looking good, and I stick some rolled-up gym socks in my shoes, make myself about two inches taller. Oh, I'm really looking cool.

Now the hair. Love solution number nine: Dixie Peach Pomade, Elmer's white glue and, of course, mint jam. That should fix it. My hair was lacquered in the perfect look of a big curl coming right down in

front and in the back, a D.A., a Duck's Ass. Cool.

Now I'm with Kay Casselli and we're playing Canasta. Her folks are out, "Moonglow" is on the 45 machine, she's wearing a white angora sweater that looks like cotton candy, and she's chewing Juicy Fruit gum with Milk Duds. Oh my God, Jerry Granelli and Marge are already on the porch swing and it's swinging away. He's getting a hickey. Oh I'd do anything for one of those.

Plan. Put my plan in motion. This is it, my chance to do IT. I present Kay Casselli with my track pin, ask if she'll go steady and she says Yessss!

"Ouch." I stick my finger; it doesn't matter. And she puts the pin on herself next to her heart as she says, "Oh my God."

Then she rolls up the bottom of her sweater, her tan stomach, and now – A Living Bra. I've never seen a real bra before. There it is, just floating and looking at me like some great temptation, oh goodness gracious. I've got to get that thing off! Reach behind her, unzip it; I got to feel – How does this thing work?

I got both hands behind her and I'm poking and trying to figure this thing out and then I decide. I'll bite it off! I'll bite that bra that separates me from glory. I'm biting and bouncing against her breasts when I realize, I've got a hard-on!

And my hair, my hair is stuck to her sweater! I'm stuck with a hard-on. And then she yells Canasta!

Not what I expected it would be like at all. My pants are sticking out in front, I've cut my finger, swallowed my gum, and lost one of my shoes in the excitement.

I wobble home, fall in the creek and a thousand mosquitoes stick themselves in my hair. I'm lying in bed pretending to sleep, when my mom comes in and says, "Ronnie, you look really zorched."

"Mom – Cool! I wanna look cool."

She tells me there will be lots of nights like this.

"I hope not, Mom."

But I'm lying there in the middle of a summer's night, listening to "Blueberry Hill," thinking, "I've got to find myself a bra and figure out how that thing works. If I could do that I could solve lots of problems."

And less glue, a lot less glue. But mint jam. Yeah, that mint jam really works. I was, oh yeah! I was cool! Yeah. Cool!

Painters teach us

that the curve beckons,

and woman,

an infinitude of curves,

beckons man

infinitely.

MARCK T. WILDER

Planned Parenthood

We traipse the length of the clinic, searching its wall of mirrored panels for the entrance, and finally find it on our second pass; but when I lean into it, it won't budge. I try to peek through the glass, but all I can make out are my eyes. I curl my knuckles, ready to knock, when she stops me.

"Hey." Her fingertips touch just below my wrist.

"Yeah?"

"I'm kinda nervous."

"Oh, Cubby." That's how we address each other when we're alone – a lexicon of bear cub synonyms. I smooth the hair by her temples, looping strands behind her ears, then pull her close and kiss her forehead. "It'll be fine."

"It's just kinda weird. Nobody else has ever really seen me, uh...." She gives me this quick, nonchalant head dip while flicking her eyes down at herself. "You know, down there."

The reason we're here, at this clinic, is because of a talk she had with a coworker during a smoke break. I imagine the conversation went something like this:

"So, naturally, you know, I'm lying there kind of tense on the, uh – on the table thing, you know, with the stirrups and all that – and the doctor guy, he's all up in there, and I'm thinking, like, 'Oh my Jesus, your hands are like icicles!' And I must have, like, flinched or something because he stopped for a second, brought his hands up to his mouth and breathed on them – like, haaaaah – and then he, like, rubbed them together, you know? Like he was some hobo trying to keep warm by a

trashcan fire. Maybe he thought he was being cute or funny or something, but it totally came off as creepy."

"Whoa, what a weirdo. That sucks, dude." Marci calls everyone dude, boy or girl. "Kinda makes me grateful I've never had one of those, uh … you know, visits."

"Yeah, girl, trust me, you do not, ever, want some guy to … wait, what? What do you mean?"

"I just…. I've never gone to see a stuff-doctor before. It just seems kinda awkward."

"Yeah, but, like, never never? Oh no, girl, you definitely should. You have to. It's so important. Don't let my little creepster horror story put you off. Like, for instance, did you know…?"

When Marci got off work, she came over and told me about the conversation. I looked up the clinic info and held her hand while she booked her appointment.

I knock on my reflection in the mirror glass and there's an electronic squawk, like the feedback blast of a megaphone, then a girl's voice, small but amplified, coming at us from this little slotted speaker box in the doorframe. "What is the purpose of your visit, please?"

I clear my throat and overenunciate each word like I'm placing a drive-through order. "Oh, yes, hi. I, uh, I mean, we, that is, my girlfriend here, she has an appointment."

Silence. No response, no door unlatching.

The feedback screech again. "Sir, you'll need to hold down the button when you wanna talk."

I hold it down. "Oh, yeah, sorry. My girlfriend here, she has an appointment."

"What's the name?"

"Marci."

"That's Marcella for three o'clock?"

"Yeah, uh-huh. That's correct."

"You know it's past three, right?"

"Yeah, sorry. We had some trouble finding your…."

Somewhere inside she's cutting me off, pressing a button that causes

the door to unlock with a grinding, electric buzz.

My shoe isn't even flat against the linoleum before the inside air hits me like it's something I could bump into. The walls are that same blah shade of green that the army wears and the key source of light in the room seems to be from what little trickles in through the darkly tinted windows. As dim as it looks in here, and even though I can close my eyes and feel the AC's recycled breath, it's still at least as hot as it was outside.

The only explanation is the number of people crammed into this waiting room. Chairs in rows, against walls, squeezed into corners, almost all filled.

The general level of enthusiasm of the people waiting – lifting their heads in living-dead unison to see who entered – never exceeds a frown. The room rustles at a volume that barely rises above a chorus of whispers. The potato-chip crackle of women flipping through brittle copies of *Cosmo, Us Weekly* and *Rolling Stone*, their pages stiff from the dried hand-sweat of late-stage pregnancy and hot flashes, rides below the sizzling hiss of mothers scattered throughout the room, locked in the same futile loop of reminding their kids to stop that and come here and sit down.

The girl who buzzes us in sits behind a pane of plastic thick enough to stop a rifle bullet, the kind that separates you from bank tellers, depending on your neighborhood.

"Jeez, what do you think it is with all this security?" Marci's idea of whispering is curling her fingers in front of her mouth when she talks.

"I don't know. Pro-lifers with pipe bombs, I guess."

Given her petite frame, egg-smooth skin, and silver bling looping down her chest with the word "Temptress" spelled out in girly rhinestone loops, I'd say the receptionist is our age. Her eyelids droop so far, they half block her pupils, like she's tired or stoned, and her eyebrows are plucked clean, penciled into bold auburn arches that would put McDonald's to shame.

"Marcella for three o'clock?" Between her expression and eyebrows, she looks simultaneously amazed and bored.

"Uh huh, yeah, that's her right there."

She wilts her head to one side so her ear practically touches her shoulder, juts out her lips, and glares at me like she's looking over a pair of imaginary glasses. "Yes, and thanks for that, sir, but unless you're her interpreter, I'd like to hear it from her, please?"

"Oh, sorry…." the words die in my throat.

I usher Marci up to the counter with a tiny hand flourish. Maybe she heard what the receptionist said or maybe I'm carrying it on my face. Marci looks from the receptionist to me, eyes huge and jaw drooped so low I can see her bottom teeth, letting me know she's on my side with a look that says, *Whoa, what's this chick's problem?*

While she checks in, I'm riffling through the pamphlet display on the counter. One with a segmented wheel of pastel pills on the cover reads: "It's your life. Live it on your terms." Another lists signs and symptoms of STDs. Curious, I pluck it out, open it to glance at the pictures inside, and knock the display on its side trying to put it back too quickly. Naturally, I pick it back up and reorganize it, apologizing to the receptionist, who, of course, doesn't even notice.

Pinned on the office door is a poster printed so large I have to take two steps back to read its simple white words on a black background: "We Support A Woman's Right To Choose."

I was raised by a single mother, but I can be a little thick when it comes to lady issues, so reading that poster, it takes me a couple of seconds – thinking, *Choose what, exactly?* – before it clicks.

Oh. Right. That.

A 360 scan around the room, and the idea creeps up and clubs me over the head that, even filled to fire-hazard capacity, I'm the only man, and that makes Marci the only woman with her man in the room.

The lady behind the bulletproof glass passes Marci a pen and a few sheets of paper on a clipboard through the sliding steel drawer fused to the window. She tells Marci something while touching her fingertips to her chest, then points her to the only seat left, in the back corner. I let Marci take it, naturally, and lean against the wall next to her.

Except for the neat stack of leaflets on the table next to Marci, the only reading material is a Highlights children's magazine, with headlines like "Jokes for Road Trips" and "Hidden Pictures." I can't be sure if flipping

through it will make me more or less conspicuous than I already am, but I do know if I don't grab it, one of these little kids, one of these bacteria baths running around, will snatch it up and make the choice for me.

I flip straight to "Hidden Pictures." There's this optical illusion that consists of six-by-six rows of solid black squares segmented by white lines. In the negative space where the lines intersect, vague gray dots appear, but if I focus on one intersection at a time, that dot vanishes while the other imaginary dots throb in my periphery.

I glance up, making a weird connection between the optical illusion and the stares I'm getting. From the corner of my eye, I feel somebody gawking at me, but by the time I look at her, she's flipping through a Cosmo. Or bobbing to headphone music. Or bottle-feeding a baby. When I close my eyes, it's like I'm an only child again, the center of attention. I open them, and everywhere I look is a face-shaped blur of someone not looking at me.

Sitting across from Marci, a lady with the same penciled eyebrows as the receptionist, lips outlined in that stark, not-quite-black shade of purple, bumps her screaming infant up and down on her gut, squinting into the baby's face saying, "Shush, shush, shush, shush, shush," with no effect. There's a little boy in the aisle between us – I'm guessing her son – with a Moe haircut and a perma-smile etched into his face. With no objections from his mother, he pushes an empty stroller into my foot, then backs it up, and bump, backs it up again, and bump. After each bump, he stops for a beat and looks up at me, giving a laugh that sounds like a hiccup.

Every couple of minutes, Marci takes a deep breath in through her nose and looks up from her clipboard to ask me a question.

"Do I have any medical allergies?"

And bump. And bump.

"Do you think I have trouble sleeping?"

And bump. And bump.

The only person I catch eyeballing me is a girl whose face, shoulders, and hips would look skeletal if it weren't for the balloon-smuggling bulge of a baby bump jutting out from the top of her jeans. She's got these deep raccoon circles around her eyes that would send up red

flags if the rest of her weren't already so pale. Her dyed red hair and lip-stick-bright tank top give her the look of a cherry impaled on a cocktail sword.

And Marci says, "Would you say that I still drink too much?"

And bump.

Tank Top Girl gazes at me long enough for me to flip through the entire magazine. I glance at her after every page, but she never looks away, doesn't blink, as far as I can tell. It's freaking me out like when Marci's cat comes into the room while we're doing it and won't break eye contact with me.

And Marci says, "There's a question here about drugs. Do you think weed counts?"

And bump.

Tank Top Girl though, there's something in her expression, the way she's looking at me, the basset-hound slant of her eyes, that I recognize on some intuitive level. I know this look. It sends me back to a time be-fore I had the words to say "bye bye."

Mom had this same hopeful look at the onset of every potential stepdad. The times I caught her beaming over his shoulder when he sat me on his lap and tried to relate to me, tickling my tummy and making Jim Carrey faces until I peed. It's the same look she gave him at dinner after the check arrived and he shooed her hand away from it, saying, "Sweetie, please, don't be silly." The same look as when she knelt down to my eye level and asked me, "Hey, kiddo, how would you feel about someday calling him 'Dad'?" It's the same look that preceded every promise she made me that things are finally going to get better. It's a look that says, Real men are still out there.

Marci slides her pen under the clip and stands. Her entire walk to the reception counter and back, every eye in the room traces her path like she's some red carpet celebrity.

Maybe I was wrong about these looks I've been getting. Maybe these women haven't been staring at me this whole time. Maybe they've been analyzing Marci's every gesture, twitch, and unconscious scratch of scalp, trying to unfold the secret of how to attract a man who would

symbolize a devotion as simple yet meaningful as moral support, someone who would hold a hand and keep her mind off things with sweet talk and inside jokes before a stranger with frosty, antiseptic hands starts spreading this and swabbing that. Maybe to these women, Marci's some kind of lady-Moses, leading her people away from the guys that daytime talk shows warned them against, towards the promised man.

There's an electric snarl and the door to the exam rooms clicks open. A woman in turquoise shirt and pants stands there. She lifts the top sheet of paper on her clipboard and reads Marci's name out loud, then scans the room. Marci stands and the doctor motions, *right this way.*

Marci flashes me a smile so tight and tense that for the first time I notice she has dimples. I smile back, give her a dual thumbs-up, and mouth, *I love you, bear cub, you'll be fine.* She's focusing more on her shoes than me, but when she looks back up, to cement the image of what a supportive boyfriend looks like in the minds of these lobby ladies, I blow her a two-handed kiss. Still holding the same, strained smile, she nods at me, then turns into the hall.

As soon as the office door clicks shut, I hop into Marci's seat, setting some distance between my legs and Stroller Kid. I drop the magazine on the table and scan the room, but something feels off. I'm getting the same looks I was getting before, only now none of them look away when I face them. I wouldn't call what they're doing "looking" any more. It's not even staring, really. They're glaring, eyebrows low and bunched together, making pug wrinkles over their noses. If their expressions are anything to go by, they want to kill me and eat me.

I grab a fat stack of leaflets, flipping through them for some kind of barrier between their eyes and mine. The first one has a pencil sketch on the front, a young girl frowning at her swollen belly, and reads: "Even if the daddy's gone, you are not alone. Know your rights as a pregnant or parenting teen."

Stroller Kid takes a few steps in, closing the gap between us, rolls the stroller back, and then hits into my foot again.

And bump.

His mother, still bouncing the screeching bundle on her chest, has stopped shushing the baby and now squints at me. The girl who,

moments ago, was flipping through *Cosmo,* one knee crossed over the other, smacking her gum, holds her place in the magazine with a finger and tilts her face slightly away so she can scowl back at me out of the corner of her eyes.

And bump. And bump.

The next leaflet shows a girl sporting a rib cage-length leather jacket and oil slick miniskirt, blowing a pouty kiss at whoever took this picture. Beneath that, the caption reads: "Better safe than statutory. Don't risk it, know the law."

If you listen close to my stomach, it's echoing the words from the poster, "A Woman's Right To Choose," through its gurgles and whines. They resonate inside every drop of sweat racing down my spine. It's the monotonous pop song hook that replays in my head: a woman's right to choose a woman's right to choose a woman's right to choose.

The two of us – Marci and me – we're old enough to smoke, but not old enough to drink.

This one time, maybe a little more than a year ago, we were out smoking Camels on my patio when my upstairs neighbor shouted down, asking if we had a light. We tossed it up and the three of us got to talking. He was this gnarled old dude who fought in Vietnam even though, deep down, he's a Dylan-loving hippie. At some point into our second smoke, Marci asked if we could give him cash to buy us booze. He obliged and even gave us back our change, a better deal than we were getting from the local winos, collecting his tax instead in the form of a couple shots from our bottle. We liked the arrangement, and called on him the next night, and the next night, and the next, and on.

We were fun drunks, and made a conscious effort never to drink past the point of having fun, which generally coincided with the point where we would black out, pass out, or barf it all up.

Then this other time, not too long after, Marci told me she was a couple weeks late. I asked her how that was possible and she told me condoms are only, like, 98 percent effective. We planned on heading up to the store to grab a home pregnancy kit but, before we left, I made a quick call to see if my neighbor was around.

When we got back, I paced outside the bathroom door, gripping the

bottle by its neck, never letting it dip down below my belt before taking another good pull. There hadn't been a sober day between us in months, and we burned through a pack of smokes a day, easy. I'd heard the stories, read the articles, and I could see how it would play out as clear as the STD pictures in that pamphlet. Our baby, mine and Marci's little miracle, was going to come out retarded and mush-faced, with too many fingers and not enough toes, all twitching and panting, the noises from its mouth sounding less like crying and more like the shrieks of a Texas Chainsaw victim, if it came out breathing at all.

In the four minutes it took to see a plus or a minus, I must have set a new Guinness record for fear-drinking.

When Marci finally shuffled out of the bathroom, she huffed out a long sigh, flashed me her sucked-in smile and shrugged. "Just a fluke, I guess. Anyway, it's negative."

I could breathe again.

The night was quiet after that. She didn't feel like drinking and I was drunk past the point of conversation. We watched TV and nuked cans of soup for dinner.

In bed later, she told me I had nothing to worry about. I could relax. She wouldn't have kept it. Not after seeing the way I reacted. Not after how scared I got.

I didn't say anything right away. I couldn't.

I heard her breathing, felt it on the back of my neck, and after some minutes passed with no response, she said, "Hello?"

The best I could give her was, "Uh huh."

Lying there, curled fetus-tight into myself and still spinning from the drink, I thought in circles about how easily my life could become something so unrecognizable. I would never get used to calling it mine again, and hated myself more than anything for the capacity for selfishness that allowed me to think and feel this way. Like I was really the one this was coming down on. I thought about the words she had used: "keep it," like our baby's tiny, retarded life was some ratty orphaned wallet she'd found in a restaurant booth. I thought about the fragile, mutant existence I almost brought into this world, born with too many of my fear genes and shame chromosomes to ever lead a normal human life.

Hovering close to something as big as that, feeling its weight, the pull

of its gravity, I felt punier than our imaginary fetus. Then I cried like our hypothetical embryo was growing in my own womb, and then torn suddenly from inside me.

Marci pulled me in and held me close, telling me, "Shush, shush, shush, honey. Don't feel bad. Please." She rubbed my chest and squeezed my shoulder, kissing my neck and spine.

When I could talk again, I made Marci the same promise I made myself: I will be better than this.

The truth is, no one in this room knows why I'm here. The only theories anyone might have are based on their experiences. Sure, maybe some are thinking the truth: I'm only here as moral support, a hand to hold during a time of anxiety and discomfort. Maybe that's what they're thinking, but with the looks they're stabbing into me, I doubt it.

To them, maybe I'm an enforcer, some brute to keep Marci from chickening out of what I want her to do. What I want her to get done. Those goofy gestures of support I made when she walked into the office were distorted into some ugly parody of real affection. And her, letting a man make a woman's choice for her. If that's what they think, I don't know how any of them can bear looking at me.

The woman bouncing the little screamer – her other kid ramming the stroller into my foot – I can practically read it scrawled in the stretch marks crawling up her arms and down the collar of her V-neck that it was some man, or men, like me who pocketed the best years of her life and ran off with them. Cosmo Girl still gnaws on her gum, but maybe also thinks about some cheating asshole – à la yours truly – who gave her whatever it is she's here to get checked out. The baby-bump skeleton in the blood red top is still looking at me, but – even if I'm the only one who can see it – it looks like she's shaking her head. As if to say, *So sad.*

And bump. And bump.

Maybe I had her look all wrong before. It's familiar, sure, but maybe instead, it's the look Mom had at the end of every would-be stepdad. The look that followed his eyes when they stared a little too long at somebody younger, slimmer, funnier, smarter. A look she had some nights when she stayed up drinking, thinking I'd gone to sleep. Maybe

it was the look Marci wore that one night, lying next to me in the dark. The shaking head and sucked-in lips that said, there will always be men like you out there.

And bump. And bump.

I want so badly to stand up and make an announcement. *Say, listen please, you've got it all wrong. This is just a routine hygiene visit. Sure, maybe I'm not perfect, but I have never, ever laid a hand on her, cheated, or forgot a birthday. I don't even leave the toilet seat up. I want to let everyone know about the times I walked to the supermarket at 5 AM to buy Pamprin and Tampax, because her cramps don't always run on our schedule.*

And yet, in another way, fuck all that. More than proving what I've done for her, I want to share with them everything she's done for me. How it's through her I've learned to care about somebody more than I care about myself, and want more than anything for that person to be okay. I want to walk person-to-person around the room, telling them how my single mother raised me, the bone-deep distrust of men she instilled, how all of us are maybe more alike than we are different. I want to stand on my chair and scream to everybody, *Please, just relax, I'm only here to be moral support for the woman I love.*

That's when the office door grinds open and Marci emerges.

And bump. And … miss. As Stroller Kid stumbles, I grab Marci's hand and we're out the door before it stops buzzing.

The sun has dipped behind the hills, washing the sky a pale blend of pinks and blues. It's cooler outside than it was in the clinic.

"So?" I say, catching my breath. "How'd it go?"

"Oh, it went fine. My doctor was this super funny Jamaican lady. Like, as much as I was dreading it before, I'm actually kind of – oh, shoot!" She's the only person I know who says shoot, and god, do I love that.

"What's wrong?" She's stopped a couple steps back, both her and her reflected doppelgänger in the mirrored windows glancing between me and the clinic.

"We gotta go back. I forgot to grab a bag of condoms."

"It's fine," I say. "I can pick some up. Let's just go."

A man is honest, kind, and courageous, protects women, is humble, bold, moral, seeks truth, loves children and fights for what is right.

CAPTAIN BUZZ SMITH[18]

Sharpie Stones

Connor Durham wrenched the backpack out of his locker.

"Hey man," Blake said, "you ready to go?"

Connor closed the locker, and they walked down the hallway toward the exit. He pushed through the doors and headed for the sidewalk.

Blake chased him outside. "Where you headed?" he asked. "Practice starts in ten minutes. I don't wanna spend the first half hour doing push-ups."

"Then you'd better get going."

"You're not coming?"

"Sorry man. Something's come up."

Blake lifted his eyebrows. "Hey, you okay? What's wrong?"

Connor didn't answer.

Blake took a couple of steps closer and stood beside his friend. "Hey, c'mon man. You can tell me. What's up?"

Connor didn't want to talk about it, but he didn't want to keep it to himself. He looked around, checking if anyone was within earshot, and then said quietly, "Daphne's pregnant."

Blake's eyes widened. Connor glared at him, willing him not to react. Blake looked around, placed his hand on Connor's shoulder, and led him toward their neighborhood.

"How'd you find out?" he whispered.

"She told me Monday morning."

"When did she find out?"

Connor shook his head. "Not sure. I didn't have time to ask before the bell rang. Haven't really seen Daphne since. Been avoiding her, I guess."

Blake nodded. "You think she's telling the truth?"

Connor stopped and squinted at him irritably. "Yes."

"Sorry," Blake said. "How are you feeling?"

"I dunno," Connor said. "Been thinking about it all week, trying to figure that out. Scared, I guess. It's a lot of … I know I'm not ready to be a dad."

Blake nodded. "Well at least you'll be out of here by the time the baby comes."

Connor's brow furrowed. "What do you mean?"

"We'll be at college."

"I don't think I'm going to college next year."

"Sure you are, man. Playin' football. Livin' the college life. Florida State, baby! We had scouts comin' in all this fall. They know our work; they've seen us play. And it works out perfect. Daphne's still got another year of school left. Her mom won't let her go anywhere. You got an easy out."

"An easy out?"

"Yeah, from bein' a dad."

"Are you serious?"

"Yeah, I mean, if I were you I'd get out now, save her the heartache. You know, make it easier on everyone."

"Shut up."

Blake looked up at Connor. His friend's eyes were hard, unblinking, his mouth thin and level. They had been friends for a long time, but Blake had never seen Connor this angry. He waited for him to speak. No sound came. "All I meant was…."

"Shut up," Connor said. "I'm not gonna ditch my pregnant girlfriend to train for college football. I mean, the fact you would even think that I would do that. You know what, forget it. I don't have time for this. You gotta go to practice, and I'm going to Daphne's. We'll talk later." He turned and walked away.

He shouldn't have been surprised at Blake's reaction. His friend had applauded when he and Daphne had started dating; she was hot, after all. But Blake had never really understood the relationship. Connor knew him well enough that he should have seen his reaction coming,

but that didn't soften the offense. The more he thought about Blake's suggestion, the more the idea disgusted him. He crossed the street.

Connor's anger was a welcome distraction from the terror that would have otherwise dogged his journey to Daphne's, a terror that had plagued him the past week. He had played out the impending conversation a hundred different ways in his head. She would be angry with him, confused, and hurt that he had been too scared to talk to her since that morning. He had meant to, but he needed that first day to let the facts sink in. And he needed the rest of the week to begin letting go of the dream. Hopefully skipping practice would lend him some credibility.

Blake was right about one thing: Connor had wanted to play football. He was good, too, and sure he'd made a good impression in training camp that September. He recalled what it felt like watching scouts scribble on their clipboards every time the team ran a good play. He loved the rush of adrenaline that came after a catch, the mad bolt down the field, weaving around tackles, ball tucked in the crook of his arm like a treasure. And Daphne, whooping with joy and shouting his name from the sidelines.

It was all he wanted in the world right now. But it didn't matter. He couldn't go.

Connor had wandered through his classes in a daze, trying to reconcile football with fatherhood. For a moment he'd wanted to believe it wouldn't be that hard, but immediately checked the thought. He'd heard his parents talk about how jarring the change was for them when he was born. It sounded exhausting. Still, he'd spent that first evening trying to come up with a way to go to college and be a dad at the same time. He'd struggled with the problem all week, but his solutions had him making demands of Daphne that he knew would never fly. Even if he played football locally, the sport would eat up too much of his time. Daphne had to come first. Daphne and the baby.

He had tried to imagine – at home, at school, working late at the grocery store – what it would be like to be a father. No school, football or leisure time. Vomit, shit, claustrophobia, pressure, responsibility.

Connor arrived at Daphne's house and walked up the empty driveway.

Her mom wasn't home – she'd been away all week. She wouldn't know yet.

He mounted the porch and rang the doorbell. A minute passed. No response. He rang again. Finally, the door opened, and he found himself staring at the angry face of Daphne's older sister, Vicki.

"What do you want?"

"Is Daphne here?"

"Why?"

Connor hesitated. He didn't want to talk to anyone else about it. He had barely wanted to talk to Blake.

"Look, I'm not here to do anything stupid, all right? I just…. I just want to talk to her. Please?"

Vicki glowered, then opened the screen door and let him in.

"Thanks," he said, trying to sound as sincere as possible. In the kitchen, Daphne, in a tank top and sweat pants, hair tied up, was sitting at the table, staring at the fridge. Vicki walked behind him, still glaring.

Connor looked at Daphne and swallowed as he realized how easy it was to spend a week in emotional turmoil over a problem and emerge resolved to make the right choice. It was a lot different when she was sitting in front of him for the first time since he had heard the news. It made his situation all the more real. He looked at her carefully, silently. Her eyes were dead with resignation. He felt a sickening weight in his gut shoving against his conscience, like a linebacker against a line of scrimmage. He thought about how easy it would be for him to wash his hands of all this. He hated himself for it.

"Hey," he breathed.

She said nothing.

"I'm … sorry I haven't talked to you since you told me. I … I dunno, I guess I just got scared."

"You should have said something."

He paused. "Yeah. Yeah, you're right. That's no excuse. I should have talked to you about it sooner, and I didn't. That's my fault, and I'm … I'm sorry."

She relaxed in her chair a little. A good sign, Connor thought. "You tell anyone else?"

She nodded. "Two or three people."

More silence.

"C'mon. Talk to me, Daph. What are you thinking?"

She turned her head and locked her reddened eyes with his. "I'm not ready to be a mom," she said quietly.

Connor nodded. "Yeah," he said. He sat down on a nearby chair, pulled it up beside her, and slid his hand over hers. "Yeah, I know. Baby, I'm sorry. I'm so sorry this happened."

"My mom's gonna kill me," she said, trying to hold in a sob. "We don't have the money to raise another kid. And people at school are gonna know sooner or later. I can't be a mom and do school, I can't drop out, I have to go to college. Damn it, I can't...." Her head fell toward his shoulder.

He moved closer and wrapped his arm around her. He had done it a million times before, but this time felt different, like a pair of handcuffs snapping into place. A dry, dead feeling cracked across his tongue.

"I know," he said. "Me too. But I want you to listen to me, all right? It's gonna be okay. We're gonna get through this. You and me, we're gonna make it work."

She looked at him, confused. He kept talking. He was scared he might change his mind if he stopped. "We're gonna be parents, and in eight months we're gonna have a baby."

She looked up at him and shook her head. "No, you have to go to school. Florida State. Connor, you have to play football...."

"I took the time to think about it," he interrupted. "I ... skipped practice. I'm not going to Florida State. I'm not going anywhere. I'm gonna stay here. Help," he swallowed, "help raise our baby." The words tasted like concrete in his mouth.

"I can't owe you that."

"You won't owe me anything. I'm doing it. My choice."

Still, Daphne shook her head. "I can't, I can't...."

"You can," Connor countered, forcing as calm a tone as he could manage. "You and I, we're gonna do this. Together. And you know what? We're gonna rock it." He forced a smile. "We're too awesome not to. It's gonna be okay. I promise."

She paused. For a moment he was afraid that he'd made a promise he wouldn't be able to keep. Still, he thought, it had to be okay. He had

to stick with her.

"Just think about it," he said. "You have a life inside you right now. And I mean … we both know we want kids someday. Maybe that's now. Maybe one day, years from now, we'll look back, and this will be the story of the best thing that ever happened to us."

She nodded. It looked to him like she was putting on a brave face. For now, he was okay with that. He was doing the same thing.

The following Monday he walked into Coach Claiborne's office to quit the football team. It wasn't a fun conversation. The coach raised an eyebrow and asked him why.

"Do I have to give a reason?" he mumbled.

"You made a commitment at the beginning of the year to play for us, Connor, a commitment to me, Coach Braddock and every other member of this team. If you're going to quit right before finals, you'd better have a good reason for it."

Connor nodded, and stared at the tips of his shoes. "I need more hours at the grocery store."

The coach nodded. "If you need money for school, there are plenty of scholarships that'll take care of you."

"It's not for school, sir."

"All right. Then what?"

Connor didn't answer. His chest knotted. The silence rang in his ears. He hated the sound, but at this point, he knew speaking would make everything worse.

"Well," Claiborne said, sounding disappointed, "I can't force you to play."

"Thank you, sir." Connor turned to leave.

"You okay, Connor?" the coach asked. "Anything wrong?"

"I'm fine," he answered, then ducked out of the office and made for his locker.

Daphne's mother came home that evening. Daphne was reluctant to tell her, but Connor insisted it would be better to get ahead of the story and make sure she didn't feel they were keeping it from her. He tried to take the lead, shoulder the blame for their irresponsibility as

much as he could.

The kitchen rang with her mother's lengthy, curse-heavy lecture about how hard she'd tried to raise her kids right, how often she'd told them to be better than she was at that age, and how Daphne and Connor had made a mistake that threatened their future.

He told his parents a day later. He would have preferred to put it off, but he understood they would want to know why he wasn't at football practice. They took it with slow, stern silence, the sort of disapproval too strong to be put into words, the only kind he'd ever received from them since he turned thirteen. It was a disapproval topped with expectation, clear in his mother's eyes as she looked across the dinner table: *You will take care of this girl.*

For the next month, Connor divided his time between homework, the grocery store, and preparation for parenthood. He spent lunch breaks holed up in the library, as much to avoid the inevitable questions about why he'd quit the team as to get ahead in classes. The few conversations he did share with friends started to scare him, and there was always the unsettling possibility that Blake had told someone Daphne was pregnant. At work, fighting for shifts took constant haggling with his manager and coworkers, but he was making it work as best he could. When he wasn't stocking shelves or checking carts, he was doing research. He spent hours scrolling through articles about gestation and clicking through pages of X-rays, photographs, and diagrams on the internet. They helped, he realized, made it easier to be okay with being a father.

Winter break was a welcome relief. Connor didn't have to see anyone he didn't want to see. Little was said at Christmas with his family. Or Daphne's. None of them really wanted to talk about it more than they had to. Daphne's mom was embarrassed. She didn't want the rest of the family to know. Daphne told him stories about being sent upstairs some mornings to put a hoodie on over her top.

By the first week back at school from winter break, people had started talking. No one claimed to know for sure, but at lunch Thursday Connor overheard someone talking in hushed tones to a cluster of seniors

gathered around a locker as he and Daphne walked past. His first instinct was to lash out, lay into them, but he couldn't be sure they were talking about her and, even then, a shouting match or a fight would only confirm the suspicion. They knew people would find out sooner or later, but apart from the select few they'd already told, they hoped to delay the announcement as long as possible.

After work the next night, Connor went by to see how she was doing. Vicki and Daphne were standing against the counter talking when he walked in. Daphne looked like she'd been crying.

"Hey," he said quietly. She raised her hand in greeting. "Where's your mom?"

"In bed," Vicki said. "It's been a long day."

Connor nodded.

"How's it going?" he asked Daphne.

"They know."

"Who knows?"

"People at school," she said. "Somehow it got out. They know. People know I'm a teen mom."

Connor swallowed and walked over to give her a hug. "We knew that would happen sooner or later," he whispered.

Daphne pulled away and nodded. "I know," she said.

"You okay?"

"Yeah," she sniffled, "I'm okay. Um, Vicki and I have been talking, and Mom too, and I … Connor, I don't think I can do this."

"Baby, it's okay," he said. "It's gonna be okay. We're gonna make it through this together, you and me…."

"No," she interrupted. Her eyes started to water again. "No, I mean … I can't. I can't have a baby. I can't be a mother."

Connor stared at her, stunned, trying to decide what to say. "So … so what, you want to put it up for adoption?"

She shook her head again. "No, I mean … I can't have a baby."

"You … you what?"

"I thought I could, I thought I could be ready for this, that it would be okay, but I just … I can't."

"We already made an appointment," Vicki said dispassionately.

"Appointment for what?" Connor asked. "For ... for an abortion?" His chest tightened as he said the word. "You wanna kill our baby?"

Slowly, Daphne walked towards the stairs.

"Daphne," he said, following her. "Daphne please." His breath caught in his throat. "Please don't do this. If you're not willing to raise the baby, give him to someone who will." She walked softly upstairs. "I meant what I said, I'll stay here and raise it with you. I'll raise it alone if that's what it takes. Give me that at least, Daph, it's my kid too. Please. Just please don't kill this kid."

Vicki inserted herself between Connor and the staircase. "I think you should go now."

"Please, Vicki. I know you don't like me very much, but please, for the love of God, don't let her do it. That's a little kid in there, just as much mine as it is hers. At least give me a chance to talk to her out of it, please."

"Shut your mouth, Connor," she said, stepping closer to him than he was comfortable with. "It's bad enough you suckered my sister into sleeping with you, but you do not get to tell her what to do with her body. This is her decision. Not yours. Back off and get out."

He pursed his lips and looked back towards the front door. "What to do with her body," he gasped. "What to ... what, and you do? You and your mom? How is that not what you've just done?"

"Shut up."

He threw his arms up in frustration. "It's been what, about three months that I've known I might be a father, and what I want to happen to that kid is written off just because you don't like me?"

She crossed her arms. "I'm not going to force my sister into a world that'll see her as a slut six months from now. Especially when there's no guarantee she'll be stable enough to take good care of the baby when it comes."

"I'll help her!"

Vicki grunted in frustration.

"When have I ever given you a reason to believe that I won't?"

She looked away from him.

"Look. I know you've got trust issues. You've known some bad guys,

and you don't want your sister to get hurt like you were. I get that. It's why I'm glad you're her sister. I'm glad she's got you looking out for her. But if you're not willing to trust me, at least let me be the reason for that. I'm doing everything I can to make sure that kid's provided for. I'll say it was all my idea if that's what it takes. Take the fall for her pregnancy. I don't know what else you expect me to do."

"You really think the world will let you do that, Connor? She's the one who'll carry a brand on her belly. Not you. There's nothing else you can do."

"So, so what, just … just kill it? That's the solution?"

"Best one I've got," Vicki whispered.

"That's a human life in there! A little kid!"

"A clump of cells."

Connor tried to keep calm. He couldn't think of anything else to say. He walked down the hallway. His hand touched the doorknob. Then he looked back at Vicki. "What if the situation were reversed?" he said. "What if she was the one who wanted it and I was the one who wanted out? You'd call me a deadbeat. A coward. Too afraid of taking responsibility for my actions, that I left my girlfriend out in the cold with a baby because I put my plans before hers. You'd see me as a monster. Oh, but when it's the other way around – when I'm in it for the long haul, ready to put my dreams on hold, I'm just as much a monster for wanting to stick with her and do the right thing."

"So my sister's a monster now?"

"I didn't mean that. I just … "

"Get out, Durham."

He glowered. He didn't want to leave, but he knew staying would get him nowhere. He turned and left, slamming the door.

Connor didn't sleep that night. He didn't do much of anything, besides try and think of ways he might convince Daphne to keep the baby. Nothing worked. She was scared. He'd seen it in her eyes. And Vicki would interpret any encouragement, any promise, any offer he might make as a means to control her sister. There was nothing he could do.

That didn't stop him from trying. He tried talking to her several times the next week, in school and out. He didn't need to win an argument, he figured; with every attempt, the goal was always to put off

her decision. He had no success. He wrote her a letter telling her he still loved her and would hold her hand through the procedure if she wanted him to. He slipped it into her locker during the morning bell.

There was no response. She was always with someone, usually the two or three girls she'd told on day one. And neither she nor they were interested in what he had to say. At least they weren't judging her the way everyone else was, Connor thought.

He hated the way she looked at him. Or maybe it was the way that she didn't. She seemed to swing back and forth between contempt and disinterest. Mostly disinterest. With every day of silence he felt an increased gnawing on the inside – a thinning, a wasting away, like what he imagined starvation felt like. It soured most of the time he spent at school and robbed him of any joy in getting a paycheck.

It wasn't just the baby, either. He missed her. He missed telling her funny stories, anticipating which kind of laughter would follow each one. He missed the fake bickering back and forth they did in public sometimes, just to make other people uncomfortable. He missed the times she called him out for doing something stupid, just to give him the opportunity to smile and shrug his shoulders as if they both knew he was invincible. He missed the sound of her cheering him from the football field sidelines.

He sometimes walked alone in places that were special to them. When they'd first started dating, before Connor got the job at the grocery store, they'd gone on walks for hours along a creek trail running through a patch of woods. He wandered through it alone now, throwing pebbles in the creek, trying to imagine what it would be like taking his own kid there to throw pebbles. He imagined the child with every walk: a little boy, with dark hair and big brown eyes like his dad's. Stumbling along in yellow rain boots, head tilted upward everywhere he went, hoping he might unlock the secrets of the universe if he could watch closely enough. Sometimes Connor took a Sharpie and wrote baby names on the flatter, smoother stones, then threw them in.

There was no life in those walks, he realized. But he felt like it was his duty to take them.

Two more weeks. Daphne stopped wearing makeup and kept wearing

hoodies. Connor wondered if she had done it by now. He rarely saw her at school. Sometimes he would go looking for her during lunch hour, without success. She was even distant from the girls who had shunned him on her behalf. Sometimes he would pass her in the halls between classes, and he thought he saw sorrow in her eyes, hidden to anyone who wasn't looking for it.

Connor and Blake reconnected, sort of. Connor hadn't expected it, hadn't really thought about Blake much after they had their argument. He hadn't had time. Blake had begun by asking if he would still play college ball. Connor hadn't answered. It seemed wrong to go, as if going would prove he hadn't wanted to keep the baby. Or maybe if he went, it would be skipping out on the penance he had forced on himself. But he didn't think Blake would understand that.

A month and a half after he and Daphne parted, Connor was down at the creek again, throwing pebbles. He had run out of good names, and the Sharpie was lost in his backpack somewhere. The ink had gone dry.

After an hour, he saw someone, a figure in his periphery. Daphne was coming from the opposite end of the trail, wearing a black windbreaker and a thin scarf around her neck. Instead of throwing his next pebble he relaxed his arm and watched her approach. She stopped and stared at him. He stared back. A long silence.

"I miss you," she said finally.

"I miss you too," he said, nodding, turning over the pebble in his hand.

They stood in silence for a while, before she took a few steps closer and said, "I wish I hadn't done it."

Connor nodded, biting his lip in an attempt to keep from asking why. "Me too," he said.

She took a deep breath, and then asked, "Can things be okay?"

He nodded slowly, unsure he meant it. He walked towards her.

Soon he stood in front of her and she whispered, "I want to get back together."

Connor moved his hands towards her waist. He held her, and mourned for the baby he would never hold. Hot, streaming tears trickled out of his eyes. He let the unnamed pebble slip out of his hand.

JOHN BIESECKER

April 3rd

The first time your mother didn't come home, I worried about her. When it happened a second time I worried about me. The third time I spent the night staring at the red numbers of the clock, I worried about you.

She never gave us a fourth time. I haven't seen her since.

Before you go getting all upset at her for leaving us, you should know that if it wasn't for her, you wouldn't be here. Your existence came from her stubbornness. You probably share that trait, along with the blue eyes and little nose. I wonder if you look like her now. If you've got the same dirty blonde hair. The same way of talking with your eyes.

She sure picked a bad time to tell me she was pregnant. The Broncos had just lost to the Raiders by a last-second field goal. I was only eighteen, still thought the way a bunch of strangers played a game was something personal. Like their loss was my loss. So I already felt empty and pissed for what amounts to no reason.

That's when she decided to tell me. She stood by the couch with this weird look in her eye. Guess she knew what my response would be.

"I'm pregnant." I'll never forget the way she said it, head tilted up, sticking out her chin. Daring me to get pissed.

Which I did.

"How'd you let that happen? Aren't you on the pill?"

"Yeah."

It's funny. All those years of Sunday school, all those years of lessons on morality and what is supposedly right, all the things I thought I believed in, went right out the window in that little moment. First, I just

stared. Then I asked, "Are you going to take care of it?" Like you were some kind of curable condition. Something she could take two aspirin for.

That was as close as I could come to saying what I meant.

She didn't answer with anything other than that glare of hers. She spun around, stormed into the bedroom, and slammed the door. I knew her mind was set. There'd be no talking her out of it. I turned off the TV and stared at the wall. Drank the rest of my beer.

We never mentioned my suggestion again.

So you see, if she hadn't been so strong and pig-headed, you wouldn't be here. I thank her for that.

Once your mother started getting bigger, things got difficult. Not that they weren't already, two young kids playing house in that tiny apartment a thousand miles from home. But things got worse. She was not a big woman to start with, about five foot two on her tippy-toes. So toward the end of the pregnancy, she seemed as wide as she was tall. Couldn't get her jacket around her. Hell, she couldn't get *my* jacket around her.

She couldn't sleep, either, so she got cranky. I already was cranky. Had been since the moment she told me. Hell, I was scared shitless. I guess she was too; I just didn't know it then. But our playing house became too real. No longer a game, no longer pretending we were grown up, out there in the big world. It was *real*. We tried to figure out how we would buy a crib and diapers and all the things we never knew we would need.

I worked landscaping in those days, throwing dirt with a shovel, which didn't exactly pay a lot. She worked as the evening desk clerk at the Hotel Boulderado, helping rich folk get checked into rooms bigger than our entire apartment. She worked right up to the day her water broke. Strong woman. I want you to know that. She had strength in her. More than I ever had. Or ever will.

That first night we took you home I'll remember till the day I die. The wind blew like crazy, your typical Colorado spring. Not real cold, but enough that we were in a panic, had you bundled up till you were just this tiny face peering out with unfocused eyes, a round ball of pink

blankets. We put you in that car seat I found at a garage sale. It was stained, but still worked. I installed it in a hurry, with your mother standing in the wind, holding you. I don't think I did it quite right, now that I look back on it. Probably could say that about a lot of things.

We got home, driving ten miles an hour the whole time. Your mother sat in the back with you. Talked to you, soft and tender. I remember watching her in the rearview, catching glimpses of her smile, her hair down across her blue eyes. She never looked up, only watched you.

That night, you cried. And cried. And *cried*. To the point your mother cried. I didn't cry. Not because I didn't want to, Lord knows I was overwhelmed, but because I had some crazy idea that being a man meant not crying. Now I cry at cheesy commercials. Shows you what thirty some years and three more kids will teach you.

They never mentioned swaddling at the hospital. You'd think they would have said something to two young, wide-eyed, new parents. But they didn't. Probably figured we would have *our* parents around to help. That being so young there was no way we were doing it by ourselves. No way we *should* have been. But our parents were parents in name only. Neither your mom nor I grew up with any idea what the word really meant. Your mother was partially raised by her aunts, bouncing around from relative to relative in her teen years before we ran away. My parents were worse. I'd rather not tell you about them.

Anyway, it was the three of us against the world. You, me, and your mother. It tied us together. Made us closer in a warm, wonderful way.

At least at first.

After about a month, she started sleeping through your cries more. Or she pretended to. She'd tap me on the shoulder, then roll over with a pillow over her head. And after work, I'd come home to find your diaper overflowing, her sitting on the couch, staring at nothing. I'd yell, she'd yell. It got so bad we hardly spoke. She wouldn't talk and I didn't know what to say. I had no patience. No empathy for her. That probably didn't help matters, so it's my fault, too. Worse, she stopped talking to you. Stopped the soft, high voice I would hear in the middle of the night as she fed you. Stopped the long looks, standing over your crib, just

smiling. Stopped the kisses on your forehead. Stopped being a mommy.

I didn't know why. I'd never heard of postpartum depression.

Then came the first night she didn't come home from work. She was still gone in the morning. I had to call in sick so I could stay home with you. I called her work. I called her friend Michelle. Nobody knew where she was.

She stumbled in the next evening, just past supper. I was too relieved to be angry, but she scared me. The way she loved on you, slurring, with big, exaggerated movements. After she fell asleep on the couch I pried you from her arms, brought you into the bed with me. Built a wall of pillows around one side of you, me on the other.

Everything went back to normal. I didn't ask what happened, and she never volunteered the information. We just pretended it never happened. As if it were that easy.

Then she started not being there, even when she was there. About a week later, she didn't come home again. I remember sitting in that old, wooden rocker we found in the dumpster and cleaned up. Holding you after your bottle till you fell asleep. I couldn't sleep. I stared at the clock on the microwave – you could see it from the living room, the damn apartment was so small – too angry to sleep. She was leaving me to do all the heavy lifting. You and I slept in the chair, through two feedings, till I had to go to work.

I didn't know what to do. I called in sick again. Got a warning about missing too much time. Summer was starting. Landscapers' busy time. They couldn't afford to get behind. I couldn't afford to lose my job. I talked it over with the old lady in the apartment below us, about what I should do. She loved you, was nice enough, but had seven cats and smelled like pine litter and cigarettes. She smoked a *lot*. I didn't want to leave you with her, but didn't know what else to do.

After one morning with her, I ended up paying for two days of daycare at a place that would take you early in the morning. It cost me about three days worth of wages. Three days of wages for two days of daycare.

Your mother came back on a Thursday morning. Didn't say a thing to me. Or to you. Just walked in the door and went to bed. You were

already in the crib sleeping, so I went to work. When I got home she acted like nothing had happened. She had given you a bath. Dressed you up in some pink onesie with a kitty on the front she must have bought that day. Even gave me a giant kiss.

For the next week, she was the mother I always thought she would be. She worked hard at making you healthy and happy. Got a book on parenting from the library, would read it at the desk when her work was slow. We even started talking again. Things felt right. Like we were a family. Like we were going to make it.

But then she started getting cranky again. I should have suggested help. Maybe some counseling. I didn't know that stuff existed. But I should have done something and I didn't. And then she started talking to me less again. Talking to you less again. I'd come home to dirty diapers and dirty dishes and a hungry you.

I knew it was coming. The night she wouldn't come home. I watched her fold in on herself. Withdraw. From me. From you. From us. I would lie beside her, watching through the missing section of blinds as the moths incinerated themselves in the porch light. I wanted to say something to her. *Anything.* Maybe it's all my fault, because I never did.

And then she left and never came home. A Thursday. You spent Friday downstairs again, inhaling God-knows how much secondhand smoke. I enrolled you in a daycare. I knew she wasn't coming back. I didn't even try to find her.

Between daycare and diapers, you cost more than I made. There's help out there, but I didn't know about it then. I didn't know anything. I managed to get food stamps for formula, but everything else still cost a fortune. I started running up my credit card.

I'd come home and clean you up. Feed you. Fall asleep beside you on your little play mat with those things that hung down, the blue hippo with the big smile, the purple elephant. You *loved* that elephant. But I'd fall asleep and wake up an hour later with you crying, half rolled off the mat, with a quarter that must have fallen out of my pocket in your hand. You could have easily choked on it. Scared me half to death.

Then one morning you were sick. Really sick. Coughing like there was a tornado in your throat. It was scary to hear such a noise coming

from such a little girl. I thought you had pneumonia. You coughed so hard you couldn't breathe. I panicked. Didn't know what else to do, so I drove you to the hospital. They said you had the croup, that you'd be okay. The doctor was some old lady – at least she seemed old to me at that age, she was probably forty – who looked at me with this weird look. I knew what she was thinking, *what's this teenage boy doing with a baby?* She asked where your mother was, and I lied, said she was working. She asked if I had any help. I lied again, said my parents lived in town, came over almost every day. She stared a long time at me, then patted you on the forehead and laid you in my arms.

Then charged me $700.

We came home and sat on the toilet with the shower going full blast, filling the room with steam. You coughed. Pinched up your face like an angry old man and cried. I cried. I cried because you cried. I cried because I didn't know how I was going to take care of you. If I *could* take care of you.

You finally fell asleep out of sheer exhaustion. I laid you in your crib and collapsed on the couch. I remember I turned on the news. And an answer came to me. They were talking about some law they had just passed in Colorado. The "fire-station law" or something. For people like me. Drop off your infant, no questions asked. They'll take care of it. See to it that it is put in a foster home, put up for adoption. Everything.

I saw it on the news, and knew what I had to do.

That night, I bundled you up. Pink fuzzy pajamas covered with tiny blue kittens. Put you in the car seat. I waited till the middle of the night, thinking there wouldn't be any people around. No one to see the scared kid sneaking through the dark with a baby in a car seat.

It wasn't easy, Audrey. I stood near the front of the firehouse, in the dark, outside the reach of the lights, wondering what I should do. I probably stood there twenty minutes. Three times I started walking back to the car with you. Then you started coughing. That deep, racking cough that made me feel helpless. Useless. Like I was a teenage boy in way over his head. Like every thought that doctor had was right. So I kissed you on the forehead and put the car carrier on the walk in front

of the door. And ran like hell.

Half way home I stopped the car. Pulled out the base to the car seat and threw it as far as I could down this weed-covered embankment. I stood and watched it roll to a stop, stark in the moonlight. I realized I was no better than your mother. I ran when the going got tough. I abandoned my baby.

Who does that?

Did I do it to give you a better life? I tell myself that, but sometimes I'm not so sure. Maybe I did it to give myself a better life. An easier life anyway, cause it sure as shit wasn't better, sitting in that quiet apartment, by myself. Wondering.

Took me a few years to sort things out. As much as I could anyway. A few years to deal with what I'd done. Not get over it. I never got over it. Just to learn to live with it without alcohol.

I still have your picture, you know. One little picture your mother took of me, holding you. You're asleep, with these little round cheeks, like an angel. I look exhausted. But happy.

You're probably wondering why I'm writing this. So am I. I'll never be able to send it. I wouldn't know where to. Hell, I don't know your name, if it's still Audrey. Or where you live. I just thought you should know that we loved you. We really did. I still do. I would love to find out that you're happy and well-adjusted, with a little family of your own. Maybe an accountant or something. Not doctor or lawyer, just something stable and decent. Something better than had you stayed with a teenage dad.

I'd just like to know – after thirty-five years of waking up in the middle of the night, of celebrating your birthday in my head because even my wife and kids don't know about you – did I do the right thing?

MICHAEL MORGAN

A Premeditated Starving

When the teenaged girl's physician joined us, I knew it was no ordinary transport to another hospital. At first I thought he wanted to keep us on our toes, but he ignored us. He hovered over his tiny patient. She was too tiny for a 17-year-old. He watched the girl as we loaded the gurney. We counted "one, two, three" and lifted her with precision and gentleness. That was easy to do because the gurney was so light it felt empty.

The elderly doctor climbed into the ambulance and sat on the bench next to me.

"Riding along?" I asked.

He shook his head.

A car with a bad muffler annoyed us with a rough idle. To shut out the noise my partner closed the rear doors from outside. He went to the driver's seat and put the key in the ignition, leaving it off while the doctor struggled to make small talk with the young woman. He did not tell us how long he would be on the bench and we did not ask. Men grow quiet when we sense problems peculiar to women.

Our patient had a brown, pretty face that would have been prettier had it not been gaunt. Safety straps crossed the linen and blanket, slack because of her size. She made little downward movements to bury herself. That prompted the doctor to say, "In no time at all you'll be back on your tennis team."

She wriggled deeper into the stretcher pads. "I feel secure here," she said. Except for her head, she was ensconced in bedding; all we could see was her face and the long, brunette hair that flowed over the sterile covers.

The doc chatted with her, smiled, and kept his crinkled eyes focused on her face with laser beam intensity. He did not look at me, but pointed in my direction, so the girl glanced my way. "He's a really nice guy."

He didn't know me from Adam. I was 21, longhaired and looked young for my age. Nonetheless, he passed the ball to me.

In life as in sports, men do not need to look at each other to pass the ball. It was my job to catch it and move it forward. If you fumble the ball in sports, your athletic reputation diminishes. You can restore your reputation with a successful catch later on. If you drop the ball in life, you don't get a second chance. Though opponents in sports may be your teammates in another game, opponents in life do not play games. This day my opponent was *anorexia nervosa*, an eating disorder that, unchecked, leads to starvation.

After the doc hurled the ball into my chest, he opened the doors. The muffler racket had ceased. There was a hush. He turned and managed to speak some final words of comfort to his patient. I listened to the softness of his voice, but heard no words. I was too busy squeezing the ball into my chest and into my heart. No way was I going to drop it.

The doc closed the doors, and I locked them from inside. My partner started the engine and the journey began. It was spring and he avoided the potholes, which was not an easy thing to do in Detroit. Some never got patched and could shake an ambulance and the people inside. We swerved a few times, but it was a smooth transport.

The girl stared at the corner cabinetry stocked with white towels and bandages. She scrunched up her nose.

"We'll get to the hospital in no time at all," I said. I tried to make my voice sound reassuring like the doctor's, but it sounded forced.

The girl did not reply. The juxtaposed doe-like eyes and sharp cheekbones revealed the indignity of her medical condition. Not much was known about *anorexia nervosa* in the late 1970s. Most men had never heard of it. Worse, we couldn't wrap our minds around it. It was impossible to hold onto hunger. How could thin young ladies premeditate starving?

Music is a useful topic in the back of an ambulance. To break the ice, I rattled off the names of some contemporary teen heartthrobs. I schooled myself with music magazines so that I could rely on all genres

for all sorts of patients. Many disliked sports, but almost all, male and female, wanted to teach me music appreciation.

She was beyond the teen idol phase and into Detroit native, Stevie Wonder.

"When you get well, you can see him live in concert," I said.

She smiled at me.

"Maybe you're ready for a sandwich," I said. "When we reach the hospital…."

Her smile crumpled into grimace as she gazed off.

My shoulders tensed. When women suffer, men lose courage, which is often replaced by exasperation.

The girl should not fear food. She should complain about the greasy grub for lunch in her high school cafeteria, and she should pig out on chocolate fudge brownies at night. In the morning she should huddle in a corner of homeroom locked in a race with the bell to squeeze in a new day's gossip. She should decide which girls to invite to her next slumber party. In place of cot straps in an ambulance, she should be strapped up in a bikini at a beach flaunting her suntan. Her skin was the type to achieve a Coppertone hue. She was the girl from Ipanema. She should shop at the mall with a gaggle of girls – or shop at the mall alone, turning the heads of young men. She should babysit some lucky little kids. They should play Twister and make "ants on a log" with raisins, cream cheese and celery.

"You should eat some food," I told her.

"I know," she said in a flat voice.

"What's your favorite song from Stevie Wonder's new album, *Songs in the Key of Life*?" I asked.

Her smile returned. "As," she answered. She half-sang some lyrics in a fragile voice. "Listen to the fade-out at the end," she instructed. "It goes on and on." She hummed the ending to "As" three times. Her voice strengthened as a cause and consequence of music.

She turned her head from side to side when I talked about Joni Mitchell's album, *Court and Spark*. She firmly told me why Joni Mitchell couldn't hold a candle to Stevie Wonder. My agreement broadened her smile.

If she does not eat, she will not be able to flash that smile. Doesn't

she know how lovely her smile is? She will never dress up for the high school prom. She will never wear a corsage or slow dance with her date. She will never walk the stage at her graduation ceremony. She will never flip a tassel to the left side of her graduation cap. She will never work part-time jobs to help with college. She will never charm customers into buying her recommended music, the latest fashion accessory, or the special of the day.

"You'll never see Stevie Wonder in concert if you don't eat," I told her.

"I know," she said.

She flicked her hair off her pointy chin, revealing the plucked chicken skin of her neck. She was at once adorable and repulsive to me. Her illness was a decision, not an infection. Any fool could see she regretted it.

This fool had to make a last-ditch attempt to compel her to fill a plate with food. Why?

Because she must eat for the energy to choose which battles were worth fighting and the energy to fight them. She must appreciate constructive criticism from her tennis coach. She must mentor a younger girl and teach her to challenge barriers without declaring war on men. She must fall in and out of love. She must experience the bitter sweetness of kiss and make up. She must forgive others. She must find the strength to forgive herself so she can eat again.

"You must eat some food," I said.

I waited. "Okay?" I pleaded.

She did not reply.

We arrived at the hospital and I pulled the blanket up around her neck. That precious smile reappeared.

"Thank you," she whispered. The ambulance stopped. The smile flickered out.

The last thing I remember that day was sitting in the ambulance cab staring over my shoulder through the interior window at the empty gurney in the back. I wondered what the old doctor would have thought. I knew I had not dropped the ball. There was never a ball in the first place. The only thing that had been passed between two men, one old and one young, was ignorance over a pretty girl starving herself to death.

A man is the face behind the mask in your worst nightmare, but also, ironically, your protector.

<div align="right">HALEY ZILBERBERG[19]</div>

Along with all the terrible things men do, we do great things, too, like rescuing people from the terrible things other men try to do to them.

<div align="right">JOEL STEIN[20]</div>

Michael Estabrook

It's Always About the Girl

I'm afraid I'm beginning to live more and more
 in my head, back 50 years into the past
 back in high school and college:

taking the prettiest girl in the school on a real date
 to a Duprees concert, asking her to go steady
 with me on that very first date

stealing my first kiss from her in the auditorium spotlight booth
 during a rehearsal of "The Sound of Music"
 nearly missing her mouth but a kiss is still a kiss

honored that she sang "I've Got a Lot of Living to Do"
 on stage to a photo of me for her talent portion
 of the New Jersey Junior Miss Pageant

holding her hand, carrying her books
 so the other guys know
 she's my girl

not even having to fight this punk
 because as he was smirking while I was warning him

to leave my girlfriend the hell alone, two
of my tough-guy friends came out of nowhere
and slammed him up against the wall

backing Mr. Smart Alec Popularity track star Donnie
 into a corner of the locker room, advising him
 to keep his fucking hands off her and
 stop sending her notes in class
 because she's my girl

coming back to school two weeks too early
 after my spinal fusion surgery
 so the other guys would know
 she wasn't fair game
 because I was still around

taking classes in Shotokan Karate just in case Don
 the big football star who'd become her favorite study-buddy
 decided to study something other than math

finding a college
 only four miles from her college
 when her father said we couldn't go to the same school

 so I could stay close to her
 and hold onto her
 to this day.

3. Men & Sports

Men are competitive.[21] Some say competition is the overriding male impulse, begun shortly after we emerge from Mom's womb and start competing with Dad for her love.[22] Parents who have raised both boys and girls know competitiveness is in their sons' genes, pointing to their wrestling and roughhousing natures.

Men compete in our speech, ideas, work, and video gaming, in our blunt-elbowed ribbing of our men friends, and overzealous rooting for our children from the sidelines of their sporting events.[23] We compete for mates by competing for money and its avatars: fast cars, bright motorcycles, mega-yatches.[24] We compete with our brains, wit, charm, humor, and of course with brawn, our muscles.

Most publicly we use our muscles in playing sports, though men can get exercised just watching and rooting as well.

Watching sports can be a consuming passion for some guys: catching the home-team's home games; travelings to training camp; hanging at the sports bar to see the away games, screaming the team on. A sports fanatic's passions can become unhinged. Some fans get tattooed with their favorite team's logo,[25] branding themselves for life with love of a franchise.

Playing sports is who some men are, and through the centuries women have hero-worshiped winning sportsmen; triumphant male athletes from all cultures are successful with the opposite sex.[26] It's strong incentive to win. The high school quarterback, star of his team, dating the captain of the cheerleading squad, beauty of her school ... I witnessed that in senior high and imagine most of us have seen similar beauty–brawn matchups.

Some men especially enjoy playing contact sports, crashing into other guys, testing our brute strength, sharpening our skills, dulling our reactions to pain. But playing contact sports can have consequences. Even winners are carried off the field, sometimes concussed, sometimes dead.[27] It's a gamble some guys are willing to take: betting

health[28] on playing a game of football, for instance. But a young man, running on testosterone, sees no gamble, is blind to the risk. A young man sees an adventure, a test of strength and skill on a gridiron with a goal line.

Joel Peckham has lived football and now writes it for us. His story, "Phys-ed," is a meditation on the sport, but also on his boy-to-man journey, his father, his family name, and more. May I suggest that mothers whose sons are playing football or considering playing football might benefit from reading Joel's story.

Bill Harley's "One-on-One" follows with a courtside view to a basketball game between a boy and a man, played silently and communicated loudly.

Finally we hear Paul Hostovsky's profound "Conversations of Men" about the Boston Bruins, that city's ice hockey team, conversations that take place ... well that's the play, and Hostovsky wouldn't want me to give it away.

MEN & SPORTS
SUIT UP!

OR
GRAB THE CHIPS

Joel Peckham's "Phys-Ed" is both personal essay and story about masculinity, boys' competitions on-field and off-, knocking a man down, dominating him, identity, fitting in, family, sons and fathers, sex, beer, and rock 'n' roll. He tumbles these subjects in our minds and sieves them for his truths, covering as much guy-territory as any piece in this anthology.

In the tradition of the personal essay, we see Peckham struggling to answer the questions he poses himself. In the tradition of the story, he brings the tale back to its beginning.

JOEL PECKHAM

Phys-Ed

1

No one taught me what to do. I clamped my fist and eyes, and reached back, flailing, pulling as if I could tear the curtain of the New England sky down on us all.

I remember fear, the cries of gulls and Beneventi's high-pitched girlish giggle. The cold stinging rain and the sense of waiting. And Kozak shoving me on the shoulder, then the chest, then backing away like a boxer, bouncing on his toes – his bright red hair, the stubble on his chin, the rise and fall of his Adam's apple, but not what he was saying. There was a soundless roar, something building in the back of my head, my fingers closing to a fist.

Every school has a bully. Mine had two – Sean Kozak and Ian Beneventi – and they were at it again. Torturing me. We'd been running an obstacle course, a kind of fitness test, and Beneventi and Kozak took turns harassing me as we ran around the cones, Kozak trying to sweep my feet from beneath me, Beneventi sprinting up and shoving me, trying to knock me down. I remember their laughter – the same sounds I'd heard many times in middle school when Kozak would wind up his long, skinny arms and slap me in the middle of the back or Beneventi would kick the back of my heel so it would fly up and I would stumble into the kids in line at the lunch counter. One time, Beneventi pushed me down a steep flight of concrete steps. I remember him laughing in the echoes. He didn't even try to slip away but stood there, proud, beaming.

On the obstacle course, I was making it more difficult. I was chubby

but had good balance and was quick when scared – and I was scared – but it was also weirdly fun, like the thrill of driving too fast on a dirt road in the dark. Kozak was slow, too big for his body, and I hopped and cut, leaped and scurried to the finish, first in the class, just a little winded and surprised.

When the other kids began to disappear behind the large green doors, Kozak and Beneventi blocked my way. Mr. Holt, the ex-military phys-ed teacher, gave us a long look, sighed and shook his head. I still remember that – the dark square, the flash of his blue tracksuit, the click of a door closing, and the finality of death, my death. Except for Eric, I was alone. Little Eric Ross, trudged toward us, terrified, his hands pushed deep into the pockets of an oversized blue sweatshirt He took his place like a second in a duel, stopping two feet behind me, saying nothing. Kozak sized me up, gave a push on my shoulder. Pushed again. Looked over at Beneventi. Smiled brightly. Happy.

I got lucky. I was terrified, and it was more a spasm than a punch. But then there was the crack of cartilage, and through Kozak's trembling hands, so much blood.

When I start to think we are driven more by fear and anger, more the product of our terrors than of our love, I think of Eric's arm around my back.

"Holy shit, Joel, what the hell was that?"

And I wept. We wept. Then laughed. Then wept.

"We're fucked," he said.

"I know," I said. "I'm fucked."

<p style="text-align:center">2</p>

"Tell it again," my son would shout from the back seat, asking for his favorite story, one of the few from my childhood I ever told. Sometimes I would add a detail to fill in a scene or amplify a point, but it was basically the same each time. Sometimes he'd ask me to demonstrate the punch, that stiff-armed windmill angling right to left, the sideways tilt of the fist, slicing awkwardly down. And he would laugh in surprise and delight that such a punch could ever land and that *I* threw it. I'm

not the kind of father who would teach his son to box in the basement or watch mixed martial arts on Friday nights. But I'm still built like the defensive end I was in college, and though I've gained a little weight, I work out each day. My arms and shoulders stretch the fabric of my work shirts and the muscles in my back still fold and flex. I'm vain enough to want to look and feel strong. Because the truth is, I am all bluff. I have thrown two punches in my life, and that was one of them. I know this story makes me a hero to him, that the point about my fear is mostly lost. How I was backed into a corner, how I didn't have a choice. Not like Eric, who came to my side willingly, insanely driven by some code of loyalty I did not deserve.

Eric and I had only a few years left together. I sometimes wonder if we would have remained friends and if we had, if I might have made different choices, aspired to different things. That was before I found my way to the gym and girls. Back then we were both nerds who liked *Doctor Who* and *Star Wars*.

To our surprise, Kozak and Beneventi never killed either of us, though we were certain death waited every day as we left the bus for the five months until summer, lurking behind an open locker, in a boys-room stall or the bus stop. Sometimes I would wake screaming from nightmares of Beneventi and Kozak taking turns punching me bloody in front of the entire school. But the days passed without incident. And when the summer was over, all of them were gone, Eric to private school and Beneventi to Xavarian, a Catholic trade school in Braintree. As for Kozak, his family moved down the road to Canton. I wouldn't see his face again for two more years.

When I think of them now my memory is kinder to Kozak. Beneventi was vicious, rabid, and skittered through the hallways of our lives, never moving in a straight line, pitching from side to side, pinching girls, knocking books from skinny arms, inflicting pain for its own sake. He liked hurting people and did so randomly. I don't know what his limits were or if he had them, and when I try to imagine the man he'd become, I shudder for the people in his life: his children, if he had them. What pleasure did the man seek out, what damage did he do once he had access to the weapons and resources of adulthood? I don't think

a kid like that can change. When a child learns to take pleasure in the pain of others, he is close to lost.

Though I didn't know his family or his life outside school, I imagine much of Beneventi's need to be a cruel and violent kid stemmed from his need to prove something to himself. We all felt that. Whatever differences I had with the other boys, each one of us was measured, sized up against each other and our fathers and the action heroes we watched on Sunday afternoons – men with guns and blunt-force, monosyllabic names like Clint and Chuck and Bruce, tough guys who drove tough cars, speaking only when they had to. Women and sex were not pursued but part of their environment, their gravity. They were powerful and cool, seething with pheromones. You came to them when you had to, sought them out, or backed away, hid from them in fear, sometimes both. And except for Schwarzenegger or Stallone whose voices we'd mock when headed to the restroom, these men weren't "ripped" or "jacked." They had chest hair, grit and scars.

Still, though I was aware of those big-screen gods, I didn't need them for a model. Mine lived at home. Most memories I have of my father in those days smell like cut grass on a spring morning. They form like puffs of breath in the cold. He is huge, stalking the sideline of a football field or brooding in the dugout, his ice-blue eyes staring under a baseball cap pulled low. He is tense, like a coiled spring, and when a player makes an error or an official a bad call, he explodes, leaping up suddenly to blaspheme like a sailor. *"Godddamnit, Jesus Christ, what the hell is wrong with you?"* Or he is standing on the pitcher's mound, flannel sleeves pushed up, darting baseballs toward me in the early April cold. "Head down, Joel, you can't hit what you can't see. Come on, stay in there, I'll only hit you if I want to."

Or he is standing above me in late autumn. I am lying on my back on the dewy grass at Ames Street playground, strapped loosely into shoulder pads, helmet, football pants. My hands grip the earth. I can feel the other boy's helmet touching mine, hear his breathing rise and fall, see the gray sky broken into squares by the grid of my face mask. The drill is fairly simple. Two boys, one a blocker, one a tackler, lie down on the ground between two tackling dummies. A runner takes a football five

yards back and at the coach's signal, must run through that corridor. This drill is a one-on-one test of quickness, strength, ferocity. You must scramble to your feet and beat your "man" as the other boys watch, nervous and quiet.

A quick bleat of a whistle, then my father's voice, starting soft and low. "Down." Then a bit louder, drawn out slowly. "Set." What I always remember in that brief pause is terror, fear, shame. How much I hated football. How badly I wanted to get up, walk away, tearing off my uniform as I strode toward the chain link fence, leaving shoulder pads, arm pads, elbow pads behind me in a trail, to swing open the gate and slam it hard behind me in a satisfying clank.

Before each game, from Pop Warner through high school and college, I would throw up in the locker room. It was my ritual, standing over the commode in uniform, helmet tucked beneath my left arm, right hand gripping the top of the stall's partition. It wasn't that I wasn't good. I was fast off the line, undersized for a lineman but explosive, with what a coach would call a good motor. I started on offense and defense in high school, was a captain my senior year, making the Associated Press all-star team that season. But part of what made me good was terror. In that pause between the drawled out "Set" and "Go," I felt the adrenalin build, spidering along my spine, fanning across my shoulder blades – fight or flight. And despite my fantasies, flight was not an option.

My father was a three-sport athlete in high school and an all-American catcher in college. In the little Massachusetts town where I grew up he was a legend. People loved or hated or feared him, sometimes all at once. Carved into the bathroom stalls in anger that read like lust amid the phone numbers of girls who would do this and the names of boys who liked that, I'd read my father's name etched into the metal in rust: "Joel Peckham sucks! Fuck Joel Peckham!" I loved my father, but I got it. He wasn't a man you "liked" and he didn't seem to care very much. He once told me, "If everybody likes you, you probably have no character" – still, I believe, one of the wisest sentences ever spoken. He had no patience for people who chose to do the wrong thing when right was clear. And for him, it was mostly clear. He inspired strong

reactions. With jet-black hair, a square chin, and a presence that could push air out of a room, he seemed larger than he was, too large to be a high school guidance counselor and baseball coach. Even when he was assisting someone else – offensive coordinator for the football team or JV basketball – he seemed outsized, like a very large man forced into a skinny suit. When those teams didn't win, anonymous letters would come in saying he should take over. It sometimes hurt his friendships.

To his credit, my father was not self-consciously macho. A trained counselor who read poetry and who drove through the 1970s in a VW bus with an enormous sunflower decal on the side, he never seemed to need to prove his manhood or pressure others to do so. Though he could be brutally harsh on his players, I can't remember him ever emasculating them. Unlike my other football and baseball coaches growing up, he never told a child that he threw or hit "like a girl," never called anyone a "pussy," "homo," or "fag."

There were no shortcuts with my father. Where other boys could prove their manhood by hitting the gym and working their abs, lying about sexual adventures, telling dirty jokes in the locker room or by ruining someone's dental work in the visitors parking lot opposite the high school, I had to live up to something more abstract and complex, something bound up in concepts of power that involved visceral sexual appeal but also intelligence, raw emotion and emotional restraint.

My father combined a potent combination of explosive anger *and* tenderness. What mattered to him wasn't about being a man, but being a Peckham, being part of his family, living up to the expectations he set for himself and for us.

I often think my image of him, the myth of my father, was driven as much by those around me as by anything I saw in him. The image of my father as a man, as "The Man," like all images, was based on what people saw in the glimpses they caught in the high school corridors and on ball fields. Images and symbols are representative though, and as such they both expand and reduce their subjects. When a man comes to represent something, he immediately grows in stature, becoming an object of lust or fear, admiration or envy. But he also shrinks, his personality simplified for easy definition and use, a

cartoon of himself, reduced to his most repeatable characteristics – a steady gaze, a lifted chin, a slow swagger, shoulders squared.

My best friend, Neil, loved to impersonate his tilt of the head when he talked, his wide kick of the infield dirt when angry, his heavy Boston accent: "Jeeeeeesuz Joel, what the hell ah yah doin'?" And I laughed with them, at him, but uncomfortably. As much as I told everyone who would listen that I was "nothing like my father," and to stop calling me "Jo Jo," short for Joel Jr. ("Joel, it's Joel"), I secretly enjoyed being a junior, being *this* man's son, The Man's son.

Even when I try to focus on the complicated, fragile elements of his personality, I feel myself watching him as if he were in a scene from an old noir film. Identity slips and changes, not over time, but in a moment, like a halfback turning on a dime. And masculinity as a concept, as cultural currency, as a way of understanding how boys and men should find their way through the world, is fluid and messy while seeming, at the same time, rigid and inescapable. There's little evidence to prove any biological basis for traits we often identify as masculine, but masculinity feels essential to the person experiencing it even as he struggles after its unattainability. Certainly it seems obvious that the fact of male biology – the testosterone, the adrenaline rushes, the requirement of penetration to achieve sexual intercourse, the phallus etc. – all seem to naturally lead to traits of strength, power, violence and anger. But I'm always nervous about things that *seem,* ideas that move from assumption to assumption with only the appearance of reason and logic. It's an unsafe structure on which to build a man.

What I as a heterosexual white American male can say about masculinity, is that the ideal man is a myth we create and recreate every day out of our fathers, celebrities, leaders, the very language we use. We construct the concept through association and opposition. What's not feminine (read soft, weak), and what is most like the powerful and attractive men we see or know at any point in time, is masculine. So masculinity is mythological, which is not to say that it is in any way unreal – any more than my image of father was unreal. When I say that, I feel sorry for him. It must be exhausting to have a real, flawed, human being under all of that.

Sometimes I believe we're all animals trying to be human, expected to be angels. The few who are asked to be gods bear a heavy burden. For psychological purposes the myth is real in the same way hope, longing, love and greed are real. It operates as a fundamental part of our psychology, as part of what we want, and know we are supposed to want, have, and be.

3

Most of what I learned about being a man back then came from watching my father, and my sense of inadequacy came from a belief that I could never live up to the man I saw in him. But that wasn't the only source. Very few boys really see or understand their fathers beyond their own image of them. For all the public service announcements about how parents should talk to their kids about sex, alcohol and drugs, we learn most about what we know or think we know about the adult world, not from our parents or television, but from each other: from our friends, to whom we can confide desires and longings, from whom respect and admiration are more easily won.

Peer pressure is more powerful than parental expectation because our friends are usually not asking us to do things that are difficult. At parties, in locker rooms, on buses on the way home – places where adults enter only briefly – kids propel each other, encourage each other to go down that alley, get in that car, turn off those lights and do things we are curious about. Actions that lie beyond the line of what is allowable – sex, drinking, breaking curfew, cheating – take little courage and even less encouragement, just the suggestion that we might not be caught and might not be alone in those desires.

When others participate – when a group becomes a mob – individual ideas, words and thoughts, consciousness and conscience, fall away. Everybody's doing it. No one is responsible. To a young man or woman, crossing that line feels like freedom, feels illicit and taboo. Tell any child about the one thing they can't do, on pain of eternal damnation, excommunication and family shame, and it will become all the kid can think about.

I've been an athlete all my life. Every Saturday and Sunday afternoon, I watch the games on television. I love the drama of team sports, the strategy, tension, beauty and grace. Yes there is violence, a barely contained surge. It's mesmerizing, entertaining, sometimes even artful. There are rules and chaos, power and finesse. I played the game from six years old to twenty-one. I could say I hated it, and I did much of the time. I could say I played because I felt I had to, or was afraid how my quitting would upset my family or my friends. And I can tell you about the nausea, fear, and sometimes rage that drove me off the line, crashing into bodies, through bodies. But I know my reasons for playing were more complex. There were times when I enjoyed it. I still remember the sheer thrill of contact, the pleasure of knocking a stranger on his back, then holding him there for a second, making him look me in the eyes before I let him up. I find myself gleefully recalling the times I hit another player with a forearm "shiv" across the face mask or came in through the line clean to square up on a running back. There is joy in feeling your momentum carry you through another person, hitting him so cleanly in the chest that you barely feel it. Sometimes when I hit someone hard enough he'd whimper as he dropped.

The ugly truth is, sometimes it felt good to hurt someone, to beat someone that fundamentally. And the fact that most of the time I didn't know my opponent made the violence impersonal. The fact that it was part of the game and within the rules, morally unobjectionable. I liked being good at an unquestionably tough game. I liked working out and seeing the muscles grow on my shoulders and chest. I liked how my T-shirts stretched around my arms. I grew guns. I was ripped, stacked.

I was a monster.

For a kid who was mercilessly picked on in junior high by boys *and* girls for being fat and shy, for a child so completely in the shadow of his father, the respect I felt from peers for being captain of the football team – the sudden interest of girls, the pats on the shoulder at the barber shop – were confusing but also thrilling. It didn't matter that the girls I liked – dancers, writers, "theater chicks" – weren't impressed by any of it. It hardly mattered that I couldn't wait for the season to end and spent

most minutes on the field checking the clock, wishing seconds could tick by faster. It didn't matter that I felt like a fraud. At least I belonged.

I was looked up to.

Until I entered the locker room, that is. Because I couldn't pull it off completely. Couldn't speak the words or play the role. For every rousing half-time Knute Rockne-esqe speech I heard, for every prayer for strength made in a circle on one knee, there are, in those dank spaces slick with condensation, those bright metal surfaces, tile, concrete floors, and steam smelling of sweat, a thousand words no mother wants to hear directed at her child, or worse, come out of his mouth. It was in the locker room where I'd hear what every girl in school would and would not do and with whom and how many times, where I'd listen to my fellow captains scream at each other in the middle of a loss: "Are we just going to bend over and take it like fags, like women?" Where overweight kids and freshman were called bitches as in, "You're my bitch today, fat boy."

If hidden video cameras were put in football locker rooms across America and the footage played back for every mother to watch, football would no longer exist. As I say that, I also know that moment is not so very far off. Every child with a cell phone has a chance to blow the cover off, open the door. It will happen.

I wish I could say that, having been bullied, I stepped in to stop the bullies. But it was years before I developed the courage to act, to do the right thing without worrying about how those actions implicated me. That kind of courage, the kind Eric had, the kind that seemed not only to be about loyalty but about integrity, was beyond me because, like most young men, I didn't have an identity. I understood myself in terms of who I wasn't and who I wanted to be with no real sense of who I was. I'd look in the mirror and see bad hair, bad skin, a nose that was too pointy and ears that were too small.

Looking at photos from those days, I'm surprised that even under all that hair goop I was a good-looking kid, even handsome. By fourteen I'd lost the weight and my complexion was just a little mottled, no more than your average teenager. As my face thinned out, my mother's high cheekbones and my father's square chin emerged. And with

my letterman jacket on I could have passed for Emilio Estevez in *The Breakfast Club*. But no matter how much I worked out, how many trophies I accumulated, I was still the fat kid who wanted, more than anything else, to fit in and measure up. It was bad enough that when everyone else was screaming along to the Beastie Boys or snaking to Def Leppard, I was humming along to Elvis and the Beatles. I actually enjoyed the books I read in English classes and was writing a poem to impress Danica Connors, the dancer and lead in the school musical, with her short, punk haircut, razor smile and lean, strong arms. I didn't want any trouble. I was satisfied I wasn't the target any longer and, for once, had a chance of almost being cool, of having a girlfriend, maybe "getting laid."

Like most boys around of sixteen, I wore my virginity like the embarrassing and uncomfortable clothes our mothers picked out at the bargain racks in Filene's Basement. I was desperate to get it off me as soon as possible. The way the other guys talked about girls so openly and easily, frightened and fascinated me. I tried to tune it out, while at the same time listening intently, hoping to pick up some of what I thought they knew. When they'd look my way, I'd blush, throw on my football pants, grab my shoulder pads, walk toward the practice field. I handled my discomfort by avoiding it – moving through spaces quickly, keeping mostly to myself. But silence gets read, too. It wasn't long before a rumor got around that I was gay.

"Well, people talk. I mean, it's kind of strange," my friends would say. "You don't talk to girls, or talk about them. You hang out with those theater kids and everyone knows your buddy, K., is a fag."

"Look, I like girls. They just don't like me," I'd say, and try to laugh it off. Even my sisters worried a little, awkwardly asking me if I thought this or that girl on the gymnastics team was cute. So I loaded up on bad advice: "Girls don't want you to be nice to them," I was told by friends who knew less than I did. "They don't want poetry and flowers. They like it when you're an asshole. Be an asshole." So in the hallway between classes when a pretty girl walked by in a short skirt, I blurted "Nice legs, Natalie." Then later in the cafeteria, "Amy, you could bounce a quarter off that sweater." My head felt light, blood

pounded, and I tried to smile and laugh like the popular guys. The girls would blush or stare, confused, or shake their heads and walk away. By the end of a week, my buddy Freddy Kaplan pulled me aside: "Jo Jo, what the hell is wrong with you? You're acting like a creep." So I dropped the act, embarrassed, ashamed, and even more confused.

When I finally had sex, I didn't tell anyone – possibly out of embarrassment or disbelief at how upsetting, anticlimactic, and utterly clichéd it was. My first experience amounted to an awkward and somewhat frantic five minutes in my father's steamed-up Chevy Cavalier by the softball diamonds at the Sacred Heart playground parking lot. I even kicked the car horn as I struggled out of my jeans and my girlfriend helped me with the condom. She was a good girl, waifish with long hair that flew about her shoulders in the lightest breeze. She went to my church and wore a tiny cross on a silver chain that seemed to float across the pale skin just below her neck. We'd been together almost three months when I told her I loved her and maybe I convinced both of us I did.

"So have you done it yet?" other boys would ask.

"Hah."

"'Hah?' That means no. What's amaatta Jo Jo, scared? Can't get it up?"

That wasn't the problem at all. The fact was we were both excited all the time, and scared but in the way of thrills and shocks, making any excuse to sneak off into basements and empty rooms, trying to figure out whose parents would be out and how late they would return.

We were conspirators and it was fun at first, like an adventure. There was laugher too. "It's like magic," she'd giggle as she reached for me and felt me grow beneath her palm. I thought she was magic too: her body a mystery, charged, sweet and unsolvable. I was restless and relentless and sometimes she'd laugh, saying how just once she'd love to watch a movie with her bra still clasped. She'd paw the air like a puppy scrambling over the top of a dune and pant, "I hardly have anything there to grab."

I'd joke, "Well, it isn't like you ever try to stop me."

It was true; she'd wait breathlessly and moan a little at my touch,

fingers in my hair, pressing on my arms. "There's no stopping Joel B. Peckham, Junior." She'd poke me in the bicep or chest and smile, dancing off.

I didn't know, still don't know if she liked the thought that I might be unstoppable. I wasn't really. I was not the type of boy to push through a door that wasn't open, run through a stop sign. And yet, I know how sometimes it can be almost a relief to simply let things happen, let the tide wash over you, let nature take its course. It's so confusing, desire and fear and expectation. When you want what you don't want. When your body responds in ways beyond your conscious control. When you come to the edge and back off in relief only to wonder and want to go back, longing to fall.

She put herself in my hands and let them travel where they wanted. So I was the one to try to take things just a little further than before, stopping when she asked or lightly pushed my hands away, but waiting for another time, another night, another chance to take a chance as if it were a game I could win by simply playing long enough, wearing her down over time – until there was no further we could go and I found myself inside a girl in a car in an empty parking lot.

When it was over, we buttoned up our jeans and I started to apologize for being clumsy and too quick – that I'd get better. I just needed practice. I heard her start to gulp for air, like she was having trouble breathing. Then she started to cry.

I never asked her why she was crying. I didn't ask her if it hurt, or if she wanted this, or if the girls at school had made her think she should. I think that was the first time I looked at a girl who wasn't one of my sisters and felt something other than fear or desire, the first time I thought maybe she was just as subject to the pressures and doubts and needs as I was. It scared me. All I could say over and over was "I'm sorry. We don't ever have to do that again." And I meant it.

"No. It's not your fault," she said. "We did this together."

In that moment though, it didn't feel that way. And though we dated six more months, we never did have sex again. I never even tried to go there. But you can't take it back. We messed around, but it had become serious and frightening, things became mechanical, hesitant and

somehow dark. The laughter stopped.

I didn't tell anyone about those five minutes in the car. When asked by other boys if I was still a virgin I was quiet because everyone knew I'd had just one girlfriend and I didn't want to hurt her. And I didn't want to lose her. I don't think I would have told those boys about it even if things had gone differently.

I was brought up by a gentleman to be a gentleman – as confusing as that seemed at times. While I was steadily being asked to be more aggressive, more male, more violent on the field, violence of any kind in any other arena was not tolerated by either of my parents. And there was no place for cruelty or disrespect towards women. My father had no patience or regard for men who'd brag about a conquest or even those who talked of women as if they were an adversary to be conquered. They were less than men to him. But at school my experience with masculinity was one that swung between the poles of homophobia and misogyny. And though I was constantly thinking about, dreaming about, and masturbating to girls, I was terrified of them and terrified of my fear of them – that my inability to look a girl in the eye or bear her returning glance was some hidden sign that I might be a "homo." My awkwardness around girls was bewildering to my friends and especially to my older sisters, who did everything they could to help, including one evening after I'd been dumped again, when they grabbed me by the arms, stood me in front of Lisa's full-length mirror, and said, "Look at yourself. You're beautiful."

But the problem was, I couldn't see it. Even if I could, beautiful was not what I was going for. At a certain point, identity is not about the way others see you. It becomes how you see yourself through their eyes. You internalize the messages, the images and the voices until it doesn't matter what "they" think or say. And there is no "you" to see or do the seeing. They have worked their way inside of you, become you.

4

Every time I hear another ex-player or father tell me he doesn't want his son to play football because of concussions, I nod my head, and wonder

if that's the entire story. It's the story I told my son, Darius, when he matter-of-factly informed me he was planning on playing football in the fall of his twelfth year.

"No you aren't," I said.

"Dad, I've already signed up at school. Hunter's playing."

"I don't care what Hunter's doing," I said. "You've got a good brain and I'm not letting you mess it up." I explained what a concussion was and what happens when the skull stops suddenly and the brain continues to drive forward, careening against bone, how no helmet can protect against that kind of damage, how I've had four concussions playing football, how I don't remember any of those games or practices, how I still get headaches and lose sleep at night.

"How many times do you laugh at me for not knowing where my keys or wallet are – or when I can't remember the names of my students or colleagues? Is that what you want for yourself?"

For two weeks we pushed against each other. Even my wife, Rachael, had begun to take his side, on occasion, telling me, "You can't stop him. He'll only resent you."

"Yes, I can," I grunted. "Watch me." Fortunately Hunter didn't end up playing after all, and Darius let it go. Maybe I instilled a little fear regarding brain damage and chronic traumatic encephalopathy, but what I wasn't saying was that my reservations were not just about the injuries.

Darius is discovering girls, and to our consternation, has even gone on his first date, albeit supervised. Rachael wrote out a contract he had to sign that hangs on the refrigerator. It stipulates no sexual contact whatsoever and reminds him he is not yet an adult and the activities he engages in during these public outings should reflect his age. When he nervously tried to tell his mother, in a mock casual voice, "I have a girlfriend." Her response was, "No you don't."

Both of us are trying to protect him from a place that seems to be pulling boys and girls into the very adult worlds of sex and violence before they could possibly understand the consequences. It's not just a matter of wanting to keep our perfect little boy perfect and little. We know we can't. But what we can't change we can resist, so that when we see another young man charged with rape or assault, I can look at the

predators *and* victims and say, "Not my son." More than that, we hope to offer a counternarrative, one more complex and harder to articulate than the one we see in the movies or hear about in the locker room.

There is something primal and beautiful about feeling the thrill of your own body, what it is and can do. I love how Rachael takes pleasure in my body. When she says she married a *man,* when she calls me *her* man, I like it and there doesn't seem anything loaded or unhealthy pressuring the words. She's responding to something visceral and honest connected to deeply-felt needs we both share – that need to feel protected, desired and cared for that may be part culture, but is also partially instinctive.

And coming up with a useful and positive definition of masculinity is nearly impossible; it requires a real comfort with ambiguity, a resistance to definition.

I have no idea what "being a man" means and no desire to define it. I am satisfied to feel it as a part of my nature and to keep an eye on it lest it become destructive. When I hear the term defined in a manner meant to excuse violence, cruelty, and misogyny, I shudder. When "boys will be boys" or "being a man" becomes code for enabling a group of people to give up the responsibilities of acting like adults and gives them license to act like animals, I want nothing to do with the idea. This allows us to stay who we are and never take responsibility for what we have been, what we have done, or for the culture we are complicit in sustaining every day.

I have a beautiful son. I want him to grow to be a good man. I want him to feel free and safe, to define what that means as he grows. It's easy to tell him being a man has nothing to do with how much you bench press, how far you can throw a ball, how many fights you've fought or won, how many women you've slept with, how many friends you have, or how much money you make. I can tell him I don't care if he plays sports or the piano or marries a boy or a girl or no one at all. I can keep telling him what isn't "being a man," but that doesn't help me define what it is. He will look to his friends, teachers and coaches for models, and he will see himself in the mirror of the internet and television screen and in the eyes of those who love and desire him. When

he makes the choices that will define him, he will be surrounded by influences and people who have made easy choices and will encourage him to do the same.

What I want to teach my son is not so much how to "be a man" but how to become an adult. If he can remember courage, compassion, loyalty, and that a sense of responsibility to each other matters, he might be able to hold onto himself even when that means being hurt. That it is okay to be afraid and even angry but not to let that darkness drive you and control you. That there are choices more complex than predator and prey.

I want to tell him, be like Eric. Walk back out into the rain when everyone else ducks for cover.

And then I want to tell him, "No, protect yourself. Run."

<div align="center">5</div>

Canton High School Practice Field, 1985

I am a freshman playing left guard on offense for the Sharon Eagles JV squad. Despite a year of intense weightlifting, I can't be more than a pound over 155, soaking wet. I'm tiny for the line – even one as undersized as this one, made up of 14- and 15-year-olds not yet large or strong enough for varsity. In September, the woods around us shimmer with heat. It must be 90 degrees and our pads droop, helmets slide down heavily, furrowing our brows, darkening our eyes in shadow. On days like this you don't win. You endure. It's a scrimmage, so the coaches prowl the field with whistles and clipboards, stepping into huddles, stopping plays, pulling one kid out, putting in another. We are interchangeable parts, pushed and pulled into different places, filling holes, gaps and passing lanes, pulled up from a pile by the shoulder pads, yanked back into the huddle to be set up once more, like dominoes.

"Okay," my father says, looking down at his clipboard. "Forty-six counter," a misdirection play in which the ball is faked to the left side of the line and every man but one blocks down in that direction to draw the defense away from the running lane before the halfback cuts back to where the tackle on that side has crossed the line, unblocked. At the same time, the left guard pulls his way and is the one man, other than

the runner, heading toward the hole as the defensive tackle sprints across, thinking he has a clear shot at the ball carrier. If things work, if the tackle is slow to recognize the counter-action and meet the blocker coming at him square, or if he simply isn't strong enough to take on the block, the guard clears him out, "blows him up." It's a sure five yards, more if the linebackers bite on the fake.

It works. At the snap of the ball I stay low, winging my right arm back as I step out, turn and fire off in one motion, exploding to my right as everyone goes left and I see the tackle come across, almost straight up and down. When I hit him I can barely feel it in my shoulder pads and arms. His legs come up. His arms fly out. He folds at the middle and I drive him through the air several feet before we hit the hard-packed dirt of the field.

The breath comes out of him. "Unh," he says. "Unh."

I wasn't ever the type of kid to celebrate a thing like that. Often, I'd help the player up as if to say, "Nothing personal. It's just my job. Sorry about that."

But this time as I climb to my feet and the tackle rolls over to his stomach, shaking the cobwebs from his head, slowly rising to his knees, pushing himself up with his arms, I see a shock of red hair peeking out beneath his helmet, and in white block letters on a green jersey, I read, KOZAK.

"Nice hit," my father says, barely looking up from his clipboard. "Okay, next play."

"Dad," I say. "I mean, Coach. Let's run it again." And for once I'm not angry or afraid. "Run it again." I feel strong. I feel joy. And I know I am smiling.

There are only three sports: bullfighting, motor racing, and mountaineering. All the rest are merely games.

ERNEST HEMINGWAY[30]

War was an exercise for sport and sport was an exercise for war.

PHILOSTRATUS[29]
{SPEAKING OF THE ANCIENT GREEKS}

Serious sport has nothing to do with fair play. It is bound up with hatred, jealousy, boastfulness, disregard of all rules, and sadistic pleasure in witnessing violence: in other words it is war minus the shooting.

GEORGE ORWELL[31]

If you listen as your read this tale, you'll hear the ping of a basketball bouncing on a driveway, the squeal of sports shoes, a man's huffing – lore from a master American storyteller.

BILL HARLEY ·

One On One

A number of years ago, we made arrangements to have a seven-teen-year-old boy spend the school year with us. His parents were moving and David wanted to finish his senior year in our area. When they brought him over for a house visit, he and I ended up playing bas-ketball. It was a friendly way of saying hello.

But it was more than that. With boys and men, one-on-one basketball is a fair measure of personality.

After we played, I knew it wasn't going to work out. I should have trusted my intuition, but telling my wife, "I didn't like the way he played basketball," didn't seem convincing. I let it pass. It was a mistake.

As a boy, anything with a ball interested me. Sometimes it was the only thing that interested me. Often, when words failed me, I found them by talking about sports. When there were no words at all, I ex-pressed myself on the field.

Sports are one way men and boys communicate. How a man plays the game and deals with victory and defeat, success and failure, says a lot about who the man is.

In my one-on-one game with David, I gave him the ball first. A small thing, but a sign of the way the game would be played, if the signal was picked up.

David turned his back to me and muscled his way towards the basket. I let him come, then stood flat-footed, not challenging him, while he tried to hook a shot in. He missed.

"Damn!" he said.

I grabbed the rebound and took it back. As he came to me, I took a shot from eighteen feet. It went in. He exhaled with disgust.

"Lucky," he said under his breath. He gave me the ball back and stood six inches from me, ready to swipe the ball.

In sports, as in any men's interaction, there are unspoken rules. Especially in informal games, there is an unwritten rule about how closely someone is covered, how much contact there is. In a one-on-one basketball game, the rule of thumb is that the game begins outside, or with a fake, then you drive towards the basket, hoping to slip by the defender. Backing in towards the basket and muscling towards the goal on the first play is bad form. You allow your opponent to shoot from the outside for quite a while before you tighten your defensive clamps. In a game to eleven, you don't start really pushing until the score is at six or seven. David was backing in toward the basket awfully early. And skin-tight defense after the first point was premature. It was not a good sign.

In pickup basketball, no words are necessary. The dynamics of the game are also complicated by the social elements of the situation. Basketball is rarely just about the game, and our game was no different. Offering him the ball was a sign that this was my house and he was welcome. But he missed the signal. I was older than he, in my early forties, and there needed to be some sign of respect coming from him. Respect for an elder is shown on the playing field too, at least initially, before the game gets close, and especially when you might be living in your opponent's house. I didn't get that from him. In fact, what I received from him was not gracious at all. It cast doubt on his ability to be a guest.

David nailed a jumper. "Nice shot," I said. He didn't say anything. He was down three by now and had no intention of losing.

I tugged on my shorts. I was winded.

He didn't pause. He dribbled hard, heading towards the basket, his elbow up to fend me off.

There is a point in a good game when you look at your opponent and you both admit with a glance that you're in the middle of something that has transcended the surroundings. Often it's just a quick grin when you both catch your breath after somebody's scored, or made a good play. It's an acknowledgment that something special has happened, that you're where you want to be, regardless of who's ahead.

When its done right, the game is bigger than the ego – it has become a test of your will and your ability, a gift given to you by the skill of your opponent. David missed that chance, too.

> I stayed outside. In a one-on-one game, age and treachery will often beat youth and speed by pounding the ball in towards the basket. I didn't want to do that. But I did clamp down on defense. His ball handling was sloppy.
> When I took the ball, he slapped at my hands and fouled me. I made no call. He got the ball back and drove to the basket.

Who calls the foul? First, you don't call little slaps or bumps in a pick-up game. The unspoken rules are "No harm, no foul" and, more importantly, "Call your own fouls" – if you clearly foul someone, you should own up to it and give him the ball. It's good etiquette, a sign you understand the rules and you know you've broken them. The game is bigger than you. If someone doesn't call a foul on himself when it clearly was a foul, and the person fouled has to call it, something has been broken. Winning has become more important than playing. That might work in the NBA playoffs, but not on the driveway. I noticed.

> I didn't call the foul. Now we were both winded, and with each basket I scored, David became wilder in his play. He pushed on both offense and defense.
> Finally, after he had shoved me one time too many, I called a foul, and he muttered under his breath.

The game had become competitive. Talk stopped. In the end, pushed into a corner, I got competitive, too. While I called no more fouls on him, and gave him the outside shot, I didn't give an inch when he came inside. It is the competitive streak that runs in men; it's hard not to answer the call. In my mind, my guest had crossed the line in his behavior. I would be polite, but damned if he would beat me.

It is paradoxical but true that unbridled competition – the petty displays of winners and losers on television or in pickup games at the "Y" – can ruin the game. It's a loss of perspective on what sports and life are about. I may not have been as bad as David – David was young, and, as

became clear through the rest of the school year, lacking in guidance about everything from ethics to courtesy to compassion – but like a Greyhound at the race track, I, too, jumped at the rabbit. In this sense, people like David are my teachers: how I respond in a sporting event is a measure of who I am. You can say it's up to me to shrug off the aggressiveness of a seventeen year old, and you'd be right. I'm not a Bodhisattva when it comes to sports.

David didn't really have a chance against me. I might be old, but I'm not incompetent. A lot of seventeen-year-olds could kill me, but David didn't have the skills.

> In the game to eleven, I was up ten-six, then pulled back and let him catch up. I hit an outside shot for the final point. He slammed the ball against the garage.
>> Back in the house, his parents were sitting with my wife.
>> "What happened, big boy?" asked his father.
>> "He got lucky, " his son said.
>> "You let him beat you?" the father asked. He shook his head.
>> David looked away.

I should have known. He learned it all from his father. The worst of it came fifteen minutes later. He was playing my ten-year-old son and didn't let him score a point. I should have stopped it right then, but I didn't say anything, and we paid for it all year long with a kid who didn't know how to play one-on-one. And he didn't want to learn from me, not on the court, or when he was having trouble at school, or when I had to pick him up at the police station in the middle of the night.

Like I said, it was all I needed to know.

David has come and gone. I tried to be there, but he wasn't interested. Thankfully, my sons have stayed, and one-on-one basketball is one of the things we do together.

And they've learned, not by my telling them, but by example. You start outside. You show respect to your opponent. You give the ball back if you foul. You acknowledge his skill.

And in the middle of the game, when it's close, you smile.

The way these guys told it, anger was the one emotion they had in abundance, the one emotion that the world had allowed them to have in abundance, so by implication it contained everything else – sorry, pain, need, shame. You name it. It was a feeling they knew well ... No [man] here was going to judge you for letting it speak.

NORAH VINCENT[32]

PAUL HOSTOVSKY

The Conversations of Men

My girlfriend says she would like to be a fly
on the wall between two urinals.

"What would I overhear?" she asks me.

I tell her the last time a man spoke to me
above a urinal, I think he said, "How about them Bruins?"

"And what did you say in return?" she wants to know.

I say I didn't know what to say because
 I don't know anything about hockey,
 and I didn't watch the game or even know
 there was one. But I didn't want him
 to know that.

So I think I said, "Goddamn!"
 because it sounded heartfelt yet noncommittal,
 because he may or may not have been a Bruins fan,
 and because the Bruins may or may not have won,
 and because he was trying to make contact
 with his gender, and if I said I didn't see the game,
 or if I said I didn't follow hockey or don't
 give a shit about the Bruins, he would probably
 feel like he hadn't made contact. And I would feel
 less of a man.

So I said, "Goddamn!" and he said
 "Unbelievable!" and shook his head in approval,
 or maybe it was disapproval – it was hard to tell, I tell her,
 because the whole thing was more or less peripheral.

4. Fathers & Sons

The most important man in my life was my father. I loved my dad though as with some fathers and sons, we had our disagreements. "Agreeing to disagree," he called it. An electronics engineer by nature and an independent by trade, he wouldn't have wanted it otherwise.

Dad expressed his love for me in many ways, most of them nonverbal. By demonstration and example he taught me how to think, use my hands – "the thumb is an amazing tool," he said – solve problems, and with two words, how to work with men. Dad taught me which end of the iron is hot, meaning the soldering iron, but also "what's what." At his workbench he taught me handyman skills and tools: Phillips- and flat-head screwdrivers, cross-cut and rip saws, nails, screws, nuts, bolts, hammers, wrenches, sandpaper, steel wool, DC and AC electricity, multi-meter, oscilloscope, soldering iron, solder, fuses, circuit breakers. We worked on his Ford Mainline together, changed the oil, gapped and installed new spark plugs, adjusted the timing.

Dad showed me how to make my wife feel safe.

He supported me in the risks I took, let me climb out on thin limbs when Mom was opposed, and quietly rooted for me, as his father had for him. In his mentoring and the freedoms he gave me was his love.

It wasn't until late in his life that he started saying, "I love you" to me, something I had long known. They were the last words we exchanged, with a hug, before his death in a horrific car crash a few weeks later. It made his passing less difficult to navigate: everything that needed to be said, had been.

Thank you, Dad, for your love and support. I miss you, bud.

I've heard some guys say regretfully, "My father never said he loved me." But when I ask them if they felt Dad's love through his mentoring, they say yes. It is an acceptance some sons must reach, that their father's love was shown, not uttered. And it is an acceptance that some women may wish to reach, that their husbands and boyfriends don't always say, "I love you." We try to show it in silent ways.

Of the 500 pieces I received in response to my call for submissions, some half were directly about or touched on the father-son connection. Most of them were written by the son about the father. It can be the strongest bond and the most contentious relationship, sometimes both at once. As Bruce Springsteen said in his show, *Springsteen on Broadway*, "My father was my hero ... and my greatest foe."

Theses stories witness fathers with their sons. "Holding Levi's Hand," finds Craig Brooke-Weiss ignoring his friends' advice and following his own. No other submission dealt with this father-son scenario, and my hat is off to Craig for the wisdom of his life decision.

Jed Diamond, author of sixteen books on men's health, tells a story of "My Father, My Son, Myself." Jed walked a long road to reuniting three generations of Diamond boys and reconciling with his dad. This story pivots on his father's obligation to support his family.

In "Game Face" by Russell Reece, the death of a family dog triggers a father's awakening to his son. The theme here, similar to that of Jed Diamond's piece, is a man's obligation to support his family. It came back from my editor with tear stains streaking the page.

Andre Dubus III, author of *House of Sand and Fog*, awakens to fatherhood in his story, "The Door." When I posted his piece on the website, Antonia left this comment: "I was swept up into this man's journey through fatherhood.... Now I'm in tears of joy for the outcome. Beautifully written." ... Thank you, Antonia.

Mike Schneider's poem about his dad, himself, and his daughter is titled "Old Blue Volvo." What's happening here? It's your call, but to me it's the acknowledgment by the son of his father living within.

To close this section, Michael Chabon writes about himself as "A Textbook Father" for his daughter. His work ends this section and begins the next with "The Hand on My Shoulder." Both are from his 2009 essay collection, *Manhood for Amateurs: The Pleasures and Regrets of a Husband, Father, and Son*.[33] Chabon, one of America's foremost men of letters, is the only writer to appear twice in this anthology.

CRAIG BROOKE-WEISS

Holding Levi's Hand

I wasn't given a choice whether my child was born or not. I came kicking and screaming into the world of daddyhood. I'd known my baby's mother for a total of five joyful, playful, and what I believed were intimate weeks – when she began to think she was pregnant. She did a home pregnancy test and found we were. A week later she was driving away from Seattle, going back to Michigan in the van I bought for us (her?) to travel around the country. She got sick, and instead I flew her home. I waited four days to hear from her and then I called. Grudgingly and with annoyance, she told me, "We're finished. Don't move to Michigan. I'm not moving to Seattle, and I expect you to support this child of ours."

Almost everyone told me to forget about this woman and this kid I'd never know. But one close friend went against the barrage of voices that were "supporting me" and insisted I take a hard look at my priorities. When I whined about the latest insulting, demoralizing comment or action my baby's mother leveled at me, my friend reminded me I had been through tougher times, "so bear down, get a grip and go for life!" I hung in and made myself a presence in my child's life, and am grateful I did. None of it was easy. I had to change not only my lifestyle but also what I consider to be life's rewards. This has been worth every painful step of the way.

I met this woman late at night when she sold me a cookie at a concert. I could blame my lust for peanut butter chocolate cookies or the child-woman with the sweet disarming voice. I could wail in anger, curse my luck, complain, bitch, scream or cry because I fathered a child with a

person who never seemed to consider the effect her actions have on me, or on my relationship with my son, our child. However, I see her as one of the great challenges of my life. As great warriors bow to their opponents, inwardly I bow to her for reminding me of all the places in me I still need to reconcile. Also, I never forget she is a devoted, loving mother with a gift for nurturing our child and does so in a positive, fun, and structured manner.

In the years preceding Levi's birth, I had a few wake-up calls from the universe cluing me in to what is important about life. In 1989, my one and only blood brother died of a heart attack ten minutes after I laughingly teased him while we worked together at a Rolling Stones concert in Dallas, Texas.

Six months later, I was hit by a car. My leg was broken in 14 places. Not long after, the woman I was seeing left me to mend by myself. She decided she liked her best friend's lover more than she liked me. Then, half a year later, my leg fully and miraculously healed and grief around my brother resolving, I met a bright-eyed, adventurous woman. We got pregnant. She aborted me.

It's only now, in retrospect, I know how rich these years have been and how necessary these events were to deepening my perspective on life. I learned that whether or not I'm aware of the reasons, there is an inherent lesson in everything – as long as I don't close my heart or mind, some of the secrets of the good life will begin to live in me. I point my finger a lot less and sometimes I remember how lucky I am to be alive.

My brother had the same birthday as my child's mother. Could my playful, sick-humored, dead brother come back as my little boy? I loved my brother a great deal, but I was often unwittingly a bastard to him. As a father, maybe I could learn some of the hard lessons of unconditional love that I missed as a brother. The powerful feelings I have for my brother initially kept me from disappearing from my baby's life. I had a lot of anger, self-pity and excuses to leave this child fatherless.

My family told me, "Forget this child. One day you'll have a 'real' family, a wife or partner who loves you and respects your role as a father. You won't have to tear up your life to be connected with this kid.

Someday you will create a child and bring it up in love. That's what a real family is, Craig."

I had a lot of support to drop this kid. They talked like this before he was born, before they met him, before they saw the love in my eyes or felt the magic of Levi's presence.

His mom told me, "You'd better not show up until two weeks after the child is born or you'll be sorry." For part of those two long weeks I was in LA, where riots were happening. Unending suffering without release or insight, the rioting in the streets and in my body were inseparable.

I stood outside the door of my sleeping child. He was three weeks old. I remember thinking I could turn back and try to forget about him. I told myself that as long as I didn't see his face, I'd remain safe, secure in my ability to disappear if I had to. Disappearing was still an option. That changed the moment I decided to enter the room.

The moment I took a step toward Levi, I made a decision about how I was going to live my life. The priorities of a lifetime changed in that instant. For the first time, "I" was not my first concern. Levi was and still is. Having a child was one thing, but deciding to own up to the responsibilities was another. I didn't know I had joined the Parents Club and become an adult. What used to be fun, such as free weekends or uninterrupted hours of listening to music, had been traded for silly-word sing-along songs (I became an expert), or rich, quiet times of driving down the road holding hands. With Levi, I experience something so much deeper than just fun. I share my child's life. It is a religious experience of joyful sorrow, sorrowful joy, and deep belly laughs.

Levi fell headfirst off his training-wheeled bicycle the other day. When he finally lifted his head from my shoulder to feel his bloody wound, he disappeared into my arms for the next hour and a half, weeping relentlessly. I held him soft and hard, loving him for his honest tears, faithful trust of my arms, and patience with my corny humor. I loved him for me and I loved him for him and I can't tell where my love begins or ends. I was grateful to be present for his first major risk-taking wound, but it also hurt me. And I laughed hard with pride and gratefulness when he asked me after his nap and a hesitant return

to his bicycle, "Daddy, would you take off my training wheels and help me learn to ride my bicycle?"

Early in Levi's life, his mom and I briefly tried to raise him together under one roof. It didn't work. To remain connected to him, my home moves to wherever he is. I said good-bye to friends and put my belongings in storage. My existence has been fractured, my living situation unstable, my romantic life a weak chuckle, and yet these last five years have been the greatest gift of my 39 years.

Some people travel to exotic places to meet their teacher who gives them a mantra, a holy word that reminds them of the sacredness of every moment. I now live an hour from my spiritual teacher, who howls when he sees me. I hear the holy word, "Daddy!" and I am reminded of the sacred.

My Father, My Son, Myself

I was five years old when my uncle Harry drove me to the mental hospital. I was confused and afraid.

"Why do I have to go?" I asked him.

He looked at me with his round face and kind eyes. "Your father needs you."

"What's the matter with him?" I was beginning to cry, and I clamped my throat tight to stop the tears.

Uncle Harry turned away and looked back at the road. In our family, we didn't talk about difficult issues. My father was a successful writer and actor in New York; eventually he moved the family to California so he could enter the emerging television and movie industry. But he ran into the "red scare" in Hollywood, where progressive playwrights, actors, and directors were accused of being Communist Party members. Like many in Hollywood at the time, he was blacklisted and found it nearly impossible to find work.

Though I didn't understand why we were visiting my father in a hospital or what was wrong with him, I knew that as the only child it was my duty to be there. It never occurred to me to ask why my mother didn't come along. I just knew I was being her "brave little man." Looking back, I see I'd become the family "care-taker," whose job it was to take care of my parents and act as a bridge between them.

It was a two-hour drive from our home in the San Fernando Valley to Camarillo State Mental Hospital, just north of Los Angeles. The hospital looked like one of the old California missions with palm trees in front, a big bell tower in the center, and adobe buildings with grassy

lawns. But as we got closer, I noticed the windows. They weren't like ours at home. There were thick bars over these windows, which were painted puke pink, like dried-up Pepto-Bismol.

Once inside the hospital, we were told we could meet my father in the visitors' room. There he was, sitting in the back. He jumped to his feet when he saw us. Although I wanted to run to him, I held back. My father looked strange. His hair was messed up, his clothes hung loosely on him, and he had a wild gleam in his eyes I had never seen before. He looked like he had shaved himself with a pocket knife, and there were small bits of food in the corners of his mouth. He walked toward us, picked me up and hugged me, but he seemed agitated and quickly put me down.

He suggested we go for a "stroll" on the grounds. I was glad to go outside, and those words calmed me. We had often gone for strolls at a park near our home in Sherman Oaks, and I can still picture my father hoisting me on his shoulders. I felt safe and on top of the world during those strolls, but that was before he was hospitalized.

It was a beautiful day outside, with soft white clouds floating peacefully by. We sat on a bench and looked out at the mountains in the distance, but my father was anything but peaceful. "You've got to get me out of here," he implored, reaching out and grabbing Uncle Harry's shoulder.

"Take it easy." Uncle Harry tried to calm him down with his soft words and kind smile. "The doctors say you just need some time to rest and recuperate."

My father jumped to his feet and started pacing and talking rapidly. "I don't get any rest here. This is a crazy house. All I get are drugs and shots, and now they're talking about shock treatments for my brain. Get me the hell out of here! Jeezus, Harry, I got a little depressed because I couldn't find work to support my wife and son. Is that a crime I should be locked up for?"

Harry got up and put his hand on my father's arm like he was gentling a frightened colt. "I'll talk to the doctors, I promise. Just calm down. I'm sure you'll get out soon," he said quietly.

I was confused and scared. Why was my father in this place, and

what kind of place was this? Why did he call it a "crazy house?" My uncle's assurance, "you'll get out soon," didn't come soon enough for my father.

My uncle came to visit my father every Sunday, and I went with him. Being a dutiful son was something I had learned early. The story of why my father was in a mental hospital, however, emerged slowly. I came to understand from overhearing my mother and uncle talking that my father had suffered a "nervous breakdown." He had become increasingly depressed because he couldn't support his family, and finally took an overdose of sleeping pills.

In my child's mind, I saw my father as a failure because he couldn't take care of his family. In fact, I felt responsible. Since I was the newest family member on the scene, I reasoned that I must have been the cause of his breakdown. I grew up wondering what happened to my father and whether it would happen to me. I'm sure, subconsciously, I went into the mental health field in hopes of curing my father and warding off any "craziness" I may have inherited.

It took me years to understand that my father wasn't a failure. In fact, he was a hero. He was the sole breadwinner of the family but couldn't find work no matter how hard he tried. His breakdown was the only way he could escape the impossible predicament he faced: being middle-aged, unemployed, his family's sole support, and blacklisted in the red-scare era.

When I was forty, I found his personal journals, with entries leading up to his hospitalization. They chronicled his struggle, desperation, and eventual despair. It helped me understand what he was up against and to understand my own struggles with depression over the years.

> JUNE 4TH: Sunday morning, my humanness has fled, my sense of comedy has gone down the drain. I'm tired, hopelessly tired, surrounded by an immense brick wall, a blood-spattered brick wall that is splattered with my blood, with the blood of my head, where I senselessly banged to find an opening, to find one loose brick, so I could feel the cool breeze and could stick out my hand and pluck a handful of wheat. But this brick wall is impregnable; not an ounce of mortar loosens, not a brick gives.

JULY 5TH: I stand naked, untrained, and my body and spirit have turned to water. I am confused and desperate. I have so much, so very much. The most gracious, lovely, tender, understanding mate any human being could ask for. I have a sweet, growing, elfin son. And I can't find bread to feed them.

AUGUST 2ND: Your flesh crawls, your scalp wrinkles when you look around and see good writers, established writers, writers with credits a block long, unable to sell their work, unable to find work, Yes, it's enough to make anyone blanch, turn pale and sicken.

SEPTEMBER 12TH: Faster, faster, faster, I walk. I plug away, looking for work, anything to support my family. I try, try, try, try, try. I always try and never stop.

NOVEMBER 8TH: A hundred failures, an endless number of failures until now, my confidence, my hope, my belief in myself, has run completely out. Middle-aged, I stand and gaze ahead, numb, confused, and desperately worried. All around me I see the young in spirit, the young in heart, with ten times my confidence, twice my youth, ten times my fervor, twice my education.

I see them all, a whole army of them, battering at the same doors I'm battering, trying in the same field I'm trying. Yes, on a Sunday morning in early November, my hope and my life stream are both running desperately low, so low, so stagnant, that I hold my breath in fear, believing that the dark, blank curtain is about to descend.

Three days after this last journal entry, he took the overdose of pills that led to his hospitalization.

Becoming a mental health professional didn't enable me to cure my dad, but it did help me understand his struggles and the stress so many men feel when society demands they be the "breadwinner," even when that may not always be preferable or even possible. My father would have been a great stay-at-home dad, and my mother loved to work outside the home, but each were caught up in roles that kept them from being themselves.

When I become a father, I thought to myself, I'm going to do things differently. The birth of my first child changed my life. I wanted to be a great father, but I was afraid I'd screw things up. My wife, Carlin, and I practiced Lamaze techniques and took birthing classes together. She wanted me to be in the delivery room with her, so I could experience the beauty and wonder of childbirth. The idea sounded good, and all our friends were doing it. But still, I worried. I passed out once when I had my teeth cleaned. I wasn't good with pain and wondered whether I could deal with my wife's pain and still remain standing.

The labor was a long one, and my wife practiced the breathing techniques we had learned in class. I did my best to coach her and gave her chips of ice to wet her dry lips. By the time we heard, "Let's get her into the delivery room," I wanted to go all the way through the birth. But I was told to go to the waiting room and they'd let me know when I could see the baby.

I was both relieved and disappointed. By then I didn't think I'd pass out. I wanted to be with my wife and see our newborn child. However, being a good boy, I followed doctor's orders and walked to the waiting room. But I didn't even make it through the doors. In the quiet of the hallway, I felt the presence of my soon-to-be-born son calling to me, "I don't want a waiting room father. Your place is here with us."

I reversed direction, found the delivery room, pushed through the doors and took my place beside my wife. She smiled through her pain and I held her hand as our son, Jemal, came into the world. Amidst tears of joy and relief, we looked at each other and at our newborn son with a love we had never known before.

The nurse handed him to me, and as I looked into his eyes, I made a vow: "I will be a different kind of father than my father was for me. I will do everything I can to help bring about a world where fathers are fully engaged with their families throughout their lives."

When I took days off from work to be with my wife and our baby, we learned the basics of child care together. We both got up at night to change our son, comfort him, or just look in wonder at him as he slept. We talked to him, played with him and fed him, though my wife had the advantage of having breasts, so in essence, "the lunch counter was

always open." I had to go back to work after a month, but even in that month, my son and I bonded.

When Jemal was a year and a half old, my wife announced that she wanted to visit a friend. "Listen," she told me. "I need some time away. I love our son, but I need a break."

I smiled and said, "Sure, I can take off some time from work. How long do you want to be away?" I was thinking a few days.

"I'd like to take two weeks," she said.

My first thought was that I'd already used up my vacation time when Jemal was born. I wondered if we could afford for me to be off work. I was also worried about whether I could handle taking care of our baby for two whole weeks by myself.

Being with Jemal when he was born helped me feel comfortable caring for a newborn. But I felt I was just filling in for my wife, that she was always there to take over, if needed. Mothers have special expertise they acquire through months of carrying the baby inside their body, expertise that dads can never learn. I saw my know-how kicking in when he was old enough to play basketball and I could teach him how to dribble with either hand, and master a jump shot.

Deep down, I felt terrified. What if he starts crying and I don't know what to do? What if something happens to him while my wife is away? What if I just freak out? The only thing that calmed me down was my wife's quiet assurances, "I trust you to take care of our son; things will be all right. You'll do fine," she said. "And I really do need to get away and see my friends."

Jemal and I both waved good-bye as she drove off. We spent the first day playing and feeding. I cleaned up both of us after a spaghetti dinner that had way too much sauce. We had fun ... although the first night was scary. What if something happens during the night? What if he cries, and I don't hear him? Gradually, as the days went by, my fears subsided. Some of my men friends came to visit, taking turns holding Jemal while he smiled and gurgled. Women friends from our baby-sitting co-op were impressed with my wife's willingness to leave our son with me, and with my skill and engagement as a new father. Somehow we made it through the two weeks my wife was away.

She came back refreshed and invigorated, though she seemed a bit surprised when I said things had gone wonderfully well. Jemal was overjoyed that she had returned. He and I shared a secret look of delight: *The boys did all right, even with mom away.* I still believe that moms have some special sauce that only women possess. But I also believe there is something unique that only dads bring to a family. When he got older, my son gave some examples. "Our play was more rough-and-tumble, and I loved that with you. When I would share my music, Mom just loved everything I did, while you were more honest in telling me what you liked and didn't like, and how I could improve." I felt proud knowing I had a unique, fatherly perspective that my son valued.

Although he never met my father while he was growing up, my son inherited his artistic talents. Jemal wrote poetry and began acting in high school plays.

After I wrote my first book, Inside Out: Becoming My Own Man, in 1983, I received a letter from a reader. "I know your father, and can tell you how to reach him." I hadn't seen my father in many years.

We reconnected, he met my family, and learned he had a grandson. I arranged for the three of us to get together. My father and my son read their poetry aloud. I read excerpts from my book. It was a magical encounter that made me proud of our male lineage that continues with the birth of my grandson, Jonovan.

Having been in a men's group for nearly forty years, I know that "male energy" is different from female. As a biology major in college, I learned that every cell in a male body has an XY set of chromosomes, and an XX pair in a female body. I love the idea that every cell in my body vibrates to a certain male frequency, and creates a symphony that is deep and beautiful, vibrant and loving.

Writing this, I think about my father. I know that his father struggled to support his family, never felt successful, and was often withdrawn and depressed. The doctors did not discharge my father from the hospital as he had hoped. In fact, he became sicker, and our family was told he would probably need to be in the hospital for years and in fact might never leave. Eventually, my mother got a divorce.

Even though the doctors had given up on my father, he never gave up on himself. After seven years in the hospital my father was given a pass

to go off the grounds for lunch with my uncle. He told Harry he needed to get stamps at the post office, crossed the street and never came back. My uncle looked but never found him, and returned alone to the hospital to tell them their patient had escaped.

My father walked for three days and eventually made it back to Los Angeles. He never returned to a mental hospital. His story had a happy ending, including our reconnection and reconciliation. He changed his name to Tommy Roberts, so the authorities wouldn't find him. He became a puppeteer in San Francisco and brought joy to hundreds of children and their parents. As a much beloved and well-known street performer, he achieved a level of celebrity he had never known in New York.

When he died at age ninety, we gathered in the visitors' room of his apartment house on Turk. A reporter from the San Francisco Chronicle attended the service and wrote an article, "Requiem for a Puppet Man," that celebrated his life. Here's an excerpt.

> Over the past 30 years, Roberts had a way of showing up on college campuses and in city parks with paper bags full of ragged homemade hand puppets. The puppets, only slightly smaller than their 4-foot, 8-inch master, would proceed to recite Roberts' poems.
>
> The crowd jammed every seat and spilled out into the hallway. They signed the memorial book. They snatched up free copies of Roberts' poems.
>
> "Because of you," said one, "old madness has new meaning. Because of you, my tongue is no longer lead."
>
> "By the standards of society, my father was not a success," said his son Jed Diamond. "He didn't make a lot of money. He was labeled as mentally ill. He liked to live among people that society pretends do not exist. Einstein said that one should strive to be not a man of success, but a man of value," his son said. "My father was a man of value."
>
> Paper cups of bright red punch were raised all around.
>
> "Him and me, we got along good," said the guy down the hall. "He was the puppet man."

I feel blessed to be the son of the puppet man, the father of Jemal and the grandfather of Jonovan. And as a psychotherapist and author of fifteen books about men's health and wellbeing, I'm doing everything I can to bring about a world where fathers are fully engaged with their families.

... the American ideal of masculinity –
generous, confident, empathetic, determined;
the one you think of when you imagine the
"Greatest Generation" who fought in the
second world war.

<div align="right">BRUCE SPRINGSTEEN[34]</div>

Game Face

She died in his arms, right there on the table. It happened before the vet even finished the exam. Todd was holding her and she collapsed against him. Gone.

"Sorry to hear that," I said when they called, or maybe it was, "Too bad." I don't remember. I needed to wash it out of my mind while I was at work. I couldn't let something like losing the family dog take me away from my job. I put on my game face and kept going, but during the drive home, it began to consume me.

Cricket was twelve. She looked like an Irish setter, but jet black with a small streak of gray on her chest. "She's a jumper," the guy had said when we picked her up. That's how she got her name and it turned out to be well deserved. Her joy was catching Frisbees, often by leaping acrobatically into the air. She would go until exhaustion set in or the Frisbee was so chewed-up it wouldn't fly. We finally began using lids from five-gallon plastic buckets – they lasted forever and it was all the same to her.

She'd been sick for several days, but last night in the den we realized it was serious. She could barely move, just stood in the middle of the room wearing a frightened, glazed look. At one point, she hobbled over and leaned her head against my knee, closed her eyes and fell asleep. I'll never forget that.

I turned into our lane as the sun disappeared behind the tree line. My tires crunched down the long gravel drive. Poor Todd, I thought. It's always tough to lose a dog, but at fifteen, and having grown up with her – it must have been very hard for him today.

The brakes gave off a quiet squeal as the car rolled to a stop against the fence. I pushed open the door and grabbed my briefcase off the back seat. Daylight was fading and dark shadows had formed along the hedgerow. In the western sky, towering clouds were backlit with traces of orange and red. Rarely home this early, I paused to enjoy the grandeur of it all.

Then I heard the sound of digging

Beyond the garden, the lamp on the barn flooded a small portion of the yard with yellow light. Todd was there, bent over a dark hole, jabbing a long-handled shovel into the ground. Cricket's body and a rumpled old sheet lay next to him. My heart went still for a moment.

Except for the scraping, clinking sounds from the shovel, the evening seemed unusually quiet. I took off my jacket, laid it over the briefcase and started across the yard. My throat tightened as I rolled up my sleeves and tried to think of what to say – something comforting, appropriate. Words never came easily.

Dry leaves crackled under my feet and Todd hesitated. He didn't look up, just started digging again.

The grave was deep and better than a fifteen-year-old would normally do. He was finishing, widening it to the right size. A large pile of soil had formed at the edge.

"Rough day," I said. "Can I give you a hand?"

He shook his head and kept working. "I'll do it," he said, lifting out another shovelful.

I squatted next to Cricket's body and stroked the hair on her neck. "She was the best," I said.

Todd stopped and looked at me for the first time. His cheek was dirty where he had brushed back tears. But it was the face of a man I saw, resolved, hard at the edge, ready to throw down a challenge. And then his face softened, and there was the boy again, hesitant and insecure. His lips parted and his tongue moved into his cheek as he struggled to hold something inside. He turned and jabbed the shovel into the dirt. A clunk. He levered and pried until something came loose. Reaching down, he pulled out a large rock and tossed it onto the pile.

"I didn't think you liked her," he said, and resumed digging.

My God, where did that come from? "Why do you say that, son?"

A shovelful of sand landed on the pile and spilled down the side. He took a broken breath and shook his head. "I don't know." He leaned on the handle, looked out across the neighbor's field.

"Todd?"

"You're always so busy. You never cared about her, never paid any attention to her." He shifted his gaze back and glared as the man stirred and the boy carefully raised his voice. "You yelled at her, and hit her sometimes."

I looked away and saw Cricket asleep with her head resting on my knee. I wanted to cry out loud, for the dog, for my son, but he was watching and I had to stay composed. I couldn't act like a child.

"There are times I've yelled at you, Todd. But I love you to death." He looked down. Wind rustled dry leaves in the oak tree next to the barn.

"I'm going to miss Cricket." I added. "I'm going to miss her a lot."

We both stared at the hole and listened to the soft electrical hum from the barn lamp. I struggled for something else to say, something that would fulfill my responsibility as the wise parent and somehow offer comfort and understanding to my son, but the words just wouldn't come.

Todd wiped his eyes and scraped up the loose gravel at the bottom of the grave. "Do you think it's big enough?" he said.

"Looks like it to me. You did a good job."

I got down and lined the moist bottom with part of the sheet. As I smoothed the wrinkles, sand spilled off the pile. Todd scooped it out with his hand.

Together we lowered Cricket's body into the grave. Todd covered her with the sheet and tucked it in around the edges. Then we both stood for a moment and looked down at the bundle. "Anything you want to do before we fill it in?" I said.

He shook his head.

"How 'bout if I get it started?"

He nodded.

I pushed the shovel into the soft pile of dirt and dropped a load into

the hole. Maybe it was my imagination or wishful thinking, but with each successive shovelful the tension that surrounded my son and me seemed to fade a little, and I was grateful for that.

Todd finished filling in, leaving nothing but a few scrapes and scratches in the soft earth and a neat, firmly packed mound.

We walked back to the house together, neither speaking, lost in our own thoughts. He went inside and I returned the shovel to the garage. Cricket's bucket-lid Frisbee lay ready on the concrete floor. I picked it up and ran my finger along the chewed edge. Too bad we didn't think to bury it with her.

I walked across the driveway waving the Frisbee around, thinking how excited Cricket would be, how she would be urging me to throw it for her if she were still here. I sailed her beloved disk out into the darkness.

As I picked up my jacket I glanced back at the barn and the portion of yard illuminated by the lamp. It looked like an empty stage at the end of a performance. I folded the jacket over my arms and leaned against the car. Todd didn't think I liked her. I guess I didn't show it like everyone else did, but I liked her a lot. She was the best dog we ever had.

She knew how I felt. I hope she did anyway. She wouldn't have rested her head against me if she didn't think I liked her – unless she was trying one last time.

I stared at my briefcase. "You're always so busy." That's what he said, and he was right. I am always busy and never around. And when I am around I don't know what to say or do. All I could think about, as I stood by that grave, was the pain of everything – of Cricket dying, of seeing my son torn up inside and being so brave, and of my own awkward uncertainty.

I wanted to put my arms around my boy, hug him as hard as I could, and let everything go. That's what I wanted to do. But I was his dad and needed to help him through it. I had to be steady and wise, chin up and all that. Didn't I?

I looked out into the darkness, feeling inept and alone. I imagined Cricket bounding toward me, happily chomping on the bucket-lid

Frisbee. I imagined calling her to me, and putting my arms around her neck to show her I loved her. It wouldn't matter if anyone were around. That's what I would do, right now, if I could.

Back at the barn, at the edge of the lighted yard, the fresh mound cast an eerie shadow. I picked up my briefcase and headed to the house. I needed to find my son.

The male tragedy, then, is that showing our love by providing takes us away from showing our love by connecting. Thus, loving our sons has taken us away from loving our sons.

WARREN FARRELL[35]

The Door

This was our first night home from the hospital, my wife recovering from her C-section, and something was wrong. Our baby cried right till dawn, only taking a breath to be fed when I carried him to his mother's breast in the darkness. Then I'd hold him to my shoulder and pat his tiny back, though he never burped or spit up. Instead, a labored grunting noise would come from his small mouth near my ear, and then he'd start crying again. What was strange was how he felt against me. I'd held babies before, most recently my youngest half-sister, and in my arms she felt soft and pliant, too pliant, and I was always careful to cradle her head and neck against my palm. I did the same with our newborn son, too, except there was something about his torso; it was his stomach; it felt as hard and bloated as a wineskin about to burst.

Early the next morning I called my brother Jeb and told him I wouldn't be in till the afternoon. We were remodeling a house in Charlestown. My younger brother, a far more skilled and experienced carpenter, was my boss.

"Everything all right?"

"Our baby needs a checkup."

"Already?"

I did not want to tell him that we feared something was wrong with our son. To say this would make it true.

Later that morning, his pediatrician examined him and told us he just needed to "pass gas."

I said: "Then why won't he?"

Our doctor shrugged. "Give him some time."

We took her at her word.

When my wife, Fontaine, got pregnant, we'd been married nearly three years. She's a modern dancer and choreographer, and those years she also worked as a part-time dance instructor and self-employed upholsterer of furniture. We lived north of Boston in a small apartment in the house of her former high school art teacher. In the basement, Fontaine had a workbench and a sewing machine and some nights when I came home from my own jobs as a carpenter and adjunct writing teacher, I'd find her down there tying down the springs of a wingback chair, or pulling buttons back through a frame to create diamond tufts in a brocaded fabric that often cost more per yard than we'd let ourselves spend on gas for our one car, an old VW. We never made much money, but it was enough.

It was a life of making things: a dance performance, a short story or novel, a chair, a deck, a new kitchen or bathroom which sometimes paid me a bonus that Fontaine and I would then blow at a restaurant with friends, many of whom spent their days making things, too. She and I made love quite often, and we ended up making this baby, Austin Christopher Dubus. The afternoon she told me she was pregnant, I was lying on the couch in our small living room trying to summon the will to get to my writing desk. It was early spring, a cold rain falling outside, and I'd already spent over eight hours demolishing a bathroom, hauling out the old sink, toilet, and bath, ripping horsehair plaster and lathe down to the studs, clearing between the bays the shredded newspapers used for insulation a hundred years ago. I wore a mask over my face for the lime dust, and I'd taken my flat bar and yanked every square-cut nail from each stud before ripping up the half-rotted floor planks over the joists, exposing ancient pipes for the plumber coming first thing in the morning.

That winter and spring I worked for Yaron. He was an Israeli who'd been in the army when the Egyptians bombed them in the desert. He had deep eyes, long black hair, and a mustache, and he would've been handsome if not for his shoulders, which were forever hunched as if he was still bracing himself to be blown to bits. He had a heavy accent, and his constant answer to any question about work or life was: "Why? It's

not worth it. It's just not worth it."

Yaron was married and lived with his wife and two young daughters in a cul-de-sac in the north end of town, an antiseptic neighborhood of nearly identical houses with matching two-car garages. Every morning at six-forty-five he would pick me up in his Taurus (No truck. "It's not worth it," he'd say. "My materials are delivered."), and we'd ride to the job site together. I was thirty-two years old, and he was ten years older than that. One gray morning, both of us sipping from Styrofoam cups of hot coffee, he told me about the black-and-white photographs he used to take in Europe, how he had an exhibition of them once in London, how that's what he'd thought his life would be, a life of art.

"What happened?"

"I fucked my wife and had two kids."

He shrugged and changed the subject. I couldn't imagine using that word when it came to making love with my wife, and he may have started talking about the job, about strapping and Sheetrock and electrical outlets, things that honestly bored me. I'd been doing construction work off and on since leaving college, but I never felt called to do it. Those years I wasn't even that good at it. When I began writing fiction in my early twenties, I made the decision to avoid jobs where there was room for advancement up some invisible ladder to greater responsibilities and more money. I was afraid they would define me and my life and would rob me of the time and energy I'd need to teach myself to write. Also, I preferred to write in the mornings, so I often took night jobs, working as a halfway house counselor, an office cleaner, a bartender, and for six months when I was twenty-two, I worked for a private investigator and bounty hunter.

The last job I'd had before I got married was as head bartender at an Irish pub in our small town on the Merrimack River. I worked four nights a week and had seven mornings to myself, but Fontaine's life happened during the day, and I did not want us to be on two different schedules, never seeing much of each other. I'd also just published my first book. It was a collection of short stories that very few people bought or read, though this did not surprise me or even disappoint me much; that manuscript had been rejected by more than thirty

publishers, and I was happy just to hold that book in my hands. I was also happy trying to write the novel my agent was in his second year of sending around. And now I was trying to write another one, a better one, though lying on that couch after another day with unhappy Yaron doing unhappy work, my body tired and heavy, I was beginning to feel my work life had taken a wrong turn. Soon it would be dark, a time I associated with going to a job after I'd spent the day writing, but now I was giving the best part of each day to ripping out toilets or hauling away old kitchen cabinets or nailing roof shingles on the gable of some lawyer's guesthouse in a misty rain. There were far worse problems to have, I knew, but I could feel the novel I was working on begin to slip away like a boat whose bowline I no longer had the strength to hold with both hands. And that's the moment my wife walked into the living room from the bathroom, smiling, her long curly black hair held back into a loose ponytail, a turquoise scarf around her neck. She looked so beautiful to me then that I did not at first take in what she had just said.

"What?"

Her eyes filled. She held up something short and white. "You're a daddy."

My body seemed to move on its own. I was up off the couch, holding her and kissing her and telling her positive words I do not now remember, though I know I felt like a liar saying them; in no time I'd be Yaron, my life of art forever behind me as I drove slope-shouldered from one job site to another, sipping bad coffee, telling the young man beside me that nothing good is worth doing, "Believe me, it's just not worth it."

I was wrong, of course. If I've ever been more wrong about anything in my life, I do not know what it is. Almost immediately, within minutes of her telling me, it seemed, I could only see this big, new thing in our lives as good; I loved my wife, she loved me, and we would find a way to make room for this baby we'd made. I brewed coffee and opened my notebook and got to work.

Daddy. It's not something I ever thought of being. I had a hunch not many other men gave it much thought either. You fall in love, you make love, and one day or night your wife turns to you in bed and says, "I want a baby."

"You do?"

"Don't you?"

"If you do."

"But don't you?"

"It's just not something I've ever thought much about."

But in one way I had. Like too many people, I come from a broken family. When I met Fontaine (and the first time I saw her she was performing on stage), I knew I would marry her. This was not so much a wish of mine as a knowledge, as if what I felt for her was music and the only dance for it was marriage, an institution that pulled me back to a dark time, my mother and father yelling at each other, throwing pots and pans, swearing, crying, this going on for months and months till that early Sunday morning in November when we four kids in pajamas followed our father out to his car before he drove away. When I heard the word marriage, yes, I thought of kids – hurt kids, lost kids, kids believing if they'd only been better kids their mother and father would still be together, kids who pretended it wasn't their fault.

"I really want a baby, honey. I want to go off the pill, okay?"

"Okay."

A few days after she told me this, I drove to my father's nine miles east. He lived alone in a small house on a hill overlooking a two-lane road and the rise of a grassy slope, its ridge a thick stand of maple trees. Six years earlier my father had pulled over on the highway to help two people hurt in an accident, and he'd been run over and suffered thirty-four broken bones, one leg pulverized, the other so damaged it had to be amputated just below the knee. It was late afternoon, and I knew he'd be finished with his day's writing and working out, exercises he did with dumbbells from his wheelchair.

He met me at the door. His hair was wet and he was naked, a towel draped over his crouch and right stump. He was fifty-six years old and had wide shoulders and a deep chest, and he was smiling, his eyes lit with love for me. "Hey, man." He held up his arms. I leaned down and hugged him. He smelled like soap, clean hair, and skin.

Soon he was dressed, and we were out on his back deck. The sun was low over the ridge of maples, their branches still bare. It was cold and I

was wearing my leather jacket, but my father sat there in a short-sleeved shirt and sweatpants, the empty right leg of which he'd tied around his stump with a red bandana. He was lighting a cigarette with his Zippo, one hand cupped around the flame. The night before, I'd called him and asked if I could stop by just before supper; I had to ask him a question. He said, "Yeah, man. I'm here."

This was new, my going to him to ask for any advice. It was my mother who raised us four kids, moving us from one cheap rented house in one mill town after another. When we saw our father, it was for two hours on a Sunday when he'd pick us up and drive us to church or take us out to a movie or restaurant he could barely afford. There was the feeling he was relaxing with us, that we, his kids, were part of his recreation, and there was also the feeling that he was doing the best he could and if we were to ask for any more than that, he wouldn't be happy.

But that was years ago. Since then, he'd married and divorced two more times, having two daughters with his third wife, who was a year older than I was. She and my half sisters lived ten miles south, and he primarily saw them on weekends, the way he used to see us. Ever since I was old enough to sit in a bar with him, my father and I had had the easy rapport of drinking buddies; we sipped and talked about whatever came up: lifting weights, a good book, politics and women and dirty jokes. But I don't remember him ever asking me what I might want to do with my time on this planet. Once, at a party at his house when he still had legs, I overheard him tell a friend of his, "I never tell my kids what to do with their lives." This, in many ways, was fine with me. I seemed to prefer to learn everything on my own the hard way anyway. And I rarely, if ever, sought out teachers.

"What's on your mind, man?"

"Fontaine wants a baby."

"Of course she does."

"But isn't it irresponsible to have one when you're as broke as we are?"

My father was looking over the railing out at the trees and sky. He took a drag from his cigarette and shook his head. He told me that lack of money will always be a problem for most people, but that shouldn't

stop anyone. "I just believe, son, when the woman wants a baby, then that's it. It's time to have that baby."

I found myself agreeing, nodding my head.

"Besides, all that shit work you have to do, when you know it's for diapers and food for your child, it makes all work holy."

Holy. This was one of my father's words. He was a Catholic, and I was not. He believed there was a God who loved him; I did not. He believed he was being watched over, while I felt strongly that I was entirely alone and the only good that would ever come to me would have to come from my own hard work and occasional good luck.

Still, driving away from my thrice-divorced father's house, I felt better, for I believe if my wife wanted a baby then that should be that. Women only had a few years to get this done, and who was I to say she could not?

Then she was pregnant, her belly growing by the week. It was a cold winter and it snowed a lot, and whenever we walked up the shoveled icy sidewalk to our apartment, I'd take Fontaine's arm and hold her close. I imagined her slipping and falling, she and the baby imperiled. I read books on nutrition for pregnant women and learned that if the fetus didn't get enough calcium, the mother's body would take it from her own bones. I made sure my wife ate yogurt and drank milk four to five times a day. When the baby began to kick, Fontaine would kneel in front of our record player, her curly black hair down and around her shoulders, her back straight, and she'd place our stereo headphones against her protruding belly and play Mozart, Motown, and Stevie Wonder. From the couch, I watched her do this. It was like watching a flower blossom into a shape you didn't see coming. We were beginning to feel less like two and more like three, and all I felt about this was joy.

Then there was the bright light of the operating room, a gloved nurse handing me our newborn son. His mother's labor had been hard and painful, more than twenty-eight hours long, her cervix never fully dilating, and now she lay conscious on the table with an oxygen mask over her nose and mouth, looking up at us, quietly weeping. Just below her breasts, there was a short curtain to keep her from seeing the surgeons

sewing up her abdomen, but seconds earlier, the moment our son was born, I had looked over that curtain and watched him being lifted from the incision, his tiny face handsome and raging just before he blurred and my voice broke and I told Fontaine, "He's a boy. He's a boy." Wiping my eyes and staring at him, I thought, *It's you.* It's you, for I recognized him from some other time and place. How was this possible? But I did, I recognized him, and now I was carrying him behind the nurse to the warming table, his fine hair wet as he cried with all the air he could summon from his small, pink chest, the stub of his umbilical cord still attached to what would become his navel. I lay him under a warming lamp, and the nurse handed me a pair of shears. I opened the blades. I was afraid to get too close to his skin.

"A little more, honey," she said. "You won't hurt him."

Snipping my son's umbilical cord felt like cutting through coated wire, an act he didn't seem to notice. The nurse began to clean our baby with a warm sponge, and I couldn't stop staring at his eyes and nose and mouth and chin, his tiny chest and nipples, his rising and falling abdomen as he kept crying, his penis and thighs and ankles and feet. I couldn't stop crying either, and I leaned in and stroked the side of his head with my thumb. I told him I was his dad and everything was going to be all right. Everything. I promise.

I first noticed the blood when I was changing his diaper on the apron of the stage. This was at the high school where Fontaine taught dance, and I was there to pick her up and drive her home. The rehearsal had just ended, and while Fontaine was talking to one of the dancers and he rest chatted gleefully while drifting up the aisles of the dark theater, it was clear our four-week-old son's diaper needed changing so I laid him down on a blanket under the colored gel lights of the stage. Maybe if I had not done this in that hazy purple light I would not have seen what I saw, a thread of orange in our son's stool. I finished cleaning and dressing him, then carried him and his open diaper out to the lighted foyer. That thread of orange seemed to be gone, but then I looked closer and saw traces of what had to be only one thing.

When I showed Fontaine, she was concerned but calm. Like my

father, she had a deep and private faith. But I was a boy again, living in a shabby house on a shabby street, getting chased down it by other boys out to get me, and now they were out to get my son, too, this sleeping infant against my shoulder I already somehow loved far more than I loved my own heartbeat, my own breaths that were shallow now as I rushed out of that theater to buckle him into his seat and drive him and Fontaine back home to where there was a phone.

Our doctor told us to bring him in first thing in the morning.

"But shouldn't we take him to the emergency room?"

"No, not yet."

Early the next morning, our doctor, a kind woman with six kids of her own, examined our infant son and said, "I still don't think this is serious, but we'll do a GI series to be sure."

I said: "Doesn't he have to drink barium for that?"

"Yes," she said. "He'll have to do it through his bottle."

Fontaine and I looked at each other. Her black hair was held back, and again, she looked calm. I picked up our nine-pound son. He grunted against me, his belly more distended than it had ever felt before.

The upper and lower GI series was scheduled for the following morning. That week Jeb and I were in his shop, close to finishing the construction of custom cabinets, and his deadline for delivery was just days away; I'd be hurting business if I did not go in to work that morning. Fontaine said she would call me just as soon as they had the results. She said this to me as we lay in bed, Austin swaddled and finally asleep in his baby basket on the floor beside us. I rose up on one elbow and peered down at him. His face was so small. On his head was the knit cap we put on him because we kept the heat low. Even in sleep, his expression was slightly strained, like he was never quite comfortable and when was someone going to notice this? I pictured being in Jeb's shop in Charlestown a few miles away from the Boston hospital where Fontaine and my son would be. It wasn't that far, but still, I imagined my wife having to feed our infant barium from a bottle by herself. This felt like abandonment to me; I was abandoning my family when they needed me most. But we also had to pay our bills, didn't we? I got paid by the hour – no work meant no money – and I couldn't let Jeb down either. Fontaine was beginning to drift off against me, but I climbed out

of bed and wrote the phone number for Jeb's shop on a piece of paper. I placed it under her car keys on the kitchen table then knelt at Austin's basket. I leaned down and kissed him lightly on his small forehead. He smelled like clean skin and wool and something sweet I couldn't name.

Minutes later, lying in the dark beside my wife, I prayed for the first time. If I'd prayed even once in my life before this moment, I do not recall doing so. But now I was silently asking God to help our son. Please, let this not be serious, and if it is serious, please – whoever you are, whatever you are – please heal our baby of it.

I felt like a hypocrite. But as I closed my eyes I also felt just a little bit better, even if I did not believe anyone or anything was truly listening or cared.

When the call came the following afternoon, I was standing at the drill press, drilling identical holes one after another into medium-density fiberboard. On the other side of the shop, Jeb was gluing and clamping together cabinet boxes, a smoking cigarette between his lips, and his partner Bob, a quiet man with two grown kids and an ex-wife, had just finished ripping maple stiles on the table saw and switching it off, and that's when he heard what I did not, the black phone on the wall ring.

My job was simple, but the holes had to be perfect, and even though I seemed to be boring into the center of each penciled X my brother had drawn for me, I kept seeing Fontaine holding our son in her arms, trying to get him to drink some chemical element that probably tasted terrible – and then what? – was our baby put into some kind of X-ray machine? I didn't know, and it felt irresponsible to me that I didn't know.

"Andre?" Bob's deep voice, his hand on my shoulder. "Your wife's on the phone."

The telephone was in a corner of the shop. Taped to the wall was a sheet of emergency numbers, a water-stained bank calendar from three years earlier, a pencil stub hanging by a string. It's the image that comes when I hear again my wife's voice in my head, high and nearly breathless, as if she's running in the dark away or toward something and there isn't much time – birth defect, malrotated, life-threatening.

"What? What do they fucking mean life-threatening?"

"Yes, they think...." She couldn't say the rest, and I couldn't hear

anymore and then I was out of the shop and driving too fast through the streets of Boston toward my wife and son and the doctors who'd just given her this news.

Our four-week-old son needed emergency surgery to correct something called a malrotated upper bowel. It happens in about one out of six thousand births, and it had happened to Austin. In his tenth week of embryonic development, Austin's organs had finished developing outside what would become his torso. His spleen, liver, kidneys, and appendix then had to do a 270-degree revolution into the cavity that would hold them, finding their rightful place, the small and large intestines fanning out in that shape most perfectly suited to easy digestion. But with Austin that revolution never occurred. The organs, while functional, went into the wrong places, and the intestines twisted and bunched and never fanned out the way they should have. Most babies who experience this die, or the diagnosis comes so late their intestines no longer work, and then these children are hooked up to medical machinery for as long as they live.

I no longer see the face of the surgeon who told us all this; I only see his assistant, a man my age then or younger, tall and pale-faced and wearing black-framed glasses. I stood there in my carpentry sweatshirt, jeans, and work boots, sawdust feathered across my chest, and he nodded at me and said, as if I needed the language made simpler: "It's life-threatening."

Fontaine was holding Austin to her shoulder, patting his back and bouncing slightly. She looked pale and focused but calm, her faith rising up from wherever faith lives. But all I felt was flaming bees hurling through my veins, for I did not trust these men or this hospital. They were just other men who'd learned another trade, and what if they were wrong? But there was no time for a second opinion, and from whom would we get it? This was one of the best hospitals for children in the world. Wait any longer and our son might not make it, or his intestines might not, and he'd be attached to a machine the rest of his life. What was there to do but trust these men? Trust them and let go and have faith they could save our son?

Hours passed before they were ready to operate. There was a waiting room with a TV and magazines and deep chairs, black night outside the hospital windows. Austin kept crying and crying; because he was going into surgery, we were not allowed to feed him, and he hadn't eaten in hours. We took turns holding him, walking him back and forth. Sometimes he'd fall quiet, and then rage again, his piercing wail in my ear. He sounded betrayed, and I felt neglectful and cruel.

A nurse finally came in and told us they were ready. She pointed to a wing of the building where the operating rooms were, and Fontaine and I hurried in that direction, Austin against my chest and shoulder. This faster movement calmed him down, and he seemed to take in the swinging doors we passed through, then the empty, quiet corridor, only a third of its overhead lights on. Against the wall in the shadows were three or four gurneys. Their mattresses were stripped, and Austin stared at them. Fontaine and I just stood there. I heard the faint buzz of the fluorescent lights above, nothing else. Fontaine may have said something about us being in the wrong place, I'm not sure, but now there were voices, low and feminine and cheerful, then soft footsteps, two women in surgical blue coming around a corner toward us. They were smiling, and they both had their hair tucked up, cotton masks hanging beneath their chins.

They introduced themselves as our son's anesthesiologists. There was the shaking of hands, their eyes on Austin, and one of them took him from my arms while the other handed me a clipboard with a form on it.

"You just have to sign this, and we'll be off."

Fontaine and the doctors began to talk about Austin's curly hair, his handsome face, but I was reading the form as quickly as you'd run barefoot over smoking embers: accidental death, not responsible, no liability, etc. I signed and handed the clipboard to the one who wasn't holding Austin. Then they were walking away before I could kiss him or touch him, both women holding him between them, his small head erect on his neck, his tiny back straight as they carried him into deep shadows through another set of swinging doors that opened and closed swiftly behind them, Fontaine and I turned to each other, holding tight, our crying echoing down the hallway.

When Austin was two days old, his troubles undiagnosed, Fontaine slept all afternoon in the bedroom recovering, and I held him swaddled in my lap in a rocking chair I'd pulled over to the gable window. Outside it was snowing, the wind kicking up every few minutes and gusting against the glass. I'd turned the heat up, and now I was rocking gently back and forth, staring down at our son's small face and hands and fingers. Sometimes I'd look out the window at the snow but not for long. I couldn't stop staring at the sleeping face of this child we'd made, this child I somehow already loved more deeply than anyone I'd ever known or loved before.

A phrase came to me, words, it seemed, for what was happening to me that afternoon when nothing felt more important or pressing or essential than what I was doing at that very moment, holding our child, keeping him safe and warm: State of Grace. I don't know where these words came from, and I did not know what they meant, but they moved through me like notes from an old cello miles away.

Hours later, when Fontaine had woken and was breast-feeding Austin in bed beside her, I took down our dictionary and looked up that phrase. The first definition I read was this: "to be surrounded by God's love."

God. Part of me resisted this. And another part, well, it just did not.

Fontaine and I sat in that waiting room, and we waited. If there were other people there, I do not remember them. If any of our families came, I can no longer summon who they were. But I see the flat light of that room, my reflection in the night windows of the hallways I'd pace every ten or fifteen minutes. It was long and empty, and as I walked it, there was the heavy-shouldered, hollow-chested feeling that I was being punished for that late afternoon nearly a year earlier when I lay on our couch and Fontaine came into the room looking so beautiful and happy to tell me of this unspeakable gift coming to us, and my very first response, before all that came after, was to reject it.

The sins of the fathers are visited upon the sons. The Bible now, a book I'd never read and had no intention of reading. But I had no words for the limitless love I felt for our son, or the shadow side of this

love, and I needed some. I remembered Hemingway: "When you have a child, the world forever takes a hostage." And there was Rilke, too: "Beauty is the beginning of terror which we are only just able to bear."

Through the waiting room window, I could see Fontaine sitting straight in her chair, her eyes closed, her lips moving almost imperceptibly.

The operation took hours. In my memory, it took all night, because when the doctor called us out to that corridor, his eyes bloodshot but warm, the early sun was shining outside the windows behind him. A cotton surgical mask still hung beneath his chin, the stubble there beginning to show. Successful. That's the word that comes. And surgery. And no complications. And congratulations. Fontaine and I holding each other, the doctor's face blurring, his big hand in mine, my hand squeezing his shoulder. And it may have been then or hours later or maybe even the next day that we got the full details of how they opened up our infant's belly. How they took out his appendix because if, years later, he ever had appendicitis the doctors would never know it because his appendix would be in the wrong place. How they could not move Austin's other organs, but they could and did save his intestines, which saved him, fanning them out the way they were supposed to be in the first place.

"And that's it?" I said. "He'll be all right?"

"He'll live a completely normal life."

Austin may have come home with us that day, or the next, I no longer know. All I know is that profound relief, joy, gratitude were shooting heat through me like kisses from the gods, and I had to do something with it all; we had been given something so good, and I had to give something, too. I kissed Fontaine and told her I would be right back. I was half-walking, half-running down that hallway, looking for the first person who could tell me where I could give blood, anything. There were kind faces and helpful faces, men and women, fingers pointing to signs and elevators and closed rooms behind glass doors, all of this on a moving current of that I can only call love. Then I was sitting at a desk filling out a form, adding my name to all those willing to give the marrow of their bones to a stranger who one day might need it. A woman took a vial of my blood, but this did not feel like enough. I wanted to

give something away right then, on the same day my son was spared. I kept looking for the blood bank but could not find it, and I wanted to get back to my wife and child. I wanted to hold him. I wanted to hold him close and never let go.

But we have to let go, don't we?

This was more than twenty years ago. Austin is now over six feet and two hundred twenty pounds and wears a size fifteen shoe. He lifts weights six days a week and reads and writes and loves serious films and good music and all sports with balls in them. When he was a baby, the scar on the right side of his abdomen was pale and an inch long. As he's grown, it's grown a bit longer and deeper, though now it's largely covered with dark hair. Every single time I see that scar, I feel only boundless gratitude.

Austin lives a thousand miles west of us, on his college campus in Ohio. He has an eighteen-year-old sister and a sixteen-year-old brother. With the birth of each, my capacity for love seemed to grow exponentially larger, opening up in me its attendant fear of loss but a deep reservoir of joy, too. So much joy, as if my deepest, truest life could only begin once I became a father.

Soon our daughter, Ariadne, a dancer and artist like her mother, will be moving to another campus, and not long after Elias, an athlete and drummer, will want to do the same. Fontaine and I will be two again. Back to where we began, for we do not own these three people that came from us. We were simply given them to love and to guide and to set free. And even though I still do not believe in an all-powerful and loving God, I know I'll pray for my children's health and safety daily and nightly, as I do now, as I will until I am no longer on this earth, for something is here among us: something I cannot see but feel; something I cannot hear but sense; something I cannot smell but know; that one late afternoon, this life will bring you to a door your lover may walk through smiling, and just because you're tired and afraid and have little to no faith, you're supposed to lift your head and breathe and walk with joy and trembling right through it.

Maternal love may be instinctive, but
paternal love is learned behavior.

MICHAEL LEWIS[36]

MIKE SCHNEIDER

Old Blue Volvo

*T*wenty horses and a crank starter –
 never made 'em better
 than the Tin Lizzie

said Grandpa, a machinist
 at the brass mill,
 the Model T a shining image,
 youth and freedom.
Henry Ford – two words jangling
 in his pocket: Living wage.
 Eight-hour day.

Dad loved the '48 half-ton
 he found for a few bucks,
 gave it fresh plugs, a bumper, played
 with the timing till it hummed.

Loved me too,
 though he couldn't say it.

With that rattly pickup showed me
 manual transmission,
 hands-on, sequenced
 pattern of the letter H, metallic
 industrial click
 of gears shifting.

Quietly
 he'd shake his head
 as that old truck bucked
 and quivered to a dead stop.

Feel the free play in the pedal.
 Let it out slow, then give it gas.

Soon, I was double-clutching
 on the downshift
 upgrade, taking raw joy
 in the engine's roar
 and surge, pulling deep
 into the furnace of itself
 to charge uphill
 like a young man
propelling himself into the world.

Now it's my daughter, sixteen,
 at the wheel.
 Our old blue Volvo jumps.
 The dashboard lights up red.
 She groans.

Quietly
 I shake my head –
 this strange voice
 on my tongue.

Let it up till it grabs, then feather it.
 Easy. That's the way.

Our neighbor down the road has a 15-year-old daughter. He said, "When a boy comes to pick her up for a date, he'll find me in the kitchen, sitting quietly at the breakfast table, cleaning my guns."

MICHAEL CHABON

A Textbook Father

Some boys were playing in the hallway: eleven, twelve years old, pushing one another around in a wheeled desk chair. Shirttails untucked, yelling, taunting, acting like idiots. Taking turns being the fortunate fool in the chair who goes careening down the linoleum and crashes into the wall and falls out and gets hurt and fakes like he's okay. They were loud, unruly, locked in to the clatter of the wheels, the delighted scream of the idiot at the moment of impact, the collective enterprise of wasting time with a hint of violence. They were, I believe, happy.

Then my daughter entered the scene, passing from one doorway to another across and down the hall. She was twelve then, going on thirteen, tall, leggy, not exactly graceful – no dancer – but with a distinct air of confidence in her gait, of knowing where she was going and how to get there. I'm not sure she even noticed the boys and their chair, perhaps because the instant she entered the hallway, they all fell completely silent and stood there gaping at her, motionless, sagging like the fingers of an empty glove. They weren't having fun anymore. She had kicked their power cord right out of the wall just by walking past.

Nobody ogled or leered at her. There was no Tex Avery business with extruded eyeballs or the unspooled flapping window shades of their tongues. Nothing unseemly or overtly sexual at all, just a bunch of boys standing around blinking as this girl sauntered by. And yet the moment, which I happened to catch sight of through a doorway, made me really uncomfortable. For a while everything about my daughter's entrance into puberty, her emerging new self and the concomitant interest of boys in her, discomfited me. And the part of it that made me squirm the most was how depressingly trite my discomfort was.

I am not a prude. I like sex; I respect sex; I have enjoyed sex, not without interruptions, losing streaks, and dry spells, for almost thirty years. I don't care to give sex any more credit than it deserves, nor do I necessarily prefer it at any given moment of the day to drugs, rock and roll, watching *The Wire,* or the sight of a paper packet filled with well-salted pommes frites still hissing with oil from the fryer. I like the dirtiness of sex, the smell of it, the measured violence and tenderness. I like thinking about sex. I don't begrudge sex or its indisputable pleasures to anyone in any variation that consenting partners can safely attempt or devise – not even to my children, when the time comes and they are of age, well informed, and emotionally ready. My wife and I vaccinated our daughter early against the human papilloma virus, a gesture that encompassed or presaged or at least sought to face up to the nature and the dangers of her eventual life as a sexual being. I believe that sexual freedom is good for all women, including my daughters, and good therefore also for the men who may one day be their partners; that sexual hypocrisy and repression are inherently evil; and that the protective ministrations and censoriousness of fathers are at best harmful to daughters and at worst the mark of the same kind of deep human ickiness that brought us the story of Lot and his daughters. And yet there I was, scowling at those boys in the hallway, feeling an obscure and altogether clichéd urge to go after them with a large mallet, because I didn't like them looking at my daughter that way – or any way at all.

Was that the kind of father I had turned out to be? Standing on the front porch with my shotgun under one arm, cartoonishly interrogating my daughters' cartoonish dates as they sat with a boxed cartoon corsage covering their cartoon boners? Fumbling with a show of jocular pedantry or saggy would-be hipness through every "little chat" with her about menarche or masturbation?

How embarrassing! and above all, in my lamentable sense of embarrassment over the whole business! when the first box of junior-size tampons made its appearance in the house – a bit prematurely, as it turned out – and in spite of my having been raised by a frank 1970s-style mother who saw to it that I understood clearly the laws and equipment of menstruation, and my having lived intimately with women and their

periods since I was not quite eighteen years old, I suffered the tritest fatherly panic imaginable.

"Do these fucking things come with instruction books?" I cried to my wife. "Oh my God, what if you die the day before she gets her period?"

"Relax," my wife said, putting her arm around my shoulder and adopting a textbook condescending-yet-patient wife cartoon tone. "It's very simple."

I have no idea what she said after that, because I was too busy pretending to pretend that I understood. I am sure it is very simple indeed, though there is still and I suppose there will always be a fundamental mystery inherent in the word applicator that I will never fully grasp. But brassieres – I'm sorry. Cup size, wires, padding, straps, clasps, the little flowers between the cups: You need a degree, a spec sheet. You need breasts. I don't know what you need to truly understand brassieres, and what's more, I don't want to know. I'm sorry. Go ask your mother.

There you have it: the most flagrant cliché imaginable. As I utter it, I might as well reach for a trout lure, a socket wrench, the switch on my model train transformer. This may be the fundamental truth of parenthood: No matter how enlightened or well prepared you are by theory, principle, and the imperative not to repeat the mistakes of your own parents, you are no better a father or mother than the set of your own limitations permits you to be. And that set is your heritage, the pinched and helpless legacy of all the limited mothers and fathers whose fumblings, evasions, and shortcomings led, by some dubious accidental magic, to the production of you. It turns out there are only nine different ways of being a father, and eight of them are distinguishable from one another only by trained experts from Switzerland, and the ninth is exactly like the others, only more so. Sooner or later, you will discover which kind of father you are, and at that moment you will, with perfect horror, recognize the type. You are the kind of father who fakes it, who yells, who measures his children with greatest accuracy only against one another, who evades the uncomfortable and glosses over the painful and pads the historic records of his sorrows and accomplishments alike. You are the kind who teases and deceives and toys

with his children and subjects them to displays of rich and manifold sarcasm when – as is always the case – sarcasm is the last thing they need. You are the kind of father who pretends knowledge he doesn't possess, and imposes information with implacable gratuitousness, and teaches lessons at the moment when none can be absorbed, and is right, and has always been right, and always will be right until the end of time, and never more than immediately after he has been wrong. And when your daughter's body begins to betray her, and her sky flickers in the distance with the heat lightning of sex, you clear your throat and stroke your chin whiskers and tell her to go ask her mother. You can't help it – you're a walking cliché.

You fathers will understand. You have a little girl. She looks up to you. You're her oracle. You're her hero. And then the day comes when she gets her first permanent wave and goes to her first real party, and from that day on, you're in a constant state of panic.

<div align="right">EDWARD STREETER[38]</div>

A wedding is for daughters and fathers. The mothers all dress up, trying to look like young women. But a wedding is for a father and daughter. They stop being married to each other on that day.

<div align="right">SARAH RUHL[37]</div>

5. Brotherhood & Friendship

The brotherhood of men is not spoken; it is felt. We feel its undercurrent with all men, but most strongly with our friends.

For most men, I imagine, our closest friends are some of our oldest; Pete and I go back decades. I know him and his life story as he knows me and mine.

But other factors define "friend."

One of these is trust. I can rely on my men friends, all of them. If one makes a promise, it is kept. As the saying has it, "Word is bond."

We support each other in deed as well. Steve is my implicit second. He would back me in a fight, and what's more, he'd push me aside and take over the fighting for me.

Men mentor and coach each other at their home workshops, on playing fields, and on the job. At a new corporate tech-writing gig, Tom, a colleague, taught me the ropes of the work and the woven politics and personalities of our department, strands that would have taken me months to unbraid. I took him to lunch.

"You don't have to buy me a meal," he said. "I was just doing my job."

He'd eclipsed his job description; he'd been a brother.

Men volunteer to help each other, especially with physical work, even when unasked. I have a downed tree in my front yard, felled three months ago. Two friends, Marc and Pat, have dropped by and offered to help me limb, buck, and split it. When I lift the hood of my car, Jay, my across-the-street neighbor, wanders over, peers into the engine compartment with me, and says, "What's up?"

We keep each other's confidences without being asked, though sometimes we do ask. We take risks and understand when our friends take risks. We tend to not judge each other.[39]

I understand that both sexes can display some of these traits and behaviors; women mentor and coach each other all the time. But I sense that many men choose their male friends on these bases.

Men's friendships are strong and deeply meaningful to us. Blogs

casting them as less than women's – less intimate, less supportive – can be found on the web.[40] But as Dr. Roger Gould, a psychiatrist, said of men's relationships: "It is true that men do not easily show intimacies and … emotional responses. It does not mean the relationships are not filled with trust, deep regard and respect, fun, and sometimes crisis support."[41]

Amen, Dr. Gould.

The stories in this section bring the undercurrent of brotherhood and men's friendships to the surface.

Here is Michael Chabon's finely observed and deftly written, "The Hand on My Shoulder." With his first paragraph, Chabon paints a masterful portrait of his father-in-law and himself. With the next, he links his in-law's face and persona in a bravura display of observation, insight, and writing.

I wasn't planning on including poetry in this anthology until Richard Schiffman's "Buddies" arrived via email, his bromantic verse changing my prose/poetry calculus.

Stephen Crane wrote in the late 1800s. In "The Open Boat," he tells a tale of shipwreck, one that reads like fiction but is in fact reportage – an exemplar of "new journalism" a half-century before the style appeared. Crane writes a ripping story about the "subtle brotherhood" of four men in a 10-foot dinghy, on the open sea, in a storm.

I asked a renowned union organizer to suggest books on men's labor. He recommended Mike Cherry's *On High Steel,* for its stories about the ironworkers who erect bridges, towers, and tall buildings. The subtext of Cherry's chapter here, "Over the Side," is the disposability of men.

Michael Chabon

The Hand on My Shoulder

I didn't play golf, and he had never smoked marijuana. I was a nail chewer, inclined to brood, and dubious of the motives of other people. He was big and placid, uniformly kind to strangers and friends, and never went anywhere without whistling a little song. I minored in philosophy. He fell asleep watching television. He fell asleep in movie theaters, too, and occasionally, I suspected, while driving. He had been in the navy during World War II, which taught him, he said, to sleep whenever he could. I, still troubled no doubt by perplexing questions of ontology and epistemology raised during my brief flirtation with logical positivism ten years earlier, was an insomniac. I was also a Jew, of a sort; he was, when required, an Episcopalian.

He was not a big man, but his voice boomed, and his hands were meaty, and in repose there was something august about his heavy midwestern features: pale blue eyes that, in the absence of hopefulness, might have looked severe; prominent, straight nose and heavy jowls that, in the absence of mirth, might have seemed imperious and disapproving. Mirth and hopefulness, however, were never absent from his face. Some people, one imagines, may be naturally dauntless and buoyant of heart, but with him, good spirits always seemed, far more admirably, to be the product of a strict program of self-improvement in his youth – he believed, like most truly modest men, in the absolute virtue of self-improvement – which had wrought deep, essential changes in a nature inclined by birth to the darker view and gloominess that cropped up elsewhere in the family tree. He didn't seem to be happy out of some secret knowledge of the essential goodness of the world, or

from having fought his way through grief and adversity to a hard-won sense of his place in it; they were simple qualities, his good humor and his optimism, unexamined, automatic, stubborn. I never failed to take comfort in his presence.

The meaning of divorce will elude us as long as we are blind to the meaning of marriage, as I think at the start we must all be. Marriage seems – at least it seemed to an absurdly young man in the summer of 1987, standing on the sun-drenched patio of an elegant house on Lake Washington – to be an activity, like chess or tennis or a rumba contest, that we embark upon in tandem while everyone who loves us stands around and hopes for the best. We have no inkling of the fervor of their hope, nor of the ways in which our marriage, that collective endeavor, will be constructed from and burdened with their love.

When I look back – always an unreliable procedure, I know – it seems to have been a case of love at first sight. I met him, his wife, and their yellow beach house all on the same day. It was a square-pillared bungalow, clapboard and shake, the color of yellow gingham, with a steep pitched roof and a porch that looked out over a frigid but tranquil bay of brackish water. His wife, like him in the last years of a vigorous middle age, had been coming to this stretch of beach since early in her girlhood, and for both her and her daughter, whom I was shortly to marry, it was more heavily and richly layered with memories, associations, artifacts, and stories than any place any member of my own family had lived since we had left Europe seventy years before. Everything about this family was like that. My future mother-in-law lived in the house in Seattle where she had been born. My father-in-law had grown up down the road in Portland. They had met at the University of Washington. Everyone they knew, they had known for longer than I'd been alive. All the restaurants they favored had been in business for years, they were charter members of their country club, and in some cases they did business with the sons of tradesmen they had dealt with in the early days of their marriage. A journey through the drawers, closets, and cabinets of their house in town yielded a virtual commercial and social history of Seattle, in the form of old matchboxes, rulers, pens, memo pads, napkins, shot glasses, candy tins, golf tees, coat hangers; years and years'

worth of lagniappes, giveaways, souvenirs, and mementos bearing the names, in typefaces of four decades, of plumbing supply companies, fuel oil dealers, newlyweds, dry cleaners, men and women celebrating birthdays and anniversaries.

God, it was a seductive thing to a deracinated, assimilated, uncertain, wandering young Jew whose own parents had not been married for years and no longer lived anywhere near the house in Maryland where, for want of a truer candidate, he had more or less grown up. They were in many ways classic WASPs, to be sure, golfing, khaki-wearing, gin-drinking WASPs. The appeal of such people and their kind of world to a young man such as I was has been well-documented in film and literature; perhaps enough to seem by now a bit outdated. But it wasn't, finally, a matter of class or style, though they had both. I fell in love with their rootedness, with the visible and palpable continuity of their history as a family in Seattle, with their ability to bring a box of photographs taken thirty summers earlier and show me the room I was sitting in before it was painted white, the madrone trees that screened the porch before two fell over, the woman I was going to marry digging for geoduck clams on the beach where she had just lain sunbathing.

Of course, they were more than a kind of attractive gift wrap for their photographs, houses, and the historical contents of their drawers. They were ordinary, problematical people, my in-laws, forty years into a complicated marriage, and over the course of my own brief marriage to their daughter, I came to love and appreciate them both as individuals, on their merits and, as my marriage began so quickly to sour, for the endurance of their partnership. They had that blind, towering doggedness of the World War II generation. I suppose it's possible that with two daughters, they'd always wanted a son, my father-in-law especially; I do know for certain that I have never been one to refuse the opportunity to add another father to my collection.

He offered himself completely, without reservation, though in his own particular, not to say limited, way (it is this inherent limited quality of fathers and their love that motivates collectors like me to try to amass a complete set). He took me down to Nordstrom, the original store in downtown Seattle, and introduced me to the man who sold him

his suits. I bought myself a few good square-cut, sober-colored numbers in a style that would not have drawn a second glance on Yesler Way in 1954. He introduced me to the woman from whom he bought jewelry for his wife, to the man who took care of his car, to all of the golf buddies and cronies whose sons he had been admiring from afar for the last thirty years. He was a bit barrel chested anyway, but whenever we went anywhere together and, as was all but inevitable, ran into someone he knew, his breast, introducing me, seemed to grow an inch broader, the hand on my shoulder would administer a little fight-trainer massage, and I would feel him – as first the wedding and, later, the putative grandchildren drew nearer – placing, for that moment, all his hopes in me. He took me to football games, basketball games, baseball games. He let me drive his Cadillac; naturally, he never drove anything else. Most of all, however – most important to both of us – he let me hang out in his den.

As the child of divorced parents, myself divorced, and a writer trained by five hundred years of European and American literary history always to search out the worm in the bud, I have, of necessity, become a close observer of other people's marriages. I have noticed that in nearly all the longest-lived ones, if there is space enough in the house, each partner will have a room to flee to. If, however, there is only one room to spare, it will always be the husband's. My in-laws had plenty of room, but while she had her office just off the bedroom (where I would sometimes see her sitting at a Chinese desk, writing a letter or searching for an article clipped from *Town & Country* about flavoring ice creams with edible flowers), my mother-in-law's appeared to serve a largely ceremonial function.

My father-in-law, on the other hand, sometimes seemed to live down in the basement. His office, like him, was mostly about golf. The carpet was Bermuda-grass green, the walls were hung with maps of St. Andrews and framed *New Yorker* covers of duffers, and the various hats, ashtrays, hassocks, cigarette lighters, plaques, novelty telephones, and trophies around the room were shaped like golf balls, tees, mashies, mulligans, and I don't know what. In the midst of all this sat an enormous black Robber Baron desk with matching black Captain Nemo

chair; an old, vaguely Japanese-looking coffee table on its last tour of duty in the house; a cyclopean television; and a reclining armchair and sofa, both covered in wool patterned with the tartan of some unknown but no doubt staunch, whiskey-drinking, golf-wild highland clan.

It is for just such circumstances, in which two men with little in common may find themselves thrown together with no other recourse than to make friends, that sports were invented. When my wife and I visited I went downstairs, flopped on the sofa, and watched a game with my father-in-law. He made himself a CC and soda, and sometimes, to complete the picture, I let him mix one for me. Like many men of my generation, I found solace when unhappy in placing quotation marks around myself and everything I did. There was I, an "unhappy husband," drinking a "cocktail" and "watching the game." This was the only room in the house where I was permitted to smoke – I have long since quit – and I made the most of it (a man's den often serves the same de-sublimating function in the household as Mardi Gras or Las Vegas in the world: a different law obtains there). We spent hours together, cheering on Art Monk and Carlton Fisk and other men whose names, when by chance they arise now, can summon up that entire era of whiskey and football and the smell of new Coupe de Ville, when the biggest mistake I ever made came home to roost, and I briefly had one of the best fathers I've ever found.

My ex-wife and I – I won't go into the details – had good times and bad times, fought and were silent, tried and gave up and tried some more before finally throwing in the towel, focused, with the special self-absorption of the miserable, on our minute drama and its reverberations in our own chests. All the while, the people who loved us were not sitting there whispering behind their hands like spectators at a chess match. They were putting our photographs in frames on their walls. They were uniting our names over and over on the outsides of envelopes that bore anniversary wishes and recipes clipped from newspapers. They were putting our birthdays in their address books, knitting us socks, studying the fluctuating fortunes of our own favorite hitters every morning in the box scores. They were working us into the fabric of their lives. When at last we broke all those promises that we thought

we had made only to each other, in an act of faithlessness whose mutuality appeared somehow to make it all right, we tore that fabric, not irrecoverably but deeply. We had no idea how quickly two families can work to weave themselves together. When I saw him sometime later at his mother's funeral in Portland, my father-in-law told me that the day my divorce from his daughter came through was the saddest one in his life. Maybe that was when I started to understand what had happened.

What was I now to him? How can it have felt to have been divorced by someone he treated like a son? These are not considerations that comfort me or make me especially proud. I try to remind myself that in the long course of his life, I occupied only a tiny span of years toward the end, when everything gleams with an unconvincing luster, moving too quickly to be real. And I try to forget that for a short while I formed a layer, however thin, in the deep stratigraphy of his family, so that some later explorer, rummaging through the drawers of his big old desk, might brush aside a scorecard from the 1967 PGA Pacific Northwest Open signed by Arnold Palmer, or an old pencil-style typewriter eraser with a stiff brush on one end, stamped queen city ribbon co., and turn up a faded photograph of me, in my sober blue suit, flower in my lapel, looking as if I knew what I was doing.

RICHARD SCHIFFMAN

Buddies

I called you after you died to hear again your ducky voice
on the answering machine.

 For weeks you continued:
 "This is Will at Bathrooms Restored, please leave a message
 after the beep."

 But I never did. What was there to say?
 Even before – what was there to say? You used to call
 first thing in the morning, "Hey Richard, it's Will,"
 and I'd say, "Hey Will, what's up?" We'd chew the bull, maybe
 plan to meet that evening. "Will, there's a concert at Carnegie,
 I can get free tickets."

 And you would trudge over
 wasted after a day of laying tiles,
 then nod off during the Beethoven.
 Who else could sleep through the "Ode to Joy"?

 Later we'd go to an all-night cafe and you would yatter
 about your nonexistent love life, and I would tell you mine.
 Guy talk, unrepeatable mostly.

 And then,
 go figure,
 you were dying,

and I sat there with the gaunt shell of you
 too stunned to speak, and you too sick to speak
(although we both knew that there was nothing left to say).

I could only hold you, but that didn't feel right either:
 two awkward and dry-eyed male animals clutching.

 Give me a break!

Later, of course, the tears did come,
 for me at least, when you moved upstate. I'm guessing
 that you had already gone beyond the veil
 where tears make sense.

On my last visit, your eyes, not exactly vacant,
 but impenetrable wells, so purged of wanting
 and of needing that they were no longer entirely human.
 Was this the enlightenment that we both pursued to India
 and beyond? Or maybe just pain, which also clears the deck
 magnificently.

Or death. That will do it too. I'd like to ask.

But it has been years since your answering machine
 stopped answering. And talk was never your thing,
 Will, nor mine, when I was with you.

We understood each other without it
 in those days before male bonding,
 when no one said the word "love," or needed to.

Stephen Crane's civil war novel, The Red Badge of Courage, *his best-known work, was written without his having had battle experience. On the other hand, "The Open Boat," his best-known short story, is based on his hellacious experience surviving the wreck of the SS Commodore off the coast of Florida on January 2, 1897. If you settle into the lingo of the nineteenth century – easy – you'll will find that Crane, though writing as a reporter, his prose dipped in poetry, is quite a yarner.*

Stephen Crane

The Open Boat

A Tale intended to be after the Fact. Being the Experience of Four Men from the Sunk Steamer "Commodore"

I

None of them knew the color of the sky. Their eyes glanced level, and were fastened upon the waves that swept toward them. These waves were of the hue of slate, save for the tops, which were of foaming white, and all of the men knew the colors of the sea. The horizon narrowed and widened, and dipped and rose, and at all times its edge was jagged with waves that seemed thrust up in points like rocks.

Many a man ought to have a bathtub larger than the boat which here rode upon the sea. These waves were most wrongfully and barbarously abrupt and tall, and each froth-top was a problem in small boat navigation.

The cook squatted in the bottom and looked with both eyes at the six inches of gunwale which separated him from the ocean. His sleeves were rolled over his fat forearms, and the two flaps of his unbuttoned vest dangled as he bent to bail out the boat. Often he said: "Gawd! That was a narrow clip." As he remarked it he invariably gazed eastward over the broken sea.

The oiler, steering with one of the two oars in the boat, sometimes raised himself suddenly to keep clear of water that swirled in over the stern. It was a thin little oar and it seemed often ready to snap.

The correspondent, pulling at the other oar, watched the waves and wondered why he was there.

The injured captain, lying in the bow, was at this time buried in that profound dejection and indifference which comes, temporarily at least, to even the bravest and most enduring when, willy-nilly, the firm fails, the army loses, the ship goes down. The mind of the master of a vessel is rooted deep in the timbers of her, though he commanded for a day or a decade, and this captain had on him the stern impression of a scene in the grays of dawn of seven turned faces, and later a stump of a top-mast with a white ball on it that slashed to and fro at the waves, went low and lower, and down. Thereafter there was something strange in his voice. Although steady, it was deep with mourning, and of a quality beyond oration or tears.

"Keep 'er a little more south, Billie," said he.

"A little more south, sir," said the oiler in the stern.

A seat in this boat was not unlike a seat upon a bucking bronco, and, by the same token, a bronco is not much smaller. The craft pranced and reared, and plunged like an animal. As each wave came, and she rose for it, she seemed like a horse making at a fence outrageously high. The manner of her scramble over these walls of water is a mystic thing, and, moreover, at the top of them were ordinarily these problems in white water, the foam racing down from the summit of each wave, requiring a new leap, and a leap from the air. Then, after scornfully bumping a crest, she would slide, and race, and splash down a long incline, and arrive bobbing and nodding in front of the next menace.

A singular disadvantage of the sea lies in the fact that after success-fully surmounting one wave you discover that there is another behind it just as important and just as nervously anxious to do something effective in the way of swamping boats. In a ten-foot dinghy one can get an idea of the resources of the sea in the line of waves that is not probable to the average experience which is never at sea in a dinghy. As each slatey wall of water approached, it shut all else from the view of the men in the boat, and it was not difficult to imagine that this par-ticular wave was the final outburst of the ocean, the last effort of the grim water. There was a terrible grace in the move of the waves, and

they came in silence, save for the snarling of the crests.

In the wan light, the faces of the men must have been gray. Their eyes must have glinted in strange ways as they gazed steadily astern. Viewed from a balcony, the whole thing would doubtlessly have been weirdly picturesque. But the men in the boat had no time to see it, and if they had had leisure there were other things to occupy their minds. The sun swung steadily up the sky, and they knew it was broad day because the color of the sea changed from slate to emerald green, streaked with amber lights, and the foam was like tumbling snow. The process of the breaking day was unknown to them. They were aware only of this effect upon the color of the waves that rolled toward them.

In disjointed sentences the cook and the correspondent argued as to the difference between a life saving station and a house of refuge. The cook had said: "There's a house of refuge just north of the Mosquito Inlet Light,[42] and as soon as they see us, they'll come off in their boat and pick us up."

"As soon as who see us?" said the correspondent.

"The crew," said the cook.

"Houses of refuge don't have crews," said the correspondent. "As I understand them, they are only places where clothes and grub are stored for the benefit of shipwrecked people. They don't carry crews."

"Oh, yes, they do," said the cook.

"No, they don't," said the correspondent.

"Well, we're not there yet, anyhow," said the oiler, in the stern.

"Well," said the cook, "perhaps it's not a house of refuge that I'm thinking of as being near Mosquito Inlet Light. Perhaps it's a life saving station."

"We're not there yet," said the oiler, in the stern.

II

As the boat bounced from the top of each wave, the wind tore through the hair of the hatless men, and as the craft plopped her stern down again the spray slashed past them. The crest of each of these waves was a hill, from the top of which the men surveyed, for a moment, a broad

tumultuous expanse, shining and wind riven. It was probably splendid. It was probably glorious, this play of the free sea, wild with lights of emerald and white and amber.

"Bully good thing it's an onshore wind," said the cook. "If not, where would we be? Wouldn't have a show."

"That's right," said the correspondent.

The busy oiler nodded his assent.

Then the captain, in the bow, chuckled in a way that expressed humor, contempt, tragedy, all in one. "Do you think we've got much of a show now, boys?" said he.

Whereupon the three were silent, save for a trifle of hemming and hawing. To express any particular optimism at this time they felt to be childish and stupid, but they all doubtless possessed this sense of the situation in their mind. A young man thinks doggedly at such times. On the other hand, the ethics of their condition was decidedly against any open suggestion of hopelessness. So they were silent.

"Oh, well," said the captain, soothing his children, "we'll get ashore all right."

But there was that in his tone which made them think, so the oiler quoth: "Yes! If this wind holds!"

The cook was bailing: "Yes! If we don't catch hell in the surf."

Canton flannel gulls flew near and far. Sometimes they sat down on the sea, near patches of brown seaweed that rolled over the waves with a movement like carpets on a line in a gale. The birds sat comfortably in groups, and they were envied by some in the dinghy, for the wrath of the sea was no more to them than it was to a covey of prairie chickens a thousand miles inland. Often they came very close and stared at the men with black bead-like eyes. At these times they were uncanny and sinister in their unblinking scrutiny, and the men hooted angrily at them, telling them to be gone. One came, and evidently decided to alight on the top of the captain's head. The bird flew parallel to the boat and did not circle, but made short sidelong jumps in the air in chicken fashion. His black eyes were wistfully fixed upon the captain's head.

"Ugly brute," said the oiler to the bird. "You look as if you were made with a jackknife."

The cook and the correspondent swore darkly at the creature. The captain naturally wished to knock it away with the end of the heavy painter; but he did not dare do it, because anything resembling an emphatic gesture would have capsized this freighted boat, and so with his open hand, the captain gently and carefully waved the gull away. After it had been discouraged from the pursuit the captain breathed easier on account of his hair, and others breathed easier because the bird struck their minds at this time as being somehow gruesome and ominous.

In the meantime the oiler and the correspondent rowed. And also they rowed.

They sat together in the same seat, and each rowed an oar. Then the oiler took both oars; then the correspondent took both oars; then the oiler; then the correspondent. They rowed and they rowed. The very ticklish part of the business was when the time came for the reclining one in the stern to take his turn at the oars. By the very last star of truth, it is easier to steal eggs from under a hen than it was to change seats in the dinghy. First the man in the stern slid his hand along the thwart and moved with care, as if he were of Sèvres. Then the man in the rowing seat slid his hand along the other thwart. It was all done with the most extraordinary care. As the two sidled past each other, the whole party kept watchful eyes on the coming wave, and the captain cried: "Look out now! Steady there!"

The brown mats of seaweed that appeared from time to time were like islands, bits of earth. They were traveling, apparently, neither one way nor the other. They were, to all intents, stationary. They informed the men in the boat that it was making progress slowly toward the land.

The captain, rearing cautiously in the bow, after the dinghy soared on a great swell, said that he had seen the lighthouse at Mosquito Inlet. Presently the cook remarked that he had seen it. The correspondent was at the oars then, and for some reason he too wished to look at the lighthouse, but his back was toward the far shore and the waves were important, and for some time he could not seize an opportunity to turn his head. But at last there came a wave more gentle than the others, and when at the crest of it he swiftly scoured the western horizon.

"See it?" said the captain.

"No," said the correspondent slowly, "I didn't see anything."

"Look again," said the captain. He pointed. "It's exactly in that direction."

At the top of another wave, the correspondent did as he was bid, and this time his eyes chanced on a small still thing on the edge of the swaying horizon. It was precisely like the point of a pin. It took an anxious eye to find a lighthouse so tiny.

"Think we'll make it, captain?"

"If this wind holds and the boat don't swamp, we can't do much else," said the captain.

The little boat, lifted by each towering sea, and splashed viciously by the crests, made progress that in the absence of seaweed was not apparent to those in her. She seemed just a wee thing wallowing, miraculously top-up, at the mercy of five oceans. Occasionally, a great spread of water, like white flames, swarmed into her.

"Bail her, cook," said the captain serenely.

"All right, captain," said the cheerful cook.

<p style="text-align:center">III</p>

It would be difficult to describe the subtle brotherhood of men that was here established on the seas. No one said that it was so. No one mentioned it. But it dwelt in the boat, and each man felt it warm him. They were a captain, an oiler, a cook, and a correspondent, and they were friends, friends in a more curiously iron-bound degree than may be common. The hurt captain, lying against the water jar in the bow, spoke always in a low voice and calmly, but he could never command a more ready and swiftly obedient crew than the motley three of the dinghy. It was more than a mere recognition of what was best for the common safety. There was surely in it a quality that was personal and heartfelt. And after this devotion to the commander of the boat there was this comradeship that the correspondent, for instance, who had been taught to be cynical of men, knew even at the time was the best experience of his life. But no one said that it was so. No one mentioned it.

"I wish we had a sail," remarked the captain. "We might try my

overcoat on the end of an oar and give you two boys a chance to rest." So the cook and the correspondent held the mast and spread wide the overcoat. The oiler steered, and the little boat made good way with her new rig. Sometimes the oiler had to scull sharply to keep a sea from breaking into the boat, but otherwise sailing was a success.

Meanwhile the lighthouse had been growing slowly larger. It had now almost assumed color, and appeared like a little gray shadow on the sky. The man at the oars could not be prevented from turning his head rather often to try for a glimpse of this little gray shadow.

At last, from the top of each wave the men in the tossing boat could see land. Even as the lighthouse was an upright shadow on the sky, this land seemed but a long black shadow on the sea. It certainly was thinner than paper. "We must be about opposite New Smyrna," said the cook, who had coasted this shore often in schooners. "Captain, by the way, I believe they abandoned that life saving station there about a year ago."

"Did they?" said the captain.

The wind slowly died away. The cook and the correspondent were not now obliged to slave in order to hold high the oar. But the waves continued their old impetuous swooping at the dinghy, and the little craft, no longer under way, struggled woundily over them. The oiler or the correspondent took the oars again.

Shipwrecks are à propos of nothing. If men could only train for them and have them occur when the men had reached pink condition, there would be less drowning at sea. Of the four in the dinghy none had slept any time worth mentioning for two days and two nights previous to embarking in the dinghy, and in the excitement of clambering about the deck of a foundering ship they had also forgotten to eat heartily.

For these reasons, and for others, neither the oiler nor the correspondent was fond of rowing at this time. The correspondent wondered ingenuously how in the name of all that was sane could there be people who thought it amusing to row a boat. It was not an amusement; it was a diabolical punishment, and even a genius of mental aberrations could never conclude that it was anything but a horror to the muscles and a crime against the back. He mentioned to the boat in general how the amusement of rowing struck him, and the weary-faced oiler smiled in

full sympathy. Previously to the foundering, by the way, the oiler had worked double watch in the engine room of the ship.

"Take her easy, now, boys," said the captain. "Don't spend yourselves. If we have to run a surf you'll need all your strength, because we'll sure have to swim for it. Take your time."

Slowly the land arose from the sea. From a black line it became a line of black and a line of white, trees and sand. Finally, the captain said that he could make out a house on the shore. "That's the house of refuge, sure," said the cook. "They'll see us before long, and come out after us."

The distant lighthouse reared high. "The keeper ought to be able to make us out now, if he's looking through a glass," said the captain. "He'll notify the life saving people."

"None of those other boats could have got ashore to give word of the wreck," said the oiler, in a low voice. "Else the lifeboat would be out hunting us."

Slowly and beautifully the land loomed out of the sea. The wind came again. It had veered from the northeast to the southeast. Finally, a new sound struck the ears of the men in the boat. It was the low thunder of the surf on the shore. "We'll never be able to make the lighthouse now," said the captain. "Swing her head a little more north, Billie," said he.

"A little more north, sir," said the oiler.

Whereupon the little boat turned her nose once more down the wind, and all but the oarsman watched the shore grow. Under the influence of this expansion doubt and direful apprehension was leaving the minds of the men. The management of the boat was still most absorbing, but it could not prevent a quiet cheerfulness. In an hour, perhaps, they would be ashore.

Their backbones had become thoroughly used to balancing in the boat, and they now rode this wild colt of a dinghy like circus men. The correspondent thought that he had been drenched to the skin, but happening to feel in the top pocket of his coat, he found therein eight cigars. Four of them were soaked with sea water; four were perfectly scatheless. After a search, somebody produced three dry matches, and thereupon the four waifs rode impudently in their little boat, and with an assurance of an impending rescue shining in their eyes, puffed at the

big cigars and judged well and ill of all men. Everybody took a drink of water.

IV

"Cook," remarked the captain, "there don't seem to be any signs of life about your house of refuge."

"No," replied the cook. "Funny they don't see us!"

A broad stretch of lowly coast lay before the eyes of the men. It was of dunes topped with dark vegetation. The roar of the surf was plain, and sometimes they could see the white lip of a wave as it spun up the beach. A tiny house was blocked out black upon the sky. Southward, the slim lighthouse lifted its little gray length.

Tide, wind, and waves were swinging the dinghy northward. "Funny they don't see us," said the men.

The surf's roar was here dulled, but its tone was, nevertheless, thunderous and mighty. As the boat swam over the great rollers, the men sat listening to this roar. "We'll swamp sure," said everybody.

It is fair to say here that there was not a life saving station within twenty miles in either direction, but the men did not know this fact, and in consequence they made dark and opprobrious remarks concerning the eyesight of the nation's lifesavers. Four scowling men sat in the dinghy and surpassed records in the invention of epithets.

"Funny they don't see us."

The lightheartedness of a former time had completely faded. To their sharpened minds it was easy to conjure pictures of all kinds of incompetency and blindness and, indeed, cowardice. There was the shore of the populous land, and it was bitter and bitter to them that from it came no sign.

"Well," said the captain, ultimately, "I suppose we'll have to make a try for ourselves. If we stay out here too long, we'll none of us have strength left to swim after the boat swamps."

And so the oiler, who was at the oars, turned the boat straight for the shore. There was a sudden tightening of muscles. There was some thinking.

"If we don't all get ashore...." said the captain. "If we don't all get

ashore, I suppose you fellows know where to send news of my finish?"

They then briefly exchanged some addresses and admonitions. As for the reflections of the men, there was a great deal of rage in them. Perchance they might be formulated thus: "If I am going to be drowned – if I am going to be drowned – if I am going to be drowned, why, in the name of the seven mad gods who rule the sea, was I allowed to come thus far and contemplate sand and trees? Was I brought here merely to have my nose dragged away as I was about to nibble the sacred cheese of life? It is preposterous. If this old ninny-woman, Fate, cannot do better than this, she should be deprived of the management of men's fortunes. She is an old hen who knows not her intention. If she has decided to drown me, why did she not do it in the beginning and save me all this trouble? The whole affair is absurd.... But no, she cannot mean to drown me. She dare not drown me. She cannot drown me. Not after all this work." Afterward the man might have had an impulse to shake his fist at the clouds: "Just you drown me, now, and then hear what I call you!"

The billows that came at this time were more formidable. They seemed always just about to break and roll over the little boat in a turmoil of foam. There was a preparatory and long growl in the speech of them. No mind unused to the sea would have concluded that the dinghy could ascend these sheer heights in time. The shore was still afar. The oiler was a wily surfman. "Boys," he said swiftly, "she won't live three minutes more, and we're too far out to swim. Shall I take her to sea again, captain?"

"Yes! Go ahead!" said the captain.

This oiler, by a series of quick miracles, and fast and steady oarsmanship, turned the boat in the middle of the surf and took her safely to sea again.

There was a considerable silence as the boat bumped over the furrowed sea to deeper water. Then somebody in gloom spoke. "Well, anyhow, they must have seen us from the shore by now."

The gulls went in slanting flight up the wind toward the gray desolate east. A squall, marked by dingy clouds, and clouds brick red, like smoke from a burning building, appeared from the southeast.

"What do you think of those lifesaving people? Ain't they peaches?"

"Funny they haven't seen us."

"Maybe they think we're out here for sport! Maybe they think we're fishin'. Maybe they think we're damned fools."

It was a long afternoon. A changed tide tried to force them southward, but wind and wave said northward. Far ahead, where coastline, sea, and sky formed their mighty angle, there were little dots which seemed to indicate a city on the shore.

"St. Augustine?"

The captain shook his head. "Too near Mosquito Inlet."

And the oiler rowed, and then the correspondent rowed. Then the oiler rowed. It was a weary business. The human back can become the seat of more aches and pains than are registered in books for the composite anatomy of a regiment. It is a limited area, but it can become the theatre of innumerable muscular conflicts, tangles, wrenches, knots, and other comforts.

"Did you ever like to row, Billie?" asked the correspondent.

"No," said the oiler. "Hang it."

When one exchanged the rowing seat for a place in the bottom of the boat, he suffered a bodily depression that caused him to be careless of everything save an obligation to wiggle one finger. There was cold seawater swashing to and fro in the boat, and he lay in it. His head, pillowed on a thwart, was within an inch of the swirl of a wave crest, and sometimes a particularly obstreperous sea came in-board and drenched him once more. But these matters did not annoy him. It is almost certain that if the boat had capsized he would have tumbled comfortably out upon the ocean as if he felt sure that it was a great soft mattress.

"Look! There's a man on the shore!"

"Where?"

"There! See 'im? See 'im?"

"Yes, sure! He's walking along."

"Now he's stopped. Look! He's facing us!"

"He's waving at us!"

"So he is! By thunder!"

"Ah, now we're all right! Now we're all right! There'll be a boat out

here for us in half an hour."

"He's going on. He's running. He's going up to that house there."

The remote beach seemed lower than the sea, and it required a searching glance to discern the little black figure. The captain saw a floating stick and they rowed to it. A bath towel was by some weird chance in the boat, and, tying this on the stick, the captain waved it. The oarsman did not dare turn his head, so he was obliged to ask questions.

"What's he doing now?"

"He's standing still again. He's looking, I think.... There he goes again. Towards the house.... Now he's stopped again."

"Is he waving at us?"

"No, not now! He was, though."

"Look! There comes another man!"

"He's running."

"Look at him go, would you."

"Why, he's on a bicycle. Now he's met the other man. They're both waving at us. Look!"

"There comes something up the beach."

"What the devil is that thing?"

"Why, it looks like a boat."

"Why, certainly it's a boat."

"No, it's on wheels."

"Yes, so it is. Well, that must be the lifeboat. They drag them along shore on a wagon."

"That's the lifeboat, sure."

"No, by…, it's … it's a bus."

"I tell you it's a lifeboat."

"It is not! It's a bus. I can see it plain. See? One of these big hotel buses."

"By thunder, you're right. It's a bus, sure as fate. What do you suppose they are doing with a bus? Maybe they are going around collecting the life crew, hey?"

"That's it, likely. Look! There's a fellow waving a little black flag. He's standing on the steps of the bus. There come those other two fellows.

Now they're all talking together. Look at the fellow with the flag. Maybe he ain't waving it."

"That ain't a flag, is it? That's his coat. Why certainly, that's his coat."

"So it is. It's his coat. He's taken it off and is waving it around his head. But would you look at him swing it."

"Oh, say, there isn't any life saving station there. That's just a winter resort hotel bus that has brought over some of the boarders to see us drown."

"What's that idiot with the coat mean? What's he signaling, anyhow?"

"It looks as if he were trying to tell us to go north. There must be a life saving station up there."

"No! He thinks we're fishing. Just giving us a merry hand. See? Ah, there, Willie."

"Well, I wish I could make something out of those signals. What do you suppose he means?"

"He don't mean anything. He's just playing."

"Well, if he'd just signal us to try the surf again, or to go to sea and wait, or go north, or go south, or go to hell – there would be some reason in it. But look at him. He just stands there and keeps his coat revolving like a wheel. The ass!"

"There come more people."

"Now there's quite a mob. Look! Isn't that a boat?"

"Where? Oh, I see where you mean. No, that's no boat."

"That fellow is still waving his coat."

"He must think we like to see him do that. Why don't he quit it? It don't mean anything."

"I don't know. I think he is trying to make us go north. It must be that there's a life saving station there somewhere."

"Say, he ain't tired yet. Look at 'im wave."

"Wonder how long he can keep that up. He's been revolving his coat ever since he caught sight of us. He's an idiot. Why aren't they getting men to bring a boat out? A fishing boat – one of those big yawls – could come out here all right. Why don't he do something?"

"Oh, it's all right, now."

"They'll have a boat out here for us in less than no time, now that they've seen us."

A faint yellow tone came into the sky over the low land. The shadows on the sea slowly deepened. The wind bore coldness with it, and the men began to shiver.

"Holy smoke!" said one, allowing his voice to express his impious mood, "if we keep on monkeying out here! If we've got to flounder out here all night!"

"Oh, we'll never have to stay here all night! Don't you worry. They've seen us now, and it won't be long before they'll come chasing out after us."

The shore grew dusky. The man waving a coat blended gradually into this gloom, and it swallowed in the same manner the bus and the group of people. The spray, when it dashed uproariously over the side, made the voyagers shrink and swear like men who were being branded.

"I'd like to catch the chump who waved the coat. I feel like soaking him one, just for luck."

"Why? What did he do?"

"Oh, nothing, but then he seemed so damned cheerful."

In the meantime the oiler rowed, and then the correspondent rowed, and then the oiler rowed. Gray faced and bowed forward, they mechanically, turn by turn, plied the leaden oars. The form of the lighthouse had vanished from the southern horizon, but finally a pale star appeared, just lifting from the sea. The streaked saffron in the west passed before the all-merging darkness, and the sea to the east was black. The land had vanished, and was expressed only by the low and drear thunder of the surf.

"If I am going to be drowned – if I am going to be drowned – if I am going to be drowned, why, in the name of the seven mad gods who rule the sea, was I allowed to come thus far and contemplate sand and trees? Was I brought here merely to have my nose dragged away as I was about to nibble the sacred cheese of life?"

The patient captain, drooped over the water jar, was sometimes obliged to speak to the oarsman.

"Keep her head up! Keep her head up!"

"Keep her head up, sir." The voices were weary and low.

This was surely a quiet evening. All save the oarsman lay heavily and

listlessly in the boat's bottom. As for him, his eyes were just capable of noting the tall black waves that swept forward in a most sinister silence, save for an occasional subdued growl of a crest.

The cook's head was on a thwart, and he looked without interest at the water under his nose. He was deep in other scenes. Finally he spoke. "Billie," he murmured, dreamfully, "what kind of pie do you like best?"

<h1 style="text-align:center">V</h1>

"Pie," said the oiler and the correspondent, agitatedly. "Don't talk about those things, blast you!"

"Well," said the cook, "I was just thinking about ham sandwiches, and...."

A night on the sea in an open boat is a long night. As darkness settled finally, the shine of the light, lifting from the sea in the south, changed to full gold. On the northern horizon a new light appeared, a small bluish gleam on the edge of the waters. These two lights were the furniture of the world. Otherwise there was nothing but waves.

Two men huddled in the stern, and distances were so magnificent in the dinghy that the rower was enabled to keep his feet partly warmed by thrusting them under his companions. Their legs indeed extended far under the rowing seat until they touched the feet of the captain forward. Sometimes, despite the efforts of the tired oarsman, a wave came piling into the boat, an icy wave of the night, and the chilling water soaked them anew. They would twist their bodies for a moment and groan, and sleep the dead sleep once more, while the water in the boat gurgled about them as the craft rocked.

The plan of the oiler and the correspondent was for one to row until he lost the ability, and then arouse the other from his seawater couch in the bottom of the boat.

The oiler plied the oars until his head drooped forward, and the overpowering sleep blinded him. And he rowed yet afterward. Then he touched a man in the bottom of the boat, and called his name. "Will you spell me for a little while?" he said, meekly.

"Sure, Billie," said the correspondent, awakening and dragging

himself to a sitting position. They exchanged places carefully, and the oiler, cuddling down in the seawater at the cook's side, seemed to go to sleep instantly.

The particular violence of the sea had ceased. The waves came without snarling. The obligation of the man at the oars was to keep the boat headed so that the tilt of the rollers would not capsize her, and to preserve her from filling when the crests rushed past. The black waves were silent and hard to be seen in the darkness. Often one was almost upon the boat before the oarsman was aware.

In a low voice the correspondent addressed the captain. He was not sure that the captain was awake, although this iron man seemed to be always awake. "Captain, shall I keep her making for that light north, sir?"

The same steady voice answered him. "Yes. Keep it about two points off the port bow."

The cook had tied a lifebelt around himself in order to get even the warmth which this clumsy cork contrivance could donate, and he seemed almost stove-like when a rower, whose teeth invariably chattered wildly as soon as he ceased his labor, dropped down to sleep.

The correspondent, as he rowed, looked down at the two men sleeping underfoot. The cook's arm was around the oiler's shoulders, and, with their fragmentary clothing and haggard faces, they were the babes of the sea, a grotesque rendering of the old babes in the wood.

Later he must have grown stupid at his work, for suddenly there was a growling of water, and a crest came with a roar and a swash into the boat, and it was a wonder that it did not set the cook afloat in his lifebelt. The cook continued to sleep, but the oiler sat up, blinking his eyes and shaking with the new cold.

"Oh, I'm awful sorry, Billie," said the correspondent contritely.

"That's all right, old boy," said the oiler, and lay down again and was asleep.

Presently it seemed that even the captain dozed, and the correspondent thought that he was the one man afloat on all the oceans. The wind had a voice as it came over the waves, and it was sadder than the end.

There was a long, loud swishing astern of the boat, and a gleaming

trail of phosphorescence, like blue flame, was furrowed on the black waters. It might have been made by a monstrous knife.

Then there came a stillness, while the correspondent breathed with the open mouth and looked at the sea.

Suddenly there was another swish and another long flash of bluish light, and this time it was alongside the boat, and might almost have been reached with an oar. The correspondent saw an enormous fin speed like a shadow through the water, hurling the crystalline spray and leaving the long glowing trail.

The correspondent looked over his shoulder at the captain. His face was hidden, and he seemed to be asleep. He looked at the babes of the sea. They certainly were asleep. So, being bereft of sympathy, he leaned a little way to one side and swore softly into the sea.

But the thing did not then leave the vicinity of the boat. Ahead or astern, on one side or the other, at intervals long or short, fled the long sparkling streak, and there was to be heard the whiroo of the dark fin. The speed and power of the thing was greatly to be admired. It cut the water like a gigantic and keen projectile.

The presence of this biding thing did not affect the man with the same horror that it would if he had been a picnicker. He simply looked at the sea dully and swore in an undertone.

Nevertheless, it is true that he did not wish to be alone. He wished one of his companions to awaken by chance and keep him company with it. But the captain hung motionless over the water jar, and the oiler and the cook in the bottom of the boat were plunged in slumber.

VI

"If I am going to be drowned – if I am going to be drowned – if I am going to be drowned, why, in the name of the seven mad gods who rule the sea, was I allowed to come thus far and contemplate sand and trees?"

During this dismal night, it may be remarked that a man would conclude that it was really the intention of the seven mad gods to drown him, despite the abominable injustice of it. For it was certainly an abominable injustice to drown a man who had worked so hard, so hard.

The man felt it would be a crime most unnatural. Other people had drowned at sea since galleys swarmed with painted sails, but still....

When it occurs to a man that nature does not regard him as important, and that she feels she would not maim the universe by disposing of him, he at first wishes to throw bricks at the temple, and he hates deeply the fact that there are no bricks and no temples. Any visible expression of nature would surely be pelleted with his jeers.

Then, if there be no tangible thing to how he feels, perhaps, the desire to confront a personification and indulge in pleas, bowed to one knee, and with hands supplicant, saying: "Yes, but I love myself."

A high cold star on a winter's night is the word he feels that she says to him. Thereafter he knows the pathos of his situation.

The men in the dinghy had not discussed these matters, but each had, no doubt, reflected upon them in silence and according to his mind. There was seldom any expression upon their faces save the general one of complete weariness. Speech was devoted to the business of the boat.

The thing which had followed the boat and waited, had evidently grown bored at the delay. There was no longer to be heard the slash of the cut water, and there was no longer the flame of the long trail. The light in the north still glimmered, but it was apparently no nearer to the boat. Sometimes the boom of the surf rang in the correspondent's ears, and he turned the craft seaward then and rowed harder. Southward, some one had evidently built a watchfire on the beach. It was too low and too far to be seen, but it made a shimmering, roseate reflection upon the bluff back of it, and this could be discerned from the boat. The wind came stronger, and sometimes a wave suddenly raged out like a mountain cat, and there was to be seen the sheen and sparkle of a broken crest.

The captain, in the bow, moved on his water jar and sat erect. "Pretty long night," he observed to the correspondent. He looked at the shore. "Those lifesaving people take their time."

"Did you see that shark playing around?"

"Yes, I saw him. He was a big fellow, all right."

"Wish I had known you were awake."

Later the correspondent spoke into the bottom of the boat.

"Billie!" There was a slow and gradual disentanglement. "Billie, will you spell me?"

"Sure," said the oiler.

As soon as the correspondent touched the cold comfortable seawater in the bottom of the boat, and had huddled close to the cook's lifebelt he was deep in sleep, despite the fact that his teeth played all the popular airs. This sleep was so good to him that it was but a moment before he heard a voice call his name in a tone that demonstrated the last stages of exhaustion. "Will you spell me?"

"Sure, Billie."

The light in the north had mysteriously vanished, but the correspondent took his course from the wide-awake captain.

Later in the night they took the boat farther out to sea, and the captain directed the cook to take one oar at the stern and keep the boat facing the seas. He was to call out if he should hear the thunder of the surf. This plan enabled the oiler and the correspondent to get respite together. "We'll give those boys a chance to get into shape again," said the captain. They curled down and, after a few preliminary chatterings and trembles, slept once more the dead sleep. Neither knew they had bequeathed to the cook the company of another shark, or perhaps the same shark.

As the boat caroused on the waves, spray occasionally bumped over the side and gave them a fresh soaking, but this had no power to break their repose. The ominous slash of the wind and the water affected them as it would have affected mummies.

"Boys," said the cook, with the notes of every reluctance in his voice, "she's drifted in pretty close. I guess one of you had better take her to sea again." The correspondent, aroused, heard the crash of the toppled crests.

As he was rowing, the captain gave him some whisky-and-water, and this steadied the chills out of him. "If I ever get ashore and anybody shows me even a photograph of an oar...."

At last there was a short conversation.

"Billie.... Billie, will you spell me?"

"Sure," said the oiler.

VII

When the correspondent again opened his eyes, the sea and the sky were each of the gray hue of the dawning. Later, carmine and gold was painted upon the waters. The morning appeared finally, in its splendor, with a sky of pure blue, and the sunlight flamed on the tips of the waves.

On the distant dunes were set many little black cottages, and a tall white windmill reared above them. No man, nor dog, nor bicycle appeared on the beach. The cottages might have formed a deserted village.

The voyagers scanned the shore. A conference was held in the boat. "Well," said the captain, "if no help is coming we might better try a run through the surf right away. If we stay out here much longer we will be too weak to do anything for ourselves at all." The others silently acquiesced in this reasoning. The boat was headed for the beach. The correspondent wondered if none ever ascended the tall wind tower, and if then they never looked seaward. This tower was a giant, standing with its back to the plight of the ants. It represented in a degree, to the correspondent, the serenity of nature amid the struggles of the individual – nature in the wind, and nature in the vision of men. She did not seem cruel to him then, nor beneficent, nor treacherous, nor wise. But she was indifferent, flatly indifferent. It is, perhaps, plausible that a man in this situation, impressed with the unconcern of the universe, should see the innumerable flaws of his life, and have them taste wickedly in his mind and wish for another chance. A distinction between right and wrong seems absurdly clear to him, then, in this new ignorance of the grave-edge, and he understands that if he were given another opportunity he would mend his conduct and his words, and be better and brighter during an introduction or at a tea.

"Now, boys," said the captain, "she is going to swamp, sure. All we can do is to work her in as far as possible, and then when she swamps, pile out and scramble for the beach. Keep cool now, and don't jump until she swamps sure."

The oiler took the oars. Over his shoulders he scanned the surf. "Captain," he said, "I think I'd better bring her about, and keep her head-on to the seas and back her in."

"All right, Billie," said the captain. "Back her in." The oiler swung the boat then and, seated in the stern, the cook and the correspondent were obliged to look over their shoulders to contemplate the lonely and indifferent shore.

The monstrous inshore rollers heaved the boat high until the men were again enabled to see the white sheets of water scudding up the slanted beach. "We won't get in very close," said the captain. Each time a man could wrest his attention from the rollers, he turned his glance toward the shore, and in the expression of the eyes during this contemplation there was a singular quality. The correspondent, observing the others, knew that they were not afraid, but the full meaning of their glances was shrouded.

As for himself, he was too tired to grapple fundamentally with the fact. He tried to coerce his mind into thinking of it, but the mind was dominated at this time by the muscles, and the muscles said they did not care. It merely occurred to him that if he should drown it would be a shame.

There were no hurried words, no pallor, no plain agitation. The men simply looked at the shore. "Now, remember to get well clear of the boat when you jump," said the captain.

Seaward the crest of a roller suddenly fell with a thunderous crash, and the long white comber came roaring down upon the boat.

"Steady now," said the captain. The men were silent. They turned their eyes from the shore to the comber and waited. The boat slid up the incline, leaped at the furious top, bounced over it, and swung down the long back of the wave. Some water had been shipped and the cook bailed it out.

But the next crest crashed also. The tumbling boiling flood of white water caught the boat and whirled it almost perpendicular. Water swarmed in from all sides. The correspondent had his hands on the gunwale at this time, and when the water entered at that place he swiftly withdrew his fingers, as if he objected to wetting them.

The little boat, drunken with this weight of water, reeled and snuggled deeper into the sea.

"Bail her out, cook! Bail her out," said the captain.

"All right, captain," said the cook.

"Now, boys, the next one will do for us, sure," said the oiler. "Mind to jump clear of the boat."

The third wave moved forward, huge, furious, implacable. It fairly swallowed the dinghy, and almost simultaneously the men tumbled into the sea. A piece of lifebelt had lain in the bottom of the boat, and as the correspondent went overboard he held this to his chest with his left hand.

The January water was icy, and he reflected immediately that it was colder than he had expected to find it off the coast of Florida. This appeared to his dazed mind as a fact important enough to be noted at the time. The coldness of the water was sad; it was tragic. This fact was somehow so mixed and confused with his opinion of his own situation that it seemed almost a proper reason for tears. The water was cold.

When he came to the surface he was conscious of little but the noisy water. Afterward he saw his companions in the sea. The oiler was ahead in the race. He was swimming strongly and rapidly. Off to the correspondent's left, the cook's great white and corked back bulged out of the water, and in the rear the captain was hanging with his one good hand to the keel of the overturned dinghy.

There is a certain immovable quality to a shore, and the correspondent wondered at it amid the confusion of the sea.

It seemed also very attractive, but the correspondent knew that it was a long journey, and he paddled leisurely. The piece of life preserver lay under him, and sometimes he whirled down the incline of a wave as if he were on a hand-sled.

But finally he arrived at a place in the sea where travel was beset with difficulty. He did not pause swimming to inquire what manner of current had caught him, but there his progress ceased. The shore was set before him like a bit of scenery on a stage, and he looked at it and understood with his eyes each detail of it.

As the cook passed, much farther to the left, the captain was calling to him, "Turn over on your back, cook! Turn over on your back and use the oar."

"All right, sir." The cook turned on his back, and, paddling with an

oar, went ahead as if he were a canoe.

Presently the boat also passed to the left of the correspondent with the captain clinging with one hand to the keel. He would have appeared like a man raising himself to look over a board fence, if it were not for the extraordinary gymnastics of the boat. The correspondent marveled that the captain could still hold to it.

They passed on, nearer to shore – the oiler, the cook, the captain – and following them went the water-jar, bouncing gaily over the seas.

The correspondent remained in the grip of this strange new enemy – a current. The shore, with its white slope of sand and its green bluff, topped with little silent cottages, was spread like a picture before him. It was very near to him then, but he was impressed as one who in a gallery looks at a scene from Brittany or Holland.

He thought: "I am going to drown? Can it be possible? Can it be possible? Can it be possible?" Perhaps an individual must consider his own death to be the final phenomenon of nature.

But later a wave perhaps whirled him out of this small deadly current, for he found suddenly that he could again make progress toward the shore. Later still, he was aware that the captain, clinging with one hand to the keel of the dinghy, had his face turned away from the shore and toward him, and was calling his name. "Come to the boat! Come to the boat!"

In his struggle to reach the captain and the boat, he reflected that when one gets properly wearied, drowning must really be a comfortable arrangement, a cessation of hostilities accompanied by a large degree of relief, and he was glad of it, for the main thing in his mind for some moments had been horror of the temporary agony. He did not wish to be hurt.

Presently he saw a man running along the shore. He was undressing with most remarkable speed. Coat, trousers, shirt, everything flew magically off him.

"Come to the boat," called the captain.

"All right, captain." As the correspondent paddled, he saw the captain let himself down to bottom and leave the boat. Then the correspondent performed his one little marvel of the voyage. A large wave

caught him and flung him with ease and supreme speed completely over the boat and far beyond it. It struck him even then as an event in gymnastics, and a true miracle of the sea. An overturned boat in the surf is not a plaything to a swimming man.

The correspondent arrived in water that reached only to his waist, but his condition did not enable him to stand for more than a moment. Each wave knocked him into a heap, and the undertow pulled at him.

Then he saw the man who had been running and undressing, and undressing and running, come bounding into the water. He dragged ashore the cook, and then waded towards the captain, but the captain waved him away, and sent him to the correspondent. He was naked, naked as a tree in winter, but a halo was about his head, and he shone like a saint. He gave a strong pull, and a long drag, and a bully heave at the correspondent's hand. The correspondent, schooled in the minor formulae, said: "Thanks, old man." But suddenly the man cried: "What's that?" He pointed a swift finger. The correspondent said: "Go."

In the shallows, face downward, lay the oiler. His forehead touched sand that was periodically, between each wave, clear of the sea.

The correspondent did not know all that transpired afterward. When he achieved safe ground he fell, striking the sand with each particular part of his body. It was as if he had dropped from a roof, but the thud was grateful to him.

It seems that instantly the beach was populated with men with blankets, clothes, and flasks, and women with coffee pots and all the remedies sacred to their minds. The welcome of the land to the men from the sea was warm and generous, but a still and dripping shape was carried slowly up the beach, and the land's welcome for it could only be the different and sinister hospitality of the grave.

When it came night, the white waves paced to and fro in the moonlight, and the wind brought the sound of the great sea's voice to the men on shore, and they felt that they could then be interpreters.

Sisterhood is powerful.

<div style="text-align: right;">KATHIE SARACHILD[43]</div>

This solidarity of sex was something that
feminism tried to teach us, and something
… that men figured out and perfected a
long time ago. … It was just something they
seemed to know.

<div style="text-align: right;">NORAH VINCENT[44]</div>

Everything that is man made was made by men. But we usually don't look at rising skyscrapers and marvel at the workers – door buckers, rough carpenters, finishing carpenters, marble cutters, electricians, glaziers, ironworkers, mail chute installers, sprinkler installers, lathers, boiler makers, plumbers, steamfitters, tin-knockers, tile workers, pipe fitters, bolters, heaters, slingers, catchers, buckers-up, and riveters – who risk their lives constructing the buildings we work and live in.

Thirty-seven of every hundred-thousand ironworkers – men who work their hands in steel on tall buildings, towers, and bridges – are killed on the job.[45] Most die by going "over the side" – falling or being pushed from the structure they're working on. The physical strength and balance, emotional control – or is it not having emotions? – and confidence required to walk an I-beam one hundred stories up, mark them as a different breed of men.

One of fifteen ironworkers is killed within ten years of entering the trade; ironworking America's sixth most fatal job.[46] If he survives the first decade of work, an ironworker has five years more on average before his limbs give out.[47] He'll retire in his forties, a worn out, scarred and ache-ridden old man, with hunched back, missing fingers, and limping gait.[48]

If you've used a radio, television or cellphone (all communicate via radio frequency waves with antennae mounted on steel transmission towers), visited a skyscraper or stadium, or driven across a bridge, you've benefited from ironworkers' labors. As Tim, a fireman who toiled on the 9/11 World Trade Center pile said, "Ironworkers are like angels on our shoulders."[49]

These men are rarely published writers, so I'm glad to have found Mike Cherry's book, On High Steel, *from which the following piece is excerpted.*

IN MEMORY OF DAN PERMIT ⌣

MIKE CHERRY

Over the Side

In the years since that night I've tried to remember what l thought about on the way home, but I've never been sure I've got it right. I've told the story of what happened on that job often, when out drinking with other ironworkers and into the miasma of fatalism that sometimes takes hold, and I've usually presented Patrick's remarks about it being a "bad" job as though they constituted an omen. But I don't really remember if I took them that way. The bare truth is simply that two days after Patrick expressed his distaste for the job, Dan Permit was knocked over the side.

The crane had been brought back to set the cooling tower. "Tower" is rather too grand a word, but the term is used irrespective of the size of the unit. It was simply a cube-shaped frame of light iron about sixteen feet on a side. Its function was to house a water tank, pumps, and related equipment. It was put together on the ground, bolted up and welded, then hoisted atop the building.

A thirty-foot jib had been added to the eighty-foot stick of the crane so that it would be possible to reach in far enough beyond the lip of the roof to place the tower where it belonged, which was well to the rear of the roof. A "jib" is simply an extension. Cranes are counterbalanced, of course, by massive weights fitted to their rear ends, and the farther out the stick is boomed, the less effective is this weight. Placing the tower where it belonged involved being able to boom out to an extreme angle, and Jack, after an argument with the operator, had us drag over a couple of tons of stuff and hang it off the counterweight. With this additional counterbalancing, the operator agreed to make the lift. Patrick

was stationed on the edge of the roof as the signalman, since the final placement of the tower was to be so far back that it would be out of the operator's sight.

The tower was hooked on, and the crane lifted it until it was nearly two-blocked.[50] Once it was up, the crane swung round until it faced directly toward its destination. Patrick then extended his arm with his fist clenched and his thumb pointing down. This means "boom out," and the operator began easing the boom forward. As the load neared the edge of the roof it of course came lower. Patrick made a twisting motion with his other hand, as though he were driving a screw into the ceiling. This is the signal to "get up" on the load. There were about four feet of space left between the blocks, and the operator began to come up through this distance with the load. He was booming out at the same time – all of this is ordinary procedure – when his cats began to leave the ground. He was no Angie, though (or perhaps the additional weights we'd hung confused his feel for his rig), and things began to happen very quickly. The balance point shot past, and the crane continued going over. He let go the load, but it was too late. The boom struck the edge of the roof, bent, and collapsed. In a sequence that no one was ever able to agree on, the rig went over on its nose, the boom folded over the roof, the cooling tower tore through the rear outside header and plunged to the ground in back of the building, and the cable that had hoisted it snapped. The breaking of the cable must not have happened until the tower had nearly reached the ground, because there were sixty-five feet of it beyond the jib sheave when the inspectors measured it later.

When all this hell broke loose, I ran like a madman for the back of the building. Dan Permit was astride a back header on the third floor, shoving bar joists around to the keel marks I had made for him. The flying cable snaked in a giant diagonal arc, took a turn around a column, and whipped him over the side. He only fell thirty-five feet, but he landed on his head in a pile of rocks that had been removed from the hole. I took one look at him and threw up.

When I finished vomiting, I took off my sweatshirt and pitched it across his face. As I started around the building, I realized that no one

else had come around back and that therefore no one else had seen Dan fall. I looked up to see Patrick climbing down the broken boom, which was curled around the roof header and led down to the crane cab at about a fifty-degree angle. Several men were helping the operator out of the rig. There was a lot of noise. As the man was lifted out, Jack kept shouting, "Is he okay?" The man answered for himself that he was. Patrick dropped from the lower end of the boom to the ground, leaned against one of the upturned cats, and lit a cigarette. He shook his head when Jack asked him if he were hurt. Jack looked at me.

I said, "Dan Permit's dead." When he just stood there, I shouted at him, "Dead, you slow-witted prick!" He and Dan Pusher, who had come up behind him, took off running toward the back of the building. Patrick pushed himself off the cat and walked slowly after them.

"Not much point in running," he said, to no one in particular.

It is traditional to take up a collection for the family of a man who has been killed. In Dan Permit's case, the money came to $212. The local deposited the money to its account and made out a check to the widow for the same amount. Freddy came out to the job and handed the check to me, saying that since I was his partner, I should be the one to give it to his wife, and for me to get some sort of card to put it in.

There was insurance coverage through the local, in the amount of $2,500. Since he was not a book man,[51] there was no coverage through the International. Had there been, his estate would have received another $10,000.

Jack, Dan Pusher, Patrick, and I attended the funeral. I tried, while attempting to give the widow the absurd lily-decorated envelope that contained the $212, to make a speech of condolence, but she seemed to hear nothing, nor did she extend her hand. I finally gave it to the elder of the two small girls beside her.

Drinking sessions for the next several days shaped themselves variously as Postmortems, Courts of Inquiry, or Symposia on The Meaning of Life. In the Postmortem phase, one man would begin by remarking that, "He only went thirty, thirty-five feet, the poor prick." All would nod. "My God, Jack himself went five floors on that job in Syracuse and

come out of it wit' nothin' more'n a pair of broken legs." It was mandatory that the next man point out that Dan Permit had landed on his head. Then someone would mention another flop, and swapping tales of who had gone how far when and with what damage might last an hour or more. Inevitably, someone would hold that since he was only a permit man, and a brand new one to boot, he shouldn't have been put where he could get hurt in the first place. Another man would snort, "And where the hell is there that a man can't get hurt?" That would open the Court of Inquiry: Should he have been on open iron anyway? Was the lift of a fairly heavy tower with a toy crane inherently unsafe? Why wasn't the man told to get out of the area while the lift was being made? What caused the tower to drop almost to the ground before the load cable parted? Had the operator done all he could?

I was surprised at the lack of agreement and the murkiness of the answers. Even after an investigation of sorts had been conducted, there was less clarity than passion, and The Meaning of Life stage of a conversation was generally made up of a series of discrete and unattended manifestos. There was lip service to When Your Number's Up It's Up, which sometimes arose in abbreviated form as You Never Know, and there was a nodding of heads when one man said that Dan Permit should have kept his job with the railroad. Patrick repeated his desire to finish the job and get out.

The accident was the main subject of conversation for about four days, gradually being replaced by expressions of hostility at the approach of winter.

I finished pushing Dan's bar joists into place, and once looked over the side at the rocks. Some still bore bloodstains. There was a mound of loose sand two or three feet from where he had landed, but it might just as well have been two or three miles away.

... the more dangerous the assignment, the more likely it is to be assigned to a man.

WARREN FARRELL[52]

It's not fish you're buying, it's men's lives.[53]

SIR WALTER SCOTT[54]

When I cross the George Washington Bridge or any of America's great bridges, I think: men have done this. Construction is a sublime male poetry.

CAMILLE PAGLIA[55]

6. Love & Desire

Men with pens have sweated reams – volumes – about our desire and love for women. In Jeff Gere's "Lei Queen Contest," we see the power a woman's love has over a man. Jeff, a renowned Hawaiian story-teller, reveals this in a conversation he had with a huge, tattooed Samoan man, a dialogue he accompanies with ukulele band and falsetto singers.

Russ Allison Loar's poem, "What Men Want," reveals truths about man's attraction to woman, and his easy bedazzlement by her.

Donna Julia, a key character in Lord Byron's epic poem, *Don Juan,* was twenty-three when she wrote "Donna Julia's Letter to Don Juan," a lament of woman's plight. Did Byron – a man writing what his character, a young woman, feels – get it right?

Julia's letter faces Shakespeare's lyrics, "Sigh No More, Ladies," from *Much Ado About Nothing.* In the second verse, The Bard rhymes "heavy" and "leavy," and in the chorus offers cheery advice to the lovelorn.

John Updike, in "The Simple Truth of Her," revisits a scene that many of us have likely lived, at least in parts. His storied powers of observation – in this tale, his eye for eyes, for example – are on full view.

To some, Philip Roth's "The Chaos of Eros," is about a man's aging. Others see an older man's attraction to a younger woman, and still others, her attraction to him. It's your call. In any case, please note Roth's *coup de littérature* in the paragraph that begins, "That first night…".

I issued a second call for submissions on the web because the first hadn't delivered a story of joyful love. "Can a guy get a happy love story around here, please?" I asked, looking skyward as I clicked the call into cyberspace. A day later, an email with Jon Pearson's "A Busload of Banjo Players" arrived, an ecstatic love story to answer my plea.

"Love & Desire" concludes with Richard Bausch's "Letter to the Lady of the House," an ode to longterm marrieds and a quiet finale to this section's glowing tango of attraction and lust.

It's hot in here. You who love and you who desire:
grab a fan
flip the page.

According to the scientists, love is just
an excess of lust, a pleasure so intense it
hijacks the mind.

JONAH LEHRER[56]

Where Love Is, There God Is Also.

LEO TOLSTOY[57]

To burn with desire and keep quiet about
it is the greatest punishment we can bring
on ourselves.

FEDERICO GARCÍA LORCA[58]

JEFF GERE

Lei Queen Contest

So there I was at 7:30 AM, master of an empty parking lot at Ala Wai Golf Course, in service to the Parks Department's Lei Queen Contest. I'd been there an hour. I was cold and grumpy. The turnout for this event was meager, as usual.

I slumped over a cup of coffee with other grumbling workers who had nothing to do as dawn edged across the morning sky. We moaned about our sad plight and how our tremendous talents were being wasted on this puny event. On and on we whined. Soon bored with that as well, I strolled down the hall to see what was going on with the contest itself.

My god, what a difference 30 yards can make. I walked into a room filled with music. Some 30 senior citizens sang a stream of Hawaiian songs. They were dressed in matching muumuus and aloha shirts with a bold print of red flowers on a white field, the ladies' hair piled high with orchids. A stand-up bass chased lots of ukuleles, and yarn leis hung on everyone.

Arica and lawai ferns bordered the room with small palm trees watching over the proceedings. The crowds of proud families, friends and ohana mingled easily in their own leis and scents, a bubbling, smiling mix of people and costumes. The air smelled crisp and sweet.

Three girls sat at tables making leis, as kupuna[59] pointed fingers and asked questions. The girls beamed with answers. Then the sun peeked over the Ko'olau Range, bathing us all in yellow light.

I sat down with a smile on my face, thinking, *I don't care about getting up early. This is magnificent! It's a privilege to be in this room with this aloha. This is just stunningly wonderful! This is what a Recreation*

Department is meant to do, something so glorious, so Hawaiian, so real!

Still, it was early, and I yawned several times as the crowd greeted each other with hugs and chuckles, the chalangalang of ukuleles, slide guitar, and falsetto singing continually pouring out of the old chorus.

To my right, I saw a huge Samoan man sitting near me, yawning. I knew he was Samoan because it was tattooed across his broad upper arm, along with lots of other things. He was covered with images. His yawn brought a yawn out of me, which he saw, and we chuckled together.

"Kinda early, yeah?" I said.

"Yeep," he said, slowly.

"I got here about 6:30. Nobody much came today."

"Yeeyep," he said. "I wuz up at seex. Me an' my girlfrien' was helping huh sistah get ready foah today. Das' her ovah deah."

I looked over, the music massaged us all, and I turned back to my sleepy companion, saying, "She's pretty. I got to bed about midnight, so it's kind of tough. Yeah, I'm sleepy today."

"Me, I getta bed 'bout ten. But no get to sleep befoah tree ... maybe two-tirdy.... Up again at six. But das OK. Dey both happy. I take one nap latah. Dis is nice an everybody happy ovah heah."

I looked around. "You're right. This is really special." We didn't talk for a long minute.

He turned to me and said, "Ya know, dis is good foah me."

"What?"

"I mean, jus' talking heah wid you. Times have changed. I have changed."

I didn't know what he meant.

After a minute he went on. "Fouah yeahs ago, if I see you jus' looking at me, maybe I jus' bust you, I hook you right heah, put my fiss 'cross youah face, an take you out, brah!"

I didn't say anything, but I was waking quickly now. We were both silent for a while.

"I grew up in KPT." He held up his big hand and I saw the three letters crudely tattooed into the valley between his thumb and first finger. Kuhio Park Terrace. Rough place. They closed its Recreation Center

because the residents kept throwing burning furniture into the pool from the tops of the looming apartment skyscrapers.

He continued slowly. "I hated everyting. I had so much dahkness in my heart, so much bad feelings inside o' me I cannot even tell you. I always stay beefing, in gangs, steal, drugs, you name it. All kinda trouble I was in. But it all wen catch up wid me. Dey catch me an' locked me up. Tree yeah, brah, is one long, long time...."

"But dat was all before, an now, now I got a new meaning fo' my life. I gonna make good my parole, go back school, learn how foah to be one counselah. Gonna pull all dat dahknes' out from my heaht, an den I can go back to KPT. I goen go back an' help dose kids, help 'em foah make bettah choices wit der lives, help 'em so dey no make da same mistakes like me, help 'em avoid da pain an' help da family too, yeah? Dat's what I gonna do. I jus' thankful I get one chance."

He said this with a slow smile that made my breath stop. Those big dark eyes and heavy lashes, the bright white teeth against the glowing deep brown skin that didn't need to shave: he didn't seem dangerous, but I didn't doubt his tale was true. I believed he had changed, too. I sat quietly, musing. The music and the sunlight and the brightly-patterned people circled gently around us.

"If you don't mind me asking, I'm just wondering: what happened to you to turn your life around? Was it religion … Jesus?"

"Nah" he chuckled. "Me 'n my bruddahs was raised in da church, but it no help me none. I still get good an' messed up. My bruddahs still go, but me no."

I waited. He said nothing. He was leaning forward, his elbows on his knees, his head drooping down. I dared to press him. "So what, then?"

His head and then his body slowly turned toward me. He seemed to be weighing his words. The old band and the aged falsetto voices struggled to reach and hold a high note. His big eyes batted and a gentle smile came over his entire being.

"What turn my life around … is da love … of a good … woman."

He turned slowly away as I moaned understanding and approval. The announcer took the mike and the Lei Queen Contest got underway.

It is not the woman who is dear to man. It is the spirit of the woman that is dear to him.

OLD SAYING[60]

[Man] is erotically fixated on woman's "shapeliness," those spongy maternal fat deposits of breast, hip and buttock which are ironically the wateriest and least stable parts of her anatomy.

CAMILLE PAGLIA[61]

RUSS ALLISON LOAR

What Men Want

When I see her
 I hold myself a little tighter,
 A little straighter,
 Appearing more attractive,
 Flexing all appropriate muscles,
 Contracting all inappropriate flab,
Making myself desirable,

For she is my sweetheart heartthrob honeybunch sex machine
 And I want her,
 This girlish saint scamp athletic fashion model intellectual.

I want her.
Now.

I am enraptured by her thin boyish sharp-shoulder-bladed frame,
 Her overexposed unashamed voluptuous fantastic flesh,

Her long short medium-length hair,
 So glossy black chestnut brown honey blonde pumpkin red
 Curling straight.

I am lost in her mysterious bold naive uninhibited forbidden
 Eyes of swimming pool blue chocolate bar brown charcoal briquette black
 London fog gray emerald chameleon green banana-tree hazel.

She walks toward me away not moving,
 This short long-legged tall small woman girl,
 So delicate and strong.

She sees me and smiles
 And I am hers,

 All over town.

Lord Byron

Donna Julia's Letter
to Don Juan

(1819)

Man's love is of man's life a thing apart,
'Tis woman's whole existence.

Man may range the court, camp,
church, the vessel, & the mart.

Sword, gown, gain & glory
offer in exchange
pride, fame & ambition
to fill up his heart,

And few there are
whom these cannot estrange.

Men have all these resources,
we but one.

To love again,
and be again undone.

WILLIAM SHAKESPEARE

Sigh No More, Ladies, Sigh No More

(1599)

Sigh no more, ladies, sigh no more;
 Men were deceivers ever;
 One foot in sea and one on shore,
 To one thing constant never;

 Then sigh not so,
 But let them go,
 And be you blithe and bonny;
 Converting all your sounds of woe
 Into Hey nonny, nonny.

 Sing no more ditties, sing no more
 Of dumps so dull and heavy;
 The fraud of men was ever so,
 Since summer first was leavy.

 Then sigh not so,
 But let them go,
And be you blithe and bonny,
 Converting all your sounds of woe
Into Hey, nonny, nonny.

JOHN UPDIKE

The Simple Truth of Her

Elsie Seidel, his high-school girlfriend, the daughter of a country feed-and-hardware merchant, had always been smartly turned out, with polished penny loafers and ribbed knee socks and sweeping skirts and broad belts in the New Look style, and with tortoiseshell barrettes gleaming in the bouncy light-brown waves of her hair. And plenty of lipstick, maroon lipstick that looked black in Kodak snapshots and rubbed off on his mouth so that afterward it stung to get it all off with spit on a handkerchief. He didn't want his mother to see; his mother didn't want him to go with Elsie at all, though the girl was respectable, more respectable locally than Owen's family, who were newcomers to this end of the county and to the school district. The district encompassed several valleys and included families whose first language was still Pennsylvania Dutch. Elsie herself spoke with a "Dutchy" care – her voice seemed older than she was.

There was a country simplicity to her, a well-fed glossiness. The first time they kissed, in the intermission of a school dance, Elsie didn't make the anxious pushing mouth that Alice Stottlemeyer had during spin-the-bottle but somehow let her lips melt into his, at this warm spitty spot where their bodies joined. She was a short girl, in a sweated-up taffeta dance dress, and he was six feet tall at seventeen, so she had to tug down at him to keep his face tight to hers; she wanted to kiss more, there behind a broken Coke machine, where the overhead fluorescent light was flickering. Her compact eager body molded itself to his; he remembered hearing how Carol Wisniewski had let herself be fucked by Marty Naftzinger standing up in the narrow space between

the rec hall and the hosiery mill, and saw that it could be done.

Not that he and Elsie ever – in a word they never used between them – fucked. He was too smart for that, too anxious to avoid wasting his one life. He knew that fucking led to marriage and he was not ready for that. In the heat and urgency of that first kiss, he recognized that Elsie had had her eye on him, as the phrase went – he had been an exotic, aloof arrival at the school, and somehow the idea of him had wormed its way excitingly into her head. So between them there was always this tilt, this unbalance: she had desired him before he knew what was up.

Owen would afterward associate Elsie with the inside of a car – its stale velour, its little dim dashboard lights, its rubber floor mats and chill metallic surfaces. Chilly at first: after they'd been driving around for hours, the heater made a torrid alcove in the dark. On dates, they took his parents' stuffy prewar Chevy. His father was generally home from work by six, and Owen was granted the car for the roaming that is, in common American wisdom, a teen-anger's right.

At first, there was only kissing, on and on, eyes closed to admit behind sealed lids a flood of other sensations, an expansion of consciousness into a salty, perfumed space quite unlike the hushed and headlong vault of masturbation. In the dark seclusion between cool tight sheets, his parents' muttering having died away, he would seem for some seconds to stand on his head, having discovered with his left hand a faithful mechanism impossibly sweet, a clench that took him back to infancy, its tight knit of newness before memories overlaid the bliss of being. Into this private darkness had come another, another seeker, and what was being found, clumsily yet unstoppably, was a core self explored by another consciousness. Elsie was both witness and witnessed. Her eyes were the wet, honey-tinged brown of horehound drops. By the particles of light that entered through the windshield, he saw the dark dents of her dimples when she smiled, and the side of one eyeball gleam as she studied him across a gap that closed in a few seconds. Huddled beside him on the front seat, a bench seat in that era, with her back gouged by the knob of the window crank and her calves and ankles roasted by the heater, she seemed cupped to receive him, a nest of growing permissions. With each date, she gave him an inch or two more of

herself that he could claim as his henceforth; there was no taking back these small territories. Beyond kissing, there was so much to touch, so many hooks and tricks among the catches and aromatic coverings, there in the shelter of the car, which sometimes was her car, for, though a year younger than he, she also had a driver's license, and when his poor old family Chevy was under overnight repair or commandeered for some adult evening errand, she would bring a car of her family's, her mother's green Dodge, or even her father's new deep-blue Chrysler, with its V-8 engine, to pick him up, at the farmhouse where his mother had not without a struggle accepted that Elsie had become his "girl," whatever that meant as the world embarked on a new half century.

Some of those evenings when Elsie did the driving, pulling up in an impressive machine, she would be invited in, into the little house's front parlor. Smartly dressed in this setting of declining gentility, Elsie spoke to Owen's mother with a lively courtesy. Her honey-brown eyes flashed; her red lips smiled. Uneasily standing by, in a flannel shirt whose sleeves were too short, in scuffed laced shoes that looked oafish compared with Elsie's polished penny loafers – much on view as she smartly crossed and recrossed her plump legs – Owen felt like a baton being passed.

When the young people, these social observances discharged, achieved freedom in a car of Elsie's, it seemed perverse, after the movie or the miniature golf was behind them and they had found a parking place, to have her seated on his left instead of on his right. Come at this way, she felt like a strange girl, with whom he must begin from scratch. Their chins and mouths made angles opposite from the usual, and his hands coped with reversed routes.

"Should we switch?" she asked, when he remarked on this strangeness. Her voice came out breathier, lower in her throat, than the polite, Dutch-flavored voice she used with his mother and the teachers at school. Her lipstick had already begun to smear and flake. Her face was waxily lit by a street lamp half a block away; they were parked in a spot he knew from childhood walks, at the back of the old Dairy Queen lot on Cedar Top. Other times, they would park up by Shale Hill, near what had been the Victory Gardens, on a dirt road made by

recent developers. Always, as the scope of her permissions widened, he searched for even safer spots, where the police would never come up and shine flashlights in their faces, as once had happened, behind the long low sheds of the old farmers' market. As she sat high behind the wheel of her father's expensive car, her mussed hair caught fire in stray loops and strands from the distant street lamp.

"Let's," he agreed. "If you don't mind my sitting behind your father's wheel."

"I don't mind, Owen. I don't like it poking me in the ribs all the time. I don't see how you can stand it."

"Elsie, when I'm with you I don't notice such things. Here I go. I'll get out and you slide over."

Thrusting himself into the public space outside the automobile, where adult morality pressed down from the stars, he opened and shut the Chrysler's passenger door (it made that sucky rich rattle-free sound) and scuttled around the broad chrome bumper and white-walled rear tires hunched over, for he already had an erection. Even behind his fly it felt scarily as if it might snag on something, until he settled behind her father's steering wheel, which wore a suede cover. The tang of the new-car smell was warmed into freshness by the heat of their bodies. As he slid across the front seat, wide enough for three, into the space where she huddled, the distant light illumined her blurred face and a small pearl earring and the fuzzy wool of her short-sleeved angora sweater. She let him slide the sweater up and sneak a finger into her bra and stroke the silky skin there, the gentle fatty rise of it. Though Elsie was plump, her breasts were small, as if still developing. When he had advanced to taking off her bra and pushing the sweater way up, her chest seemed hardly different from his own; a breast of hers in his hand felt as delicate as a tear bulging in his eye. One night, parked up by the Victory Gardens, where the street lamp was closer than on Cedar Top, he watched raindrops on the windshield make shadows on her chest, thin trails that hesitated and fell as his fingertips traced and tried to stop them, there, and there. She had dear little nipples like rabbit noses. She let him kiss them, suck them until she said, in her breathy, un-Dutchy voice, "Ow, Owen. Enough, baby," and touched his head the way the

barber did when he wanted it to move. Sitting up, he made circles with his finger and his saliva around her nipples, softly round and round, loving the sight of them so much he felt dizzy, as the parallel shadows of the raindrops faintly streaked her chest and the backs of his hands.

She never touched his prick. It was too sacred, too potent. They pretended it wasn't there, even when their bodies straightened at the angle permitted by the front seat and its heater-crowded foot space and he held her buttocks through her rumpled skirt and pressed himself rhythmically against her, all the time their mouths kissing, until he came, came in his underpants, where the dried jism made a brittle stain he later picked off with his fingernail, hoping his mother wouldn't notice it when she did the wash.

His sense of sexual etiquette was primitive, gleaned from the way men and women acted in the movies up to their huge closeup kiss at the end, and from enigmatic dialogue in a few books, like "For Whom the Bell Tolls" and "Forever Amber" and "A Rage to Live" and "The Amboy Dukes," that he had looked into, and from a pornographic poem that Marty Naftzinger's younger brother, Jerry, a runty curly-haired kid in Owen's class, could recite, if you paid him a dime. But it was developed enough to ask, after one such climax against her compliant body, "What can we do for you?"

This embarrassed her. Elsie liked to pretend that what had just happened hadn't happened at all. "How do you mean?"

This made him shy in turn. "I mean – just holding still for me isn't enough, is it?"

She said, "We can't do more, Owen. There might be consequences you don't want."

Yet there was more, both knew it, and as his senior year ran out they groped to find it without committing sins so dark and final that their lives would be forever deformed. Elsie was less afraid of this than he; he refused to test how far she would let him "go." It had become their way in the car for him to bend over and kiss the silky warm inner sides of her thighs and then press his mouth as far up as he could into the warmth, her warmth. At first, she resisted, pushing at his shoulders, and then came to expect it. In those days, even teen-age girls wore

girdles: the crotch of her underpants was guarded by edges of stiff elastic, and though she shyly edged her hips forward in the car seat his lips could not quite reach the damp cotton. Not that he knew enough to make her come with his mouth, or how girls came at all. The pleasure was his, in being this close to a secret, in having her yield it up to him, even her fragrance, which was strong enough at times to exert a counterforce, a wish to pull his face away. But he loved it there between her legs, and how hot and sticky his cheeks grew against her thighs, and the graceless awkwardness this maneuver asked of her, still wearing her knee socks and loafers.

The summer before he went off to M.I.T., their experiments took on a desperate edge. She knew he was slipping away; the baton had not been passed after all. Owen had got a summer job on a surveying crew, tending the target marks and chopping brush out of the sight lines. Elsie had gone to a Lutheran camp in Ohio, where she was a counselor, for six weeks.

After Elsie returned from Ohio, it seemed almost too much work to take a bath in the farmhouse's one tub and go out again, into the dark. He and she needed the dark now. With the freedoms they had granted each other, they needed such privacy that even a distant street light or the remotest chance of a cop with a flashlight and barking voice could not be borne. Where could they go, with their maturing needs and fears of eventual desertion? His summer had not been so distracted that he had missed the implication, in her letters from camp, that she had found companionship with the boy counselors, or the gossip, when in August she had returned, that while he was cutting brush in future housing developments she was to be seen at the township's public pool, lounging in a two-piece bathing suit on a towel on the grass, with another boy, a boy her age, in her class, who would be there with her after September.

"My father owns a hundred acres of woods not that far from Brechstown," she told Owen, after an hour of directionless cruising one evening. "There's an old road in. Nobody ever comes there."

"Sounds perfect," he said, but did it? He let her direct him, turn by turn, on narrow roads he had never driven before. He was frightened at

the road entrance, with its "No Trespassing" sign and rusting remains of barbed-wire fence; there was a sandstone boulder that with his summer muscles he rolled five feet to the side so they could get by. They were in the fragile old black Chevrolet; his father, mocking his own poverty, called it "the flivver." As branches raked the creeping car's sides, Owen felt guilt, yet less than if it had been her father's Chrysler, which was kept so shipshape and simonized. A litter of cans and wrappers in the headlights revealed that others had been here before, also pushing aside the boulder in their strength of desire. The road was rough; the old car rocked. Suppose they broke an axle or got a flat tire? The scandal, the disgrace would stain his life forever.

"Isn't this far enough?" he asked. He felt a trap closing behind him.

"It goes in for a long way but gets worse," Elsie admitted. He turned off the ignition and the headlights. Such darkness! It pounced upon them with an audible crackle; it locked around the windows as if the car had plunged into a black river. As his eyes adjusted, he saw a star or two high in the windshield, in the spaces between the great still trees overhead. Occasional headlights on the dirt road a half mile away twinkled. Elsie's face was a mere glimmer in the cave of velour, rubber, shaped steel, and shatterproof glass. His lips found hers, and they were full and moist, but the old melting, one mouth into another, met impediments, things he couldn't put out of his mind. Suppose the Chevy didn't start when they wanted to go? Suppose he couldn't back it out on this overgrown road, the bushes a solid mass behind them and he without the machete he used on the surveying crew? He felt life, a silent vegetable life, enclosing them, on this her father's land, this man present in every leaf and reaching branch. Owen was still young enough to invest the darkness with spying presences; they distracted him when he should have been purely bent on the treasure at hand, in the deepest privacy he and Elsie would ever know.

It was August; she wore shorts and no girdle. As their embraces gained ardor and flexibility, her crotch came into his hand as if rising to it. She lifted her hips on the car seat so he could slide her shorts down; through his clumsiness her white underpants came off with them, and Elsie did not try to grab them back. She seemed to stretch, elongating

her belly. Even in this darkness, he saw wet gleams upon her eyeballs, like faraway fireflies, and the pallor of her long belly descending to a small soft shadow. Frightened of that shadow, he turned his attention to her breasts; with a touch more practiced than with her underpants, he unhooked her bra and tugged up her short-sleeved jersey. She crossed her arms and pulled the jersey the rest of the way, up over her head, with the bra. Her hair, cut shorter this summer so she could be in and out of the lake at the Lutheran camp, bounced, releasing a scent of shampoo. The bony smooth roundness of her shoulders gave him the shock of her nakedness; he hid his face against the side of her neck, saying, "Oh, God. I can't stand this."

Her cheek tensed as she smiled. "Now you, Owen," she breathed into his ear. "Your shirt."

Quickly, not wanting to let go of her for a second, he pulled it off, wishing he had bathed more carefully, for the smell of his armpits joined that of her shampoo and her skin in the close air of the car. He could see more and more, as if light were leaking from the patches of sky between the trees, shedding glimmers into the woods, where faint noises were reviving and becoming less faint. He kissed her breasts, trying to be delicate, trying not to bite as the nipples grew hard, while she pressed into his ear a voice that seemed made up, enlarged and rehearsed, like something in the movies: "Owen, I used to take off my clothes in my room and walk around looking at myself in the mirror, wishing you could see me."

"You're beautiful – amazing," he told her, meaning it, but, as if her voice had swabbed out his ears, he now heard other things, whispers and stirrings around them, on the other side of the glass and metal. From somewhere not too distant there was a hoot, an owl or possibly a signal from a murderous, demented gang that lived here in caves and came out at night. Suppose the car doesn't start? he thought again. It often didn't, in rainstorms, or on cold mornings, his father frantic, flooding the engine in his panic, so the wearying starter turned it over, uncatching, cooga cooga. "Did you hear something?" he asked Elsie.

She had left her loafers on the gritty floor of the car and had risen up, bare now even to her feet, to kneel on the seat beside him, stroking

his face as he tongued her breasts; even in his state of growing terror he marveled, holding her tight, at the give of a girl's waist, at the semi-liquid space below the ribs and then, behind, the downy hard plate at the base of the spine and the glassy globes of her buttocks, smooth into the cleavage, all of it unified like the silvery body of a fish, all so simple and true, the simple truth of her, alive in his arms. He heard the distant hoot again. Something rustled near the car tires. She felt his mouth losing interest in her nipple, and began to listen with him. Behind the skin between her breasts, her heart was beating. "I don't think so," Elsie answered, her voice losing its movie-screen largeness and becoming small, with a childish quaver.

For reassurance she added, "He says nobody ever comes here except in hunting season." But she, too, must have seen the cans and wrappers in the headlights, evidence of others. He: her father, the owner, all around them, hating Owen, what he was doing to his daughter, striving in every twig and trunk to eject the two of them. They listened and heard a noise so faint it could have just been saliva rattling in their held breath. Owen's hands began to move again, gathering her tender taut nakedness closer to him, his fingertips finding a touch of fuzz in the cleavage behind. He wondered how to get his head down to kiss that soft shadow he had glimpsed; it seemed shyer, gauzier than what he had seen in dirty photographs and drawings, the few he had seen. His prick was aching behind his fly, and her hand dropped and, the first time ever, began fumbling at his belt buckle to release it, its imperious pressure, its closeted sour smell.

But he had spooked her, he had spooked them both, and the desire that dominated him, bare-chested though he was, was the desire to escape, to see if the car could start and he could back it up that narrow road without hitting a tree or a deep hole. Her father's land, and her nakedness in it like a shout: Owen was vulnerable, criminal even – trespassing, and she a minor. He must restore her intact to society. The rustling near the tires became a sudden thrashing, a distinct lunge of the unknown.

"Elsie," he whispered.

"What?" Perhaps expecting some avowal, some earthy plea.

"Let's get out of here."

She hesitated. He heard her heart beat, her breath whistle. "It's up to you," she decided in the mannerly voice that she had used with his mother. Then, catching his mood, she whispered, "Yes, let's."

Often afterward, he would remember details of this hour (her shorts and underpants in one sweep; her gleaming eye-whites; his sense of her slithering into the space above his head like a silken kite, like an angel crammed into the upper corner of a Sienese Nativity) and regret his lack of the boldness that would have let him linger with her gift of herself, and taste it, and let her continue undoing his pants. But his nerves had poisoned their privacy. Naked or not, she was a person, and now a frightened one. His retreat was cowardly, but he felt brave and cool, successfully managing its details. He started the engine – thank God, it started, drowning out all those other sounds – and backed down the overgrown road by the wan glow of the backup lights while branches scraped metal and Elsie scrambled into her clothes. He would have backed up right onto the paved road, not bothering to roll back the boulder, but she said, in a voice whose calmness sounded stern, "Owen. We should put it back the way we found it."

Her father's precious land. This had been her show, he realized. He got out angrily and in the glare of his own headlights heaved the rock into place, for the next trespassers. "Sorry, sorry, sorry," he said when the Chevy was safely running down the highway, to Brechstown, where she lived. "I chickened out."

Elsie said, after lighting a cigarette, "You're more citified than I am. Woods don't frighten me. My father and uncle hunt in the fall. There are no bears or anything, not even bobcats anymore. I felt safe."

"You should have told me that while we were in there."

"I tried to distract you, to keep you interested."

"You did, you were stunning. I loved it. You."

She was silent, putting his jerky speech together.

He told her, "It's just as well. We might have fucked."

Not a word they used, with others or between themselves: it was a kind of offering. But she held her silence. It occurred to him, his face heating in a blush, that he hadn't been prepared even physically, with

one of these rubber things he had seen years ago up by the abandoned Dairy Queen.

She at last spoke: "I wouldn't have let you, Owen. I intend to be a virgin for my husband. It was just, like I said, I wanted you to know me, to see me, as I see myself."

"You were beautiful. Are beautiful, Elsie."

Was she crying? "Thank you, Owen," she brought out. "You're a nice person."

Too nice, was the implication. Still, he couldn't blame himself. Her body like that of a slithering cool flexible fish in his arms had been a revelation, but it had been revelation enough for one night.

Were there other nights to follow? There might have been, but when he looked back, trying to recall each underlit detail, it didn't seem so. Their futures came upon them fast. Elsie had another boyfriend for her senior year, and married yet another boy, one she met at the local Penn State extension. Surprisingly, they left the region, settling in the San Francisco area. If Owen wouldn't take her away, another would.

They must have driven around that night, burning up gas, letting their heartbeats slow down, trying to talk into place what they had learned about each other and their own lives, before he drove her home to Brechstown. Her house was up a long crunching driveway, an old farmhouse like his own family's but fully, fussily fixed up. When he kissed her goodnight, again there was not that melting together, though he took the liberty of stroking a breast as she leaned toward him.

Owen felt he had failed, but no one could take from him his stolen treasure, how far Elsie had "gone," leaving him with a kind of home movie his mind could run and rerun in a rickety projector, not just in bed but in inward moments of daylight, bits and pieces of her barely seen – her heartbeat like a stranger knocking on the other side of a door.

The woman is life,
and the man is the servant of life …

<div align="right">JOSEPH CAMPBELL[62]</div>

To be a man is to have the wind at your
back.

<div align="right">ANONYMOUS[64]</div>

Women think of being a man as a gift.
It is a duty.

<div align="right">NORMAN MAILER[63]</div>

I know I'm not supposed to like [Philip Roth], because he's a misogynist and demeans women, but I can't help it.

LENA DUNHAM[65]

She likes him because he's honest.

LENONA WINTER[66]

Philip Roth

The Chaos of Eros

I knew her eight years ago. She was in my class. I don't teach full-time anymore, strictly speaking don't teach literature at all – for years now just the one class, a big senior seminar in critical writing called Practical Criticism. I attract a lot of female students. For two reasons. Because it's a subject with an alluring combination of intellectual glamour and journalistic glamour and because they've heard me on NPR reviewing books or seen me on Thirteen talking about culture. Over the past fifteen years, being cultural critic on the television program has made me fairly well known locally, and they're attracted to my class because of that. In the beginning, I didn't realize that talking on TV once a week for ten minutes could be so impressive as it turns out to be to these students. But they are helplessly drawn to celebrity, however inconsiderable mine may be.

Now, I'm very vulnerable to female beauty, as you know. Everybody's defenseless against something, and that's it for me. I see it and it blinds me to everything else. They come to my first class, and I know almost immediately which is the girl for me.

It is now eight years ago – I was already sixty-two, and the girl, who is called Consuela Castillo, was twenty-four. She is not like the rest of the class. She doesn't look like a student, at least not like an ordinary student. She's not a demi-adolescent, she's not a slouching, unkempt, "like"-ridden girl. She's well spoken, sober, her posture is perfect – she appears to know something about adult life along with how to sit, stand, and walk. As soon as you enter the class, you see that this girl either knows more or wants to. The way she dresses. It isn't exactly what's

called chic, she's certainly not flamboyant, but, to begin with, she's never in jeans, pressed or unpressed. She dresses carefully, with quiet taste, in skirts, dresses, and tailored pants. Not to desensualize herself but more, it would seem, to professionalize herself, she dresses like an attractive secretary in a prestigious legal firm. Like the secretary to the bank chairman. She has a cream-colored silk blouse under a tailored blue blazer with gold buttons, a brown pocketbook with the patina of expensive leather, and little ankle boots to match, and she wears a slightly stretchy gray knitted skirt that reveals her body lines as subtly as such a skirt possibly could. Her hair is done in a natural but cared-for manner. She has a pale complexion, the mouth bowlike though the lips are full, and she has rounded forehead, a polished forehead of a smooth Brancusi elegance. She is Cuban. Her family are prosperous Cubans living in Jersey, across the river in Bergen County. She has black, black hair, glossy but ever so slightly coarse. And she's big. She's a big woman. The silk blouse is unbuttoned to the third button, and so you see she has powerful, beautiful breasts. You see the cleavage immediately. And you see she knows it. You see, despite the decorum, the meticulousness, the cautiously soigné style – because of them – that she's aware of herself. She comes to the first class with the jacket buttoned over her blouse, yet some five minutes into the session, she has taken it off. When I glance her way again see that she's put it back on. So you understand that she's aware of her power but that she isn't sure how to use it, what to do with it, how much she even wants it. That body is still new to her, she's still trying it out, thinking it through, a bit like a kid walking the streets with a loaded gun and deciding whether he's packing it to protect himself or to begin a life of crime.

That first night we were sitting on the sofa listening to *Dvořák*. At one point Consuela found a book that interested her – I forget which one, though I'll never forget the moment. She turned around – I was sitting where you are, at the corner of the sofa, and she was sitting there – and she twisted her torso half around, and with the book resting on the arm of the sofa, she started to read, and because of the leaning, the bending forward, under her clothing I saw her buttocks,

Philip Roth

saw the shape clearly, which was one whopping invitation. She is a tall young woman in a slightly too narrow body. It is as if the body doesn't quite fit. Not because she's too fat. But she's by no means the anorexic type. You see there female flesh, and it is good flesh, abundant – that's why you see it. So there she was, not openly lying across the sofa but, all the same, with her buttocks sort of half turned to me. A woman as conscious of her body as Consuela and doing that is, I concluded, inviting me to begin. The sexual instinct is still intact – none of the Cuban correctitude has interfered. In that half-turned ass, I see that nothing has gotten in the way of the pure thing. All that we'd talked about, all that I'd had to listen to about her family, none of it has interfered. She knows how to turn her ass despite all that. Turns in the primordial way. In display. And the display is perfect. It tells me that I need no longer suppress the wish to touch.

I started to caress her buttocks, and she liked it. She said, "This is a strange situation. I can never be your girlfriend. For every possible reason. You live in a different world."

"Different?" I laughed "How different?" And right there, of course, you start the lying, and you say, "Oh, it's not such a lofty place, if that's what you're imagining. It's not such a glamorous world. It's not even a world. Once a week I appear on TV. Once a week I'm on the radio. Every few weeks I appear in print in the back pages of a magazine read by twenty people at most. My program? It's a Sunday morning cultural program. Nobody watches. It's not much of a world to worry about. I can bring you into that world easily enough. Please stay with me."

She looks to be thinking about what I've said, but what sort of thinking can it be? "Okay," she says, "for now. For tonight. But I can never be your wife."

"Agreed," I said, but I thought, Who was asking her to be my wife? Who raised the question? I am sixty-two and she's twenty-four. I merely touch her ass and she tells me she can't be my wife? I didn't know such girls continued to exist. She is even more traditional than I imagined. Or maybe more odd, more unusual than I imagined. As I would discover, Consuela is ordinary but without being predictable. Nothing mechanical about her behavior. She's at once specific and mysterious,

and strangely full of little surprises. But, in the beginning especially, she was difficult for me to decipher, and, mistakenly – or perhaps not – I chalked that up to her Cubanness. "I love my cozy Cuban world," she told me. "I love the coziness of my family, and I can tell already that's not something you like or want. So I never can really belong to you."

This naive niceness in combination with her marvelous body was so enticing to me that I wasn't sure even then, on that first night, that I could fuck her as though she were another cavorting Miranda. No, Consuela was not the goat in the clock. It didn't matter what she was saying – she was so damned attractive that not only could I not resist her but I didn't see how any other man could, and it was in that moment, caressing her buttocks while she explained that she could not be my wife, that my terrible jealousy was born.

The jealousy. The uncertainty. The fear of losing her, even while on top of her. Obsessions that in my varied experience I had never known before. With Consuela as with no one else, the siphoning of confidence was almost instantaneous.

So we went to bed. It happened fast, less because of my intoxication than because of her lack of complexity. Or call it clarity. Call it newly minted maturity, though maturity, I would say, of a simple kind: she was in communion with that body in the very way she wished and wasn't able to be in communion with art. She undressed, and not only was her blouse silk but her underwear was made of silk. She had nearly pornographic underwear. A surprise. You know she has chosen this to please. You know she has chosen this with a man's eye in mind, even if a man were never to see it. You know that you have no idea what she is, how clever she is or how stupid she is, how shallow she is or how deep she is, how innocent she is or how guileful she is, how wily, how wise, even how wicked. With a self-contained woman of such sexual power, you have no idea and you never will. The tangle that is her character is obscured by her beauty. Nonetheless, I was greatly moved seeing that underwear. I was moved by seeing that body. "Look at you," I said.

There are two things you notice about Consuela's body. In the first place, the breasts. The most gorgeous breasts I have ever seen – and I was born, remember, in 1930: I have seen quite a few breasts by now.

These were round, full, perfect. The type with the nipple like a saucer. Not the nipple like an udder but the big pale rosy-brown nipple that is so very stirring. The second thing was that she had sleek pubic hair. Normally it's curly. This was like Asian hair. Sleek, lying flat, and not much of it. The pubic hair is important because it returns.

Yes, I pulled back the covers and she came into my bed, Consuela Castillo, superclassically the fertile female of our mammalian species. And already, that first time, and at only twenty-four, she was willing to sit on top of me. She wasn't sure of herself once she was there, and till I tapped her arm to get her attention and slow her down, she was obliviously overenergetic, caroming about with her eyes shut, off in a child's game of her own. I suppose she was trying to give herself over completely, but she was too young for that and, hard as she tried, that's not what she achieved. However, because she knew how alluring her breasts were and she wanted me to be able to see them at their best, she climbed on top of me when I asked her to.

I remember I said, "Do you realize that you have the most beautiful breasts I've ever seen?"

And like the efficient, thorough private secretary taking a memo, or perhaps like the well-brought-up Cuban daughter, she replied, "Yes, I know that. I see how you respond to my breasts."

In sex there is no point of absolute stasis. There is no sexual equality and there can be no sexual equality, certainly not one where the allotments are equal, the male quotient and the female quotient in perfect balance. There's no way to negotiate metrically this wild thing. It's not fifty-fifty like a business transaction. It's the chaos of eros we're talking about, the radical destabilization that is its excitement. You're back in the woods with sex. You're back in the bog. What it is is trading dominance, perpetual *imbalance*. You're going to rule out dominance? You're going to rule out yielding? The dominating is the flint, it strikes the spark, it sets it going. Then what? Listen. You'll see. You'll see what dominating leads to. You'll see what yielding leads to.

No matter how much you know, no matter how much you think, no matter how much you plot and you connive and you plan, you're not

superior to sex. It's a very risky game. A man wouldn't have two-thirds of the problems he has if he didn't venture off to get fucked. It's sex that disorders our normally ordered lives. I know this as well as anyone. Every last vanity will come back to mock you. Read Byron's *Don Juan*. Yet what do you do if you're sixty-two and believe you'll never have a claim on something so perfect again? What do you do if you're sixty-two and the urge to take whatever is still takable couldn't be stronger? What do you do if you're sixty-two and you realize that all those bodily parts invisible up to now (kidneys, lungs, veins, arteries, brain, intestines, prostate, heart) are about to start making themselves distressingly apparent, while the organ most conspicuous throughout your life is doomed to dwindle into insignificance?

Don't misunderstand me. It isn't that, through a Consuela, you can delude yourself into thinking that you have a last shot at your youth. You never feel the difference from youth more. In her energy, in her enthusiasm, in her youthful unknowing, in her youthful knowing, the difference is dramatized every moment. There's never any mistaking that it's she and not you who is twenty-four. You'd have to be a clod to feel you're young again. If you felt youthful, it would be a snap. Far from feeling youthful, you feel the poignancy of her limitless future as opposed to your own limited one, you feel even more than you ordinarily do the poignancy of every last grace that's been lost. It's like playing baseball with a bunch of twenty-year-olds. It isn't that you feel twenty because you're playing with them. You note the difference every second of the game. But at least you're not sitting on the sidelines.

Here's what happens: you feel excruciatingly how old you are, but in a new way. If you have her, why can't you have her?

You're not getting what you want even when you're getting what you want. There is no peace in it and there can't be, because of our ages and the unavoidable poignancy. Because of our ages, I have the pleasure but I never lose the longing. Had this never happened before? No. I was never sixty-two years old before. I was no longer in that phase of my life when I thought I could do everything. Yet I remembered it clearly. You see a beautiful woman. You see her from a mile away. You go to

her and say, "Who are you?" You have dinner. And so on. That phase, when it's worry-free.

You get on the bus. A creature so gorgeous everybody is afraid to sit next to her. The seat next to the most beautiful girl in the world – and it's empty. So you take it. But now isn't then, and it'll never be calm, it'll never be peaceful. I was worried about her walking around in that blouse. Peel off her jacket, and there is the blouse. Peel off the blouse, and there is perfection. A young man will find her and take her away.

How do I know a young man will take her away? Because I once was the young man who would have done it.

Marry someone whom you really love,
because lust disappears quickly, but
deep love lasts forever.

CARL REINER[67]

JON PEARSON

A Busload of Banjo Players

Elya and I are sitting at a small patio table in a nice little breakfast place in Santa Barbara. It's our anniversary, not our wedding anniversary, but the anniversary of the day we first got together at Starbucks five years ago. It's a Sunday and the place is packed. We've ordered and I'm waiting for my massive cinnamon apple pancake. Elya, like most women, is waiting for something sensible, a spinach omelet, and I say, "Okay, I want you to imagine something, and I mean really imagine it."

And Elya, gorgeous as hell in her Jackie Kennedy-looking sunglasses, is drinking in my every word. The smell of bacon and pancakes is in the air, and roses, and I am so happy I don't have a head, the summer sky is my head.

"You're shooting a documentary," I say, "a nature film. And in the camera frame" (I frame my head and shoulders with my hands), "you have come across a rare Amazonian tree frog. And for the next thirty seconds I am going to *be* that tree frog. And your job is to watch. But watch like it's a frippin miracle, 'cause I'll be going to a place beyond all human understanding, and doing little things with my face and hands. I hope to God the waitress doesn't bring our food while I'm doing this. The people around us will think I'm having a seizure. But it'll be worth it. And then, afterward, you can do your own nature scene."

Now, many women might say, "Cut it out," or "Not another one of your crazy imagination games," or "You're gonna get us arrested?" But sweet Elya removes her sunglasses and fixes me with her big, beautiful brown eyes as if to say, *Go ahead, cowboy. Knock yourself out.*

And moments later, Elya, a former kick-ass corporate lawyer *and*

professional actress, is "doing" a Sargasso Sea glow fish, pinching her face into something scary, fishy, ugly and intense while looking gorgeouser and gorgeouser by the second. Suddenly I want to make primal love to her on the patio table as she again proves the greatest of all secrets: that real beauty is far bigger than mere pretty. Pretty paints its toes and hopes you like its purse. Pretty primps, and prays somebody's watching.

Beauty, on the other hand, could give a shit. It breaks the rules. It goes for broke. It is an all-or-nothing, radioactive busload of banjo players flying off a cliff, because beauty is a raging fire. It doesn't wish or want, worry, wait, or look back.

And that is why Elya, my now wife, is to me the most beautiful woman alive. And it is my solemn, every-single-day job to keep it that way, to stoke the fires of her deep beauty, to help her be her one-and-only self. In my wedding vows I proclaimed: "I shall love you like no man has ever loved a woman." A tall order. But when the vow first popped into my head, I felt I was riding a bicycle upside down on a cloud and everywhere I looked was Saturday and ice cream.

Every day with Elya, I learn how to be a man. I aspire to become the man-space in which Elya can be herself, where she doesn't walk on eggshells, hold back, or fit into some idealized movie in my head.

I met Elya after I had given up all hope. *All* hope. I was sixty and had never married. I figured women had too many working parts, any one of which could go wrong, and I knew no woman I would want would ever want me.

Then, Elya – brilliant, beautiful, amazing Elya. I didn't feel an ounce of neediness. All I wanted to do was love her. As if I had been storing up love my entire life, as if I were a circus wagon of tricks and surprises and all I needed was the right woman to see past my clever defenses, see the man who wanted to love her mightily in his own crazy-ass way.

"Why me," I ask her, "when you could have anyone?"

And always she says, "'Cause you bring out the silly in me."

We run through the house like seagulls, kick our legs in bed while making up poems, we switch childhood memories. I call her Bambina. She calls me Coconut Head. Every day I make her a birthday card, and every time we come into the house we hug.

It's not easy to love. It is easy to get lazy or selfish or driven or lost in a hundred ways and, when the going gets rough, to want a fantasy. I always wanted a fantasy. Now I don't.

I've had a miracle. And I've learned that just as beauty is bigger than mere pretty, intimacy is bigger than any dream. So I don't care any more about looking good. I care about being seen. I want to stop running and come home. And I want Elya to feel seen and safe. I want her to feel loved and free. I want her to feel, every single day, like I am the answer to her prayers … because she is the answer to mine.

Richard Bausch

Letter to the Lady of the House

It's exactly 20 minutes to midnight, on this, the eve of my 70th birth-
day. And I've decided to address you, for a change, in writing, odd as
that might seem. I'm perfectly aware of how you're going to take the fact
that I'm doing this at all, so late at night with everybody due to arrive
tomorrow and the house still unready. I haven't spent almost five de-
cades with you without learning a few things about you that I can pre-
dict and describe with some accuracy. Though I admit that, as you put
it, lately we've been more like strangers than husband and wife.

Well, so if we are like strangers, perhaps there are some things I can
tell you that you won't have already figured out about the way I feel.
Tonight we had another one of those long, silent evenings after an ar-
gument. Remember? Over pepper. We had been bickering all day re-
ally, but at dinner I put pepper on my potatoes and you said that about
how I shouldn't have pepper because it always upsets my stomach. I'm
bothered to remark that I used to eat chili peppers for breakfast. And if
I wanted to put plain, old, ordinary black pepper on my potatoes – as I
had been doing for more than 60 years – that was my privilege.

Writing this now, it sounds far more testy than I meant it. But that
isn't really the point. In any case, you chose to overlook my tone. You
simply said, "John, you were up all night the last time you had pepper
with your dinner."

I said, "I was up all night because I ate green peppers, not black pep-
per but green peppers."

"A pepper is a pepper. Isn't it?" You said. And then I started in on you.
I got – as you call it – legal with you, pointing out that green peppers are

not black pepper. And from there we moved on to an evening of mutual disregard for each other that ended with your decision to go to bed early. The grandchildren will make you tired and there's still the house to do. You had every reason to want to get some rest. And yet, I felt that you were also making a point of getting yourself out of proximity with me, leaving me to my displeasure with another ridiculous argument settling between us like a fog.

So after you went to bed, I got out the whiskey and started pouring drinks. And I had every intention of putting myself into a stupor. It was also my birthday, after all, and – forgive this, it's the way I felt at the time – you had nagged me into an argument and then gone off to bed. The day had ended as so many of our days end now. And I felt, well, entitled. I had a few drinks without any appreciable effect, though you might well see this letter as firm evidence to the contrary.

And then I decided to do something to shake you up. I would leave. I'd make a lot of noise going out the door. I'd take a walk around the neighborhood and make you wonder where I could be. Perhaps I'd go check into a motel for the night. The thought even crossed my mind that I might leave you all together. I admit that I entertained the thought, Marie. I saw our life together now as the day to day round of petty quarreling and tension that it's mostly been over the past couple of years or so. And I wanted out as sincerely as I ever wanted out of anything.

And I got up from my seat in front of the television and walked back down the hall to the entrance of our room to look at you. I suppose I hoped you'd still be awake so I could tell you of this momentous decision I felt I'd reached. And maybe you were awake. One of our oldest areas of contention being the noise I make, the feather thin membrane of your sleep that I am always disturbing with my restlessness in the nights.

All right, assuming you were asleep and don't know that I stood in the doorway of our room, I will say that I stood there for perhaps five minutes looking at you in the half dark, the shape of your body under the blanket. You really did look like one of the girls when they were little and I used to stand in the doorway of their rooms. Your illness last

year made you so small again. And as I said, I thought I had decided to leave you for your peace as well as mine.

I know you have gone to sleep crying, Marie. I know you felt sorry about things and wished we could find some way to stop irritating each other so much. Well, of course, I didn't go anywhere. I came back to this room and drank more of the whiskey and watched television. It was like all the other nights. The shows came on and ended and the whiskey began to wear off. There was a little rain shower. I had a moment of the shock of knowing I was 70.

After the rain ended, I did go outside for a few minutes. I stood on the sidewalk and looked at the house. The kids, with their kids, were on the road somewhere between their homes and here. I walked up to the end of the block and back and a pleasant breeze blew and shook the drops out of the trees. My stomach was bothering me some and maybe it was the pepper I'd put on my potatoes. It could just as well have been the whiskey.

Anyway, as I came back to the house, I began to have an eerie feeling that I had reached the last night of my life. There was this small discomfort in my stomach and no other physical pang or pain. And I'm used to the small ills and side effects of my ways of eating and drinking. Yet I felt a sense of the end of things more strongly than I can describe. When I stood in the entrance of our room and looked at you again, wondering if I would make it through to the morning, I suddenly found myself trying to think what I would say to you if, indeed, this were the last time I would ever be able to speak to you. And I began to know I would write you this letter.

At least words in a letter aren't blurred by tone of voice, by the old, aggravating sound of me talking to you. I began with this and with the idea that, after months of thinking about it, I would at last try to say something to you that wasn't colored by our disaffection. What I have to tell you must be explained in a rather round about way.

I've been thinking about my cousin, Louise, and her husband. When he died and she stayed with us last summer, something brought back to me what is really only the memory of a moment. Yet it reached me, that moment, across more than 50 years.

As you know, Louise is nine years older than I and more like an older sister than a cousin. I must have told you, at one time or another, that I spent some weeks with her back in 1933, when she was first married. The memory I'm talking about comes from that time. And what I have decided I have to tell you comes from that memory. Father had been dead four years. We were all used to the fact that times were hard and that there was no man in the house, though I suppose I filled that role in some titular way.

In any case, when mother became ill, there was the problem of us, her children. Though I was the oldest, I wasn't old enough to stay in the house alone or to nurse her either. My grandfather came up with a solution– and everybody went along with it – that I would go to Louise's for a time and the two girls would go to stay with grandfather.

So we closed up the house and I got on a train to Virginia. I was a few weeks shy of 14 years old. I remember that I was not able to believe that anything truly bad would come of mother's pleurisy and was consequently glad of the opportunity it afforded me to travel the 100 miles south to Charlottesville, where cousin Louise had moved with her new husband only a month earlier, after her wedding.

Because we traveled so much at the beginning, you never got to really know Charles when he was young. In 1933 he was a very tall, imposing fellow with bright red hair and a graceful way of moving that always made me think of athletics and contests of skill. He had worked at the Navy Yard in Washington and had been laid off in the first months of Roosevelt's New Deal. Louise was teaching in a day school in Charlottesville so they could make ends meet. And Charles was spending most of his time looking for work and fixing up the house.

I had only met Charles once or twice before the wedding, but already I admired him and wanted to emulate him. The prospect of spending time in his house, or perhaps going fishing with him in the small streams of central Virginia, was all I thought about on the way down. And I remember that we did go fishing one weekend, that I wound up spending a lot of time with Charles, helping to paint the house and to run water lines under it for indoor plumbing.

Oh, I had time with Louise too, listening to her read from the books she wanted me to be interested in, walking with her around Charlottesville in the evenings, and looking at the city as it was then, or sitting on her small porch and talking about the family, mother's stubborn illness, the children Louise saw every day at school. But what I want to tell you has to do with the very first day I was there.

I know you think I use far too much energy thinking about and pining away for the past. And I therefore know that I'm taking a risk by talking about this ancient history and by trying to make you see it. But this all has to do with you and me, my dear, and our late inability to find ourselves in the same room together without bitterness and pain. That summer, 1933, was unusually warm in Virginia. And the heat, along with my impatience to arrive, made the train almost unbearable. I think it was just past noon when it pulled into the station in Charlottesville, with me hanging out one of the windows looking for Louise or Charles. It was Charles who had come to meet me. He stood in a crisp-looking seersucker suit with a straw boater cocked at just the angle you'd expect a young, newly married man to wear a straw boater, even in the middle of economic disaster.

I waved at him and he waved back and I might have jumped out the window if the train had slowed even a little more than it had before it stopped in the shade of platform. I made my way out, carrying the cloth bag my grandfather had given me for the trip. Mother had said, through her room, that I looked like a carpetbagger. And when I stepped down to shake hands with Charles, I noticed that what I thought was a new suit was tattered at the ends of the sleeves.

"Well," he said, "Young John." I smiled at him and I was perceptive enough to see that his cheerfulness was not entirely effortless. He was a man out of work, after all. And so, in spite of himself, there was worry in his face, the slightest shadow in an otherwise glad and proud countenance.

We walked through the station to the street and on up the steep hill to the house, which was a small, clapboard structure, a cottage really, with a porch at the end of the short sidewalk lined with flowers. They were marigolds, I think. And here was Louise coming out of the house,

her arms already stretched wide to embrace me. "Lord," she said, "I swear you've grown since the wedding, John."

Charles took my bag and went inside. "Let me look at you, young man," Louise said. I stood for inspection. And as she looked me over, I saw that her hair was pulled back, that a few strands of it had come loose, that it was brilliantly auburn in the sun. I suppose I was a little in love with her. She was grown and married now. She was a part of what seemed a great mystery to me, even as I was about to enter it. And of course, you remember how that feels, Marie, when one is on the verge of things, nearly adult, nearly old enough to fall in love.

I looked at Louise's happy, flushed face and felt a deep ache as she ushered me into her house. I wanted so to be older. Inside, Charles had poured lemonade for us and was sitting in the easy chair by the fireplace, already sipping his. Louise wanted to show me the house and the backyard, which she had tilled and turned into a small vegetable garden. But she must have sensed how thirsty I was and so she asked me to sit down and have a cool drink before she showed me the upstairs.

Now of course, looking back on it, I remember that those rooms she was so anxious to show me were meager indeed. They were not much bigger than closets really, and the paint was faded and dull. The furniture she'd arranged so artfully was coming apart. The pictures she'd put on the walls were prints she'd cut out, magazine covers mostly. And the curtains over the windows were the same ones that hung in her childhood bedroom for 20 years.

"Recognize these?" she said with a deprecating smile. Of course, the quality of her pride had nothing to do with the fineness, or lack of it, in these things, but in the fact that they belonged to her and that she was a married lady in her own house.

On this day in July, in 1933, she and Charles were waiting for the delivery of a fan they had scrounged enough money to buy from Sears, through the catalog. There were things they would rather have been doing, especially in this heat, and especially with me there. Monticello wasn't far away. The university was within walking distance. And without too much expense, one could ride a taxi to one of the lakes nearby. They had hoped that the fan would arrive before I did, but since it

hadn't – and since neither Louise nor Charles was willing to leave the other alone while traipsing off with me that day – there wasn't anything to do but wait around for it.

Louise had opened the windows and shut the shades and we sat in her small living room and drank the lemonade, fanning ourselves with folded parts of Charles' morning newspaper. From time to time, an anemic breath of air would move the shades slightly. But everything grew still again. Louise sat on the arm of Charles's chair and I sat on the sofa. We talked about pleurisy and, I think, about the fact that Thomas Jefferson had invented the dumbwaiter, how the plumbing at Monticello was at least a century ahead of its time.

Charles remarked that it was the spirit of invention that would make a man's career in these days. "That's what I'm aiming for, to be inventive in a job, no matter what it winds up being."

When the lemonade ran out, Louise got up and went into the kitchen to make some more. Charles and I talked about taking a weekend to go fishing. He leaned back in his chair and put his hands behind his head looking satisfied. In the kitchen, Louise was chipping ice for our glasses. And she began singing something low for her own pleasure, a barely audible lilting. And Charles and I sat listening. It occurred to me that I was very happy. I had the sense that soon I would be embarked on my own life, as Charles was. And that an attractive woman like Louise would be there with me.

Charles yawned and said, "God, listen to that. Doesn't Louise have the loveliest voice?"

And that's all I have from that day. I don't even know if the fan arrived later. And I have no clear memory of how we spent the rest of the afternoon and evening. I remember Louise singing a song, her husband leaning back in his chair, folding his hands behind his head, expressing his pleasure in his young wife's voice. I remember that I felt quite extraordinarily content just then.

And that's all I remember.

But there are, of course, the things we both know. We know they moved to Colorado to be near Charles' parents. We know they never

had any children. We know that Charles fell down a shaft at a construction site in the fall of 1957 and was hurt so badly that he never walked again. And I know that when she came to stay with us last summer, she told me she'd learned to hate him, and not for what she'd had to help him do all those years. No, it started earlier and was deeper than that. She hadn't minded the care of him – the washing and feeding and all the numberless small tasks she had to perform each and every day, all day. She hadn't minded this. In fact, she thought there was something in her makeup that liked being needed so completely. The trouble was simply that whatever she had once loved in him she had stopped loving. And for many, many years before he died, she'd felt only suffocation when he was near enough to touch her, only irritation and anxiety when he spoke.

She said all this and then looked at me, her cousin, who had been fortunate enough to have children and to be in love over time and said, "John, how have you and Marie managed it?" And what I wanted to tell you has to do with this fact. That while you and I had had one of our whispering arguments only moments before, I felt quite certain of the simple truth of the matter, which is that – whatever our complications – we have managed to be in love over time. "Louise," I said.

"People start out with such high hopes," she said, as if I wasn't there. She looked at me. "Don't they?"

"Yes," I said.

She seemed to consider this a moment. Then: "I wonder how it happens."

I said, "You ought to get some rest," or something equally pointless and admonitory. As she moved away from me, I had an image of Charles standing on the station platform in Charlottesville that summer, the straw boater set at its cocky angle. It was an image I would see most of the rest of that night, and on many another night since.

I can almost hear your voice as you point out that, once again, I've managed to dwell too long in a memory of something that's passed and gone. The difference is that I'm not grieving over the past now. I am merely reporting a memory so that you might understand what I'm

about to say to you.

The fact is, we aren't the people we were even then, just a year ago. I know that as I know things have been slowly eroding between us for a very long time. We are a little tired of each other. And there are annoyances and old scars that won't be obliterated with a letter, even a long one written in the middle of the night in desperate sincerity, under the influence – admittedly – of a considerable portion of bourbon whisky, but nevertheless, with the best intention and hope that you may know how, over the course of this night, I came to the end of needing an explanation for our difficulty.

We have reached this place, everything we say seems rather aggravating mindless and automatic, like something one stranger might say to another in one of the thousand circumstances where strangers are thrown together for a time, and the silence begins to grow heavy on their minds and someone has to say something.

Darling, we go so long these days without having anything at all to do with each other. And the children are arriving tomorrow. And once more we'll be in the position of making all of the gestures that give them back their parents as they think their parents are. And what I wanted to say to you– what came to me as I thought about Louise and Charles on that day so long ago, when they were young and so obviously glad of each other, and I looked at them and knew it and was happy – what came to me was that even the harsh things that happened to them, even the years of anger and silence, even the disappointment and the bitterness and the wanting not to be in the same room anymore, even all that must have been worth it for such loveliness.

At least I am here, at 70 years old, hoping so. Tonight, I went back to our room again and stood gazing at you asleep, dreaming whatever you were dreaming. And I had a moment of thinking how we were always friends too, because what I wanted, finally, to say was that I remember well our own sweet times, our own old loveliness. And I would like to think that even if– at the very beginning of our lives together– I had somehow been shown that we would end up here with this longing to be away from each other, this feeling of being trapped together, of being tied to each other in a way that makes us wish for other times, some

other place, I would have known enough to accept it all freely for the chance at that love. And if I could, I would do it all again, Marie. All of it. Even the sorrow. My sweet, my dear adversary, for everything that I remember.

7. Men & War

When I asked women friends for volunteers to beta-read this anthology, a dozen stepped forward. But one said she would not look at this section: "I'm opposed to war in all forms."

I understand. Women are life's creators and nurturers. An aversion to killing lives in most women, and many ridicule men's penchant for war. But in the 1980s, England's Prime Minister, Margaret Thatcher, went to war in the Falkland Islands, and India's Prime Minister, Indira Gandhi, ordered her troops to storm the Golden Temple, Sikhism's holiest site. In 1863, Harriet Tubman became the first woman to lead an armed assault during the Civil War.[68] And in 1429, Joan of Arc led her troops to battlefield triumph.[69]

Women have waged war.

A man may have to come to grips with combat, because it may figure in his life or death. He might *have* to fight for what is right or wrong, *want* to fight, or want to avoid fighting. But if he lives in a country with a draft or obligatory military service, he will have to face his relationship to war, as did young American men during the War of Independence, Civil War, World Wars, Korea, and Vietnam. War was central to their thoughts and lives.

I read many war stories researching this anthology, but having never lived through battle, I'll never comprehend it. Warrior-hood is a fraternity to which non-combatants do not belong.

Women ask, "Why do men fight?"

As has been said, let's not blame war on the warrior.[70] A man usually goes to war because his country sends him. Yes, some young men volunteer to fight, seem eager to wage these wars – the thrill of fighting, of protecting the tribe, of machismo and the warrior myth, live in them – but it is the leaders who send them.

Are there "good" wars and "bad" wars?

San Francisco columnist Herb Cain (and others) referred to World War II as "the last good war." I suggested this to a Scottish veteran at Ranville, France, on the 50[th] anniversary of D-Day, June 6, 1994.

He shot back, "Nae war is a good war, and naebody kens it like an auld Tommy.[71] The Second World War was a necessary war; we had to drive the Nazis oot of Europe. But World War II was no' a good war. Ye'll be remembering that, won't ye, laddie?"[72]

Battle streams a flood of life-threatening initiations at fighting soldiers. Many return home drowning from their immersion in war's tides. Don Narkevic's story, "Polish Day, Kennywood Park," sees a World War II vet, head barely above water, schooling a 12-year-old boy in dancing.

In "A Girl Named Martha" an extract from Tim O'Brien's collection, *The Things They Carried,* a soldier brings heavy artillery into battle, as well as distracting thoughts of a girl he's never so much as kissed.

In John Crawford's "No Crying in Baseball," two stories nested inside another, we hear a soldier's phone call home to his wife, telling her of his day in the Iraq war. In both O'Brien's and Crawford's pieces, we'll see that a woman, though thousands of miles away, is central to a soldier's life. We'll witness a man's *need* for a woman in these stories.

Victor Ayscough's "My Vietnam" follows a pivotal afternoon in the writer's relationship to the war. Finally, in "What About Women?", we'll read Jonathan Gottschall's essay on women's culpability in men's fights.

"I wis never mair alive than when I wis fightin'," the Scottish veteran told me. The war writing here is similarly vibrant. But the alive role of men in war is also the most degrading they play. After reading this section, one woman said, *"Poor men!"*

I had to pass on that potential beta-reader because of her refusal to look at this section. Yes, most women are opposed to war, and cannot fathom why men fight. But as Warren Farrell wrote, "Understanding men requires understanding men's relationship to the Three Ws: Women, Work, and War."[73] Here's an opportunity to better understand men and war, and to read some brilliant writing. Please don't skip this section.

The defense of the tribe

is an

insanely

compelling idea

and once

you've been

exposed to it

there's almost nothing else you'd rather do.

SEBASTIAN YOUNGER[74]

Don Narkevic

Polish Day, Kennywood Park

Near dark, as rain stumbles in, amusement rides close one by one and kids swarm the Polish pavilion, festooned in red and white bunting. On stage, the Polka-Aires blare brassily, moving from polka to polka, as couples, hedged in by green picnic tables, round a makeshift dance floor. Under the tables children squat, hypnotized by the circling of their twirling parents. My sister and brothers scavenge through left-over foods: warm potato salad, shriveled kielbasa links, stale hard rolls, and orphaned bottles of opened soda pop gone flat. Having thrown up on the Jack Rabbit half an hour ago, my stomach is content to be empty.

In the rear of the pavilion, Dad plays poker with a group of non-dancers, whose abandoned wives dance with other abandoned wives. Dad knows how to dance. But he won't. Not when there's a chance to clip a few beer-addled pigeons at five-card stud. And no one seems to see what's going on except me. So I'm keeping my eyes glued to the man who holds Mom closer than Dad does when they hug.

The man dancing with Mom is Ted Benkowski, a friend of the family whom we call Mr. B. He lives a block from our home and delivers our milk. During the school year, his delivery truck seems to pull up just as we're leaving for school. He takes the opportunity to tease us about our height or our hair or our pitiful lack of knowing anything. His tortured conversations end in a handshake, our small hands mere walnuts in the massive nutcracker of his clenched fist.

When the band switches from a polka to a Czárdás, Mr. B's drunken promenade soon staggers out of rhythm. But Mom maintains her balance and his, propping him up like wet laundry. His sweaty face glows

red as a traffic light. But he never stops. At the end of each dance, before Mom has a chance to escape, he holds her hostage until the next song. Dad pays more attention to the ladies in his poker hand than his lady on the dance floor. As Mom tries to keep up with her palsied partner, her flowery skirt wilts in the heat. Untucked, Mr. B's long-sleeved white shirt, rolled to his elbows, clings to his damp body. A narrow black tie garrotes his neck like a short fuse, and a thick belt chokes his baggy brown trousers. The early grace of his wide wing tips surrendered long ago to several bottles of Pabst.

At the end of the Czárdás, the dancers applaud. The leader of the band grabs the microphone. As his mustache suffocates the chrome, he asks the audience, "Ladies and gentlemen, are you having a good time?"

The audience roars with more applause and yips of approval.

The leader's face plumps with pride. "Dziękuję, ladies and gentlemen," he says, bowing. Then he adds, "But as Porky the świnia says, 'Th-Th-Th-That's all, folks!'"

The crowd moans.

Like a tinny radio commercial, he shrieks, "Enjoy the rest of Polish Day here at Kennywood Park!"

Mr. B shouts back, "If y-y-you keep p-playing, we'll keep enjoying!"

The drummer badda-booms.

Everyone laughs.

Nonetheless, the musicians disband.

As Mom walks toward me, fanning herself with her palms, Mr. B clings to her like one of my Aunt Valeria's fox stoles, his long arms draped around her neck. My sister and brothers scatter like minnows. When Mom reaches our picnic table, she rolls her eyes at me. While prying him off, she says to Mr. B, "Taddzu, sit down. I'll fix you something to eat."

He grins, leans over, and whispers in Mom's ear. As she listens, she blushes and smiles, but her eyes dash at me like flash cards she uses to teach my younger brother arithmetic. I know what they add up to. After Mom pushes him away, Mr. B laughs and plops down next to me at our table. With a napkin, Mom wipes off her ear. Through my peripheral vision, I see him staring at me. His thick spectacles magnify his glass

eye as the good eye zeros in on me like a riflescope. I never know which eye of his to look at. Dad told me to always look a man in the eye when talking to him, but he never said which one. Anyway, direct eye contact will cause Mr. B to say something to me, so I avoid looking at him. He says something anyway.

"Hey, kid, you kn-know how to d-dance?"

I pretend he's talking to someone else and don't answer, but he stabs me with his elbow. "Hey, I'm-m-m talking to you!"

I look at Mom who's making him a ham sandwich. She smiles at me and nods toward Mr. B. If I lie and say, yes, Mr. B will grab me like a mannequin, maneuver me to the center of the dance floor, and force me to prove my claim. I saw him do that once to my cousin Kevin at a wedding. If I say, no, he'll make some smart remark.

I say, "No." My answer punches all the air out of his face.

He exhales loudly, like a tire going flat fast. I smell stale beer. "How old are y-you?" he asks.

"Twelve."

His face deflates further. "Th-that's no age," he says. "Th-that's how m-many eggs in a d-dozen." He laughs. I don't. When he's done laughing, he inspects me, a non-laugher. As his face contorts like some agony in Gethsemane, I can tell he finds me unsuitable as a child, let alone a Polish one. Then he indicts Mom, the party responsible.

"J-Jesus Christ, Emercine," he says to Mom, "these k-kids d-d-don't kn-know n-nothing."

Mom tries to rescue me. "He's twelve, Taddzu. He doesn't have to dance."

To appease him, Mom sets a paper plate in front of him with two slabs of ham sandwiched between slices of paska.

Looking down at the food, Mr. B frowns, his chin touching his chest. When Mom places an Iron City Beer next to the plate, he livens. "Dziękuję. Do y-you have any chrzan?" he asks.

Mom slides the bottle of horseradish across the table. After slathering the bread with horseradish, Mr. B takes a horse-sized bite. I figure I'm safe as long as he eats.

"I'll bet … you d-don't … speak Polish … either," he says between chomps.

Busy with packing, Mom stops listening to the conversation. I don't know much Polish, just a few words. But it's worth a shot. "I know that *dziękuję* means thank you," I say.

"M-My d-dog can say that much," he says, picking something from his yellow teeth with a match.

"I know that *baci* means grandmother."

"After mama and papa, that's the third word P-Polish b-babies learn."

I feel like Dad when he's drawing nothing but losing hands and knows the dealer's dealing from the bottom of the deck. So I look Mr. B dead in his live eye and say, "I know that *gromki pysk* means loud mouth."

With his left hand, he grabs the back of my neck and holds it tighter than a grenade. With his right hand, he picks up his Iron City. As he drinks, his grip tightens. I feel like an Ohio River catfish held by the gills by some weekend fisherman having his picture taken by one of his buddies. Maybe Mr. B senses the sass in my last answer because he asks me another question.

"Do you kn-know what today is?"

"Friday."

"No."

"June sixth."

"No."

"Polish Day at Kennywood."

"No."

I'm out of ammo. I know it's a trick question, but I don't know the trick answer. I surrender. "I don't know," I say.

He smirks like MacArthur staring down at the humiliated Japanese on the USS Missouri. "See," he says, "you don't know that much." He shakes me by the neck for a moment, and when his grip loosens, I wriggle out. He shouts at Mom, "These kids!"

"Don't cry to me, Taddzu. Talk to his father," Mom says, pointing at Dad, still playing cards. When Mom refers to Dad as "father," I know she's angry with him. This time, for playing cards all day and ignoring her.

"Joe Narky's a bum," Mr. B says. "Christ, I out-shot him at the sh-shooting gallery th-this afternoon. And I've only got one good

p-peeper." Looking over his shoulder at Dad, he adds, "He's got t-ten god d-damned fingers, and he still can't w-win at cards!"

Not sure if I should smile or laugh or leave, I look to Mom. Mom laughs, but I know she doesn't approve of the language. Once, during an argument over his gambling, Dad let the "f" word fly, and Mom didn't talk to him for a week. Before Mr. B can continue his editorial on the state of our nation's youth, Mrs. B arrives at our picnic table and tells her husband it's time to leave. Her voice crackles sweet as a box of Cracker Jack, yet it squeaks shrill as the prize toy whistle. As a child in the thirties, Mrs. B's leg got caught under a playground merry-go-round. She still walks with a slight limp. Childless, Mrs. B enjoys strolling the amusement park arm-in-arm with her husband, watching the faces of children as they wait in line, anticipating the wild rides.

Looking at the last piece of his sandwich like it's a religious relic, Mr. B says, "I'm n-not going. You go with Emercine."

Mrs. B looks at me, then at Mom. From behind his back, she pretends to strangle her husband of eighteen years.

"And how are you getting home?" she asks.

"I'm g-going home with Joe N-Narky."

Still standing behind him, Mrs. B cocks her fist. Her upper teeth bite her top lip. Then she explains the situation to Mr. B as though to a child. "Emercine's going home with Joe Narky. And they have four kids. Remember? There's no room for you."

Like an impudent child, Mr. B explains with equal composure, "N-Narky is still p-playing cards. You take Emercine and her kids in our car, and m-me and this kid will go with N-Narky in his car."

When Mr. B said, "this kid," he nudged me in the ribs. I do not want to ride with Mr. B. I look at Mom and try to catch her eye, but she and Mrs. B have already begun taking our stuff to the other car. I do not want to ride with Mr. B. As my older brother totes a cooler to the car, he sticks his tongue out at me and laughs. I do not want to ride with Mr. B.

When Mom leaves with Mrs. B without saying anything to Dad, I run over to where he sits playing cards. The whiskey-blank faces of the other men reveal nothing. As I circle the table, each man moves his cards closer to his chest, unwilling to let anyone, even a kid, get a

glance at his hand. A few of the men, the winners, have piles of dollar bills and change. Dad's got fifty-seven cents. After he tosses two quarters into the pot to call a raise, he's down to a nickel and two pennies. With beer bottle in hand, Mr. B, somber as a funeral visit, approaches the table. When a fat man with a cigar lays down three kings, Dad slaps his cards on the table face down like drowned bodies and gets up, leaving the seven cents behind with the rest of his losses. Mr. B laughs and slaps the fat man on the back.

Dad's not a sore loser. He always figures he'll win big next time. When he asks me where Mom is, I tell him she left with Mrs. B. I can tell he's putting two and two together and coming up with an odd number. After some pensive thought, his face animates, saying that Mom will probably be asleep in bed by the time we get home.

On the way to the car, he endures the verbal abuse of Mr. B as he details Dad's "piss poor" card playing. The rain weakens to a mist. As we cross the cinder parking lot, Dad knows just when and where to help keep Mr. B from falling down without being obvious. As I trail behind them, I figure I can hide in the back seat of Dad's car like a foxhole. But as Dad opens the back door of our Ford Fairlane, Mr. B insists I sit up front, between Dad and him. I look at Dad. He shrugs and shuts the rear door. I try to slide across the seat to the middle, but my sweaty legs stick to the hot vinyl. Mr. B thumps down on the seat like a dead man.

As we pull out of the parking lot, Mr. B wedges his bottle of beer between his legs. On the way, his image fades in and out of street-lamp light, his torso stiff as a bronze on exhibit at the Carnegie. I smell stale sweat. I keep waiting for someone to speak. After a while, Dad turns on the radio.

After a few minutes of "In-A-Gadda-Da-Vida," Mr. B grouses in a low drunken tone, "G-Goddamn hippie m-music. How do kids d-dance to th-that?"

Dad elbows me and nods at the radio. I change stations, finding the news.

" . . . at the Tomb of the Unknown Soldier, on this the twenty-fifth anniversary of the Allied invasion of Normandy . . . "

Mr. B's left arm flies in front of me, his hand knocking my hand away from the radio. His fingers poke at all the radio buttons, changing

stations like a mad piano player trying to find the right note. His furious fingers continue to pound until Dad turns the radio off. The death of the radio seems to please Mr. B. To the thud of windshield wipers, he lights a Lucky. He takes a drag and exhales, smoke rolling, banking off the windshield and spreading like a slow motion explosion. In a trance of alcohol and under a veil of smoldering tobacco, Mr. B speaks.

"D-Day we parachuted behind enemy lines." His stony face is the color of a tombstone. "As we fell, the Krauts fired into the night sky, picking some of us off like clay pigeons."

Earlier in the day, Dad challenged Mr. B to a contest at the shooting gallery. "Five bucks says I can out-shoot you, Taddzu," Dad bragged

Mr. B, walking with his wife, worked on a chocolate cone. Mom told Dad that we didn't have five dollars for foolishness.

"Good," Mr. B said. "M-make it ten, J-Joe."

Dad plunked down a quarter on the counter. Mr. B did the same. The barker snapped up the change and held out a rifle.

"You go first, Taddzu," Dad offered.

"N-No, you," Mr. B replied and continued eating his ice cream.

Dad grabbed the rifle. I had never seen Dad shoot craps let alone a gun. When Dad started firing, Mr. B watched, and Mrs. B and Mom left in a huff. When dad finished, he had only scored three hits. No prize.

With a crunch, Mr. B finished his cone and picked up the rifle. While he was still chewing, he fired off round after round, each shot pinging a target. It sounded like a car running back and forth over the ding-hose at a service station. By the time Mr. B finished, the barker had lined up several stuffed animals on the counter, all of which Mr. B ignored and stray kids fought over.

When the car stops at a red light, Mr. B takes several loud gulps of beer. Like many other vets, Mr. B never talked about the war. Dad, a younger man, served as a peacekeeper in Bad Wildungen, Germany after V-E Day, and now concentrates on Mr. B's tale of combat.

"Just before I hit the ground," Mr. B continues, "a sniper shot me in the eye."

I peek up at his eye, expecting blood. All I see is a dead marble. Without looking at me, Mr. B nudges my ribs with his elbow, sharp as a bayonet.

"It had to be a sniper," he says. "No green-ass recruit gets that lucky!"

He laughs. Dad laughs. I laugh, too, and notice that Mr. B no longer stutters.

"My buddy got caught in a tree. He dangled like a puppet. I cut his chute straps. He fell on me. That's when I saw his chest wound. I slung him over my shoulder. As he wheezed, blood splattered down the leg of my uniform."

Mr. B grabs my knee, his grip tightening, hurting me. I don't let on. I bite my lip until it bleeds, the irony taste like a mouthful of shrapnel. When he continues the story, he lets go of my knee.

"I tried to find my platoon and ran into a German soldier, a boy my age. He raised his arms in surrender. The three of us wandered in silence toward the sounds of artillery fire. By midnight I found the front, the end of a day that had no end."

Mr. B removes his glasses, the lenses, thick as a telescope's, able to pierce the past. He rubs his eye as if to erase the haunting faces of a war still being waged. Into the red ruts on the sides of his nose, he realigns his frames.

"A medic snapped off my buddy's tags. The lieutenant swore, stared at me cold, told me we weren't taking prisoners. So I marched the kid into the woods. I raised my rifle and shouted at him. He turned and faced me, his mouth open, afraid, yet knowing what I had to do. Before he could speak, I shot."

For a while no one speaks. Then, I guess, I say the wrong thing.

"You're a hero, Mr. B."

His hand returns to my knee, but his touch is gentle. "What I did," he says, his voice subdued, reminding me of mine when I confess sins in the dark of the confessional, "I am ashamed of."

Mr. B lets go of my knee. In the ashtray, he executes his cigarette. From his shirt pocket, he removes his cigarette pack. Empty. He crushes it. As he tries to draw another swallow of beer, the empty bottle huffs. He drops it like a dud grenade.

"F-F-Fuck it," he says, his stutter revived.

Dad pulls up to the curb in front of Mr. B's home. The wipers scud across dry glass, and Dad turns them off. Sitting on the porch steps,

Mrs. B waits. Their pet, a three-legged dachshund, nestles in her lap. After Dad exits, he walks around the car and chats with Mrs. B. He lost at cards and he lost ten bucks to Mr. B at the shooting gallery. He wants to delay going home to face the music Mom will make him dance to.

While still inside the car, Mr. B grabs my knee again. He squeezes while shaking it, and looks at me, his good eye bloodshot, yet focused, lucid as memory; the other, dead as his buddy.

"L-Learn to d-dance," he says to me, "n-n-now that you kn-know a little something."

You are not fighting for America. You are not fighting for the Marine Corps. You are just a bunch of 19-year-olds trying to make it to chow.

SAM SIATTA[75]

Tim O'Brien

A Girl Named Martha

First Lieutenant Jimmy Cross carried letters from a girl named Martha, a junior at Mount Sebastian College in New Jersey. They were not love letters, but Lieutenant Cross was hoping, so he kept them folded in plastic at the bottom of his rucksack. In the late afternoon, after a day's march, he would dig his foxhole, wash his hands under a canteen, unwrap the letters, hold them with the tips of his fingers, and spend the last hour of light pretending. He would imagine romantic camping trips into the White Mountains in New Hampshire. He would sometimes taste the envelope flaps, knowing her tongue had been there. More than anything, he wanted Martha to love him as he loved her, but the letters were mostly chatty, elusive on the matter of love. She was a virgin, he was almost sure. She was an English major at Mount Sebastian, and she wrote beautifully about her professors and roommates and midterm exams, about her respect for Chaucer and her great affection for Virginia Woolf. She often quoted lines of poetry; she never mentioned the war, except to say, Jimmy, take care of yourself. The letters weighed 10 ounces. They were signed Love, Martha, but Lieutenant Cross understood that Love was only a way of signing and did not mean what he sometimes pretended it meant. At dusk, he would carefully return the letters to his rucksack. Slowly, a bit distracted, he would get up and move among his men, checking the perimeter, then at full dark he would return to his hole and watch the night and wonder if Martha was a virgin.

They were called legs or grunts.

To carry something was to hump it, as when Lieutenant Jimmy Cross

humped his love for Martha up the hills and through the swamps. In its intransitive form, to hump meant to walk, or to march, but it implied burdens far beyond the intransitive.

Almost everyone humped photographs. In his wallet, Lieutenant Cross carried two photographs of Martha. The first was a Kodacolor snapshot signed Love, though he knew better. She stood against a brick wall. Her eyes were gray and neutral, her lips slightly open as she stared straight-on at the camera. At night, sometimes, Lieutenant Cross wondered who had taken the picture, because he knew she had boyfriends, because he loved her so much, and because he could see the shadow of the picture-taker spreading out against the brick wall. The second photograph had been clipped from the 1968 Mount Sebastian yearbook. It was an action shot – women's volleyball – and Martha was bent horizontal to the floor, reaching, the palms of her hands in sharp focus, the tongue taut, the expression frank and competitive. There was no visible sweat. She wore white gym shorts. Her legs, he thought, were almost certainly the legs of a virgin, dry and without hair, the left knee cocked and carrying her entire weight, which was just over 100 pounds. Lieutenant Cross remembered touching that left knee. A dark theater, he remembered, and the movie was *Bonnie and Clyde,* and Martha wore a tweed skirt, and during the final scene, when he touched her knee, she turned and looked at him in a sad, sober way that made him pull his hand back, but he would always remember the feel of the tweed skirt and the knee beneath it and the sound of the gunfire that killed Bonnie and Clyde, how embarrassing it was, how slow and oppressive. He remembered kissing her good night at the dorm door. Right then, he thought, he should've done something brave. He should've carried her up the stairs to her room and tied her to the bed and touched that left knee all night long. He should've risked it. Whenever he looked at the photographs, he thought of new things he should've done.

What they carried was partly a function of rank, partly of field specialty.

As a first lieutenant and platoon leader, Jimmy Cross carried a compass, maps, code books, binoculars, and a .45-caliber pistol that weighed 2.9 pounds fully loaded. He carried a strobe light and the

responsibility for the lives of his men.

As an RTO, Mitchell Sanders carried the PRC-25 radio, a killer, 26 pounds with its battery.

As a medic, Rat Kiley carried a canvas satchel filled with morphine and plasma and malaria tablets and surgical tape and comic books and all the things a medic must carry, including M&M's for especially bad wounds, for a total weight of nearly 20 pounds.

As a big man, therefore a machine gunner, Henry Dobbins carried the M-60, which weighed 23 pounds unloaded, but which was almost always loaded. In addition, Dobbins carried between 10 and 15 pounds of ammunition draped in belts across his chest and shoulders.

As PFCs or Spec 4s, most of them were common grunts and carried the standard M-16 gas-operated assault rifle. The weapon weighed 7.5 pounds unloaded, 8.2 pounds with its full 20-round magazine. Depending on numerous factors, such as topography and psychology, the riflemen carried anywhere from 12 to 20 magazines, usually in cloth bandoliers, adding on another 8.4 pounds at minimum, 14 pounds at maximum. When it was available, they also carried M-16 maintenance gear – rods and steel brushes and swabs and tubes of LSA oil – all of which weighed about a pound. Among the grunts, some carried the M-79 grenade launcher, 5.9 pounds unloaded, a reasonably light weapon except for the ammunition, which was heavy. A single round weighed 10 ounces. The typical load was 25 rounds. But Ted Lavender, who was scared, carried 34 rounds when he was shot and killed outside Than Khe, and he went down under an exceptional burden, more than 20 pounds of ammunition, plus the flak jacket and helmet and rations and water and toilet paper and tranquilizers and all the rest, plus the unweighed fear. He was dead weight. There was no twitching or flopping. Kiowa, who saw it happen, said it was like watching a rock fall, or a big sandbag or something – just boom, then down – not like the movies where the dead guy rolls around and does fancy spins and goes ass over teakettle – not like that, Kiowa said, the poor bastard just flat-fuck fell. Boom. Down. Nothing else. It was a bright morning in mid-April. Lieutenant Cross felt the pain. He blamed himself. They stripped off Lavender's canteens and ammo, all the heavy things, and Rat Kiley

said the obvious, the guy's dead, and Mitchell Sanders used his radio to report one U.S. KIA and to request a chopper. Then they wrapped Lavender in his poncho. They carried him out to a dry paddy, established security, and sat smoking the dead man's dope until the chopper came. Lieutenant Cross kept to himself. He pictured Martha's smooth young face, thinking he loved her more than anything, more than his men, and now Ted Lavender was dead because he loved her so much and could not stop thinking about her. When the dustoff arrived, they carried Lavender aboard. Afterward they burned Than Khe. They marched until dusk, then dug their holes, and that night Kiowa kept explaining how you had to be there, how fast it was, how the poor guy just dropped like so much concrete. Boom-down, he said. Like cement.

In addition to the three standard weapons – the M-60, M-16, and M-79 – they carried whatever presented itself, or whatever seemed appropriate as a means of killing or staying alive. They carried catch-as-catch-can. At various times, in various situations, they carried M-14s and CAR-15s and Swedish Ks and grease guns and captured AK-47s and Chi-Coms and RPGs and Simonov carbines and black market Uzis and .38-caliber Smith & Wesson handguns and 66 mm LAWs and shotguns and silencers and blackjacks and bayonets and C-4 plastic explosives. Lee Strunk carried a slingshot; a weapon of last resort, he called it. Mitchell Sanders carried brass knuckles. Kiowa carried his grandfather's feathered hatchet. Every third or fourth man carried a Claymore antipersonnel mine – 3.5 pounds with its firing device. They all carried fragmentation grenades – 14 ounces each. They all carried at least one M-18 colored smoke grenade – 24 ounces. Some carried CS or tear gas grenades. Some carried white phosphorus grenades. They carried all they could bear, and then some, including a silent awe for the terrible power of the things they carried.

In the first week of April, before Lavender died, Lieutenant Jimmy Cross received a good-luck charm from Martha. It was a simple pebble, an ounce at most. Smooth to the touch, it was a milky white color with flecks of orange and violet, oval-shaped, like a miniature egg. In the accompanying letter, Martha wrote that she had found the pebble on

the Jersey shoreline, precisely where the land touched water at high tide, where things came together but also separated. It was this separate-but-together quality, she wrote, that had inspired her to pick up the pebble and to carry it in her breast pocket for several days, where it seemed weightless, and then to send it through the mail, by air, as a token of her truest feelings for him. Lieutenant Cross found this romantic. But he wondered what her truest feelings were, exactly, and what she meant by separate-but-together. He wondered how the tides and waves had come into play on that afternoon along the Jersey shoreline when Martha saw the pebble and bent down to rescue it from geology. He imagined bare feet. Martha was a poet, with the poet's sensibilities, and her feet would be brown and bare, the toenails unpainted, the eyes chilly and somber like the ocean in March, and though it was painful, he wondered who had been with her that afternoon. He imagined a pair of shadows moving along the strip of sand where things came together but also separated. It was phantom jealousy, he knew, but he couldn't help himself. He loved her so much. On the march, through the hot days of early April, he carried the pebble in his mouth, turning it with his tongue, tasting sea salt and moisture. His mind wandered. He had difficulty keeping his attention on the war. On occasion he would yell at his men to spread out the column, to keep their eyes open, but then he would slip away into daydreams, just pretending, walking barefoot along the Jersey shore, with Martha, carrying nothing. He would feel himself rising. Sun and waves and gentle winds, all love and lightness.

What they carried varied by mission.

When a mission took them to the mountains, they carried mosquito netting, machetes, canvas tarps, and extra bug juice.

If a mission seemed especially hazardous, or if it involved a place they knew to be bad, they carried everything they could. In certain heavily mined AOs, where the land was dense with Toe Poppers and Bouncing Betties, they took turns humping a 28-pound mine detector. With its headphones and big sensing plate, the equipment was a stress on the lower back and shoulders, awkward to handle, often useless because of the shrapnel in the earth, but they carried it anyway, partly for safety, partly for the illusion of safety.

On ambush, or other night missions, they carried peculiar little odds and ends. Kiowa always took along his New Testament and a pair of moccasins for silence. Dave Jensen carried night-sight vitamins high in carotene. Lee Strunk carried his slingshot; ammo, he claimed, would never be a problem. Rat Kiley carried brandy and M&M's candy. Until he was shot, Ted Lavender carried the starlight scope, which weighed 6.3 pounds with its aluminum carrying case. Henry Dobbins carried his girlfriend's pantyhose wrapped around his neck as a comforter. They all carried ghosts. When dark came, they would move out single file across the meadows and paddies to their ambush coordinates, where they would quietly set up the Claymores and lie down and spend the night waiting.

Other missions were more complicated and required special equipment. In mid-April, it was their mission to search out and destroy the elaborate tunnel complexes in the Than Khe area south of Chu Lai. To blow the tunnels, they carried one-pound blocks of pentrite high explosives, four blocks to a man, 68 pounds in all. They carried wiring, detonators, and battery-powered clackers. Dave Jensen carried earplugs. Most often, before blowing the tunnels, they were ordered by higher command to search them, which was considered bad news, but by and large they just shrugged and carried out orders. Because he was a big man, Henry Dobbins was excused from tunnel duty. The others would draw numbers. Before Lavender died there were 17 men in the platoon, and whoever drew the number 17 would strip off his gear and crawl in headfirst with a flashlight and Lieutenant Cross's .45-caliber pistol. The rest of them would fan out as security. They would sit down or kneel, not facing the hole, listening to the ground beneath them, imagining cobwebs and ghosts, whatever was down there – the tunnel walls squeezing in – how the flashlight seemed impossibly heavy in the hand and how it was tunnel vision in the very strictest sense, compression in all ways, even time, and how you had to wiggle in – ass and elbows – a swallowed-up feeling – and how you found yourself worrying about odd things: Will your flashlight go dead? Do rats carry rabies? If you screamed, how far would the sound carry? Would your buddies hear it? Would they have the courage to drag you out? In some respects, though

not many, the waiting was worse than the tunnel itself. Imagination was a killer.

On April 16, when Lee Strunk drew the number 17, he laughed and muttered something and went down quickly. The morning was hot and very still. Not good, Kiowa said. He looked at the tunnel opening, then out across a dry paddy toward the village of Than Khe. Nothing moved. No clouds or birds or people. As they waited, the men smoked and drank Kool-Aid, not talking much, feeling sympathy for Lee Strunk but also feeling the luck of the draw. You win some, you lose some, said Mitchell Sanders, and sometimes you settle for a rain check. It was a tired line and no one laughed.

Henry Dobbins ate a tropical chocolate bar. Ted Lavender popped a tranquilizer and went off to pee.

After five minutes, Lieutenant Jimmy Cross moved to the tunnel, leaned down, and examined the darkness. Trouble, he thought – a cave-in maybe. And then suddenly, without willing it, he was thinking about Martha. The stresses and fractures, the quick collapse, the two of them buried alive under all that weight. Dense, crushing love. Kneeling, watching the hole, he tried to concentrate on Lee Strunk and the war, all the dangers, but his love was too much for him, he felt paralyzed, he wanted to sleep inside her lungs and breathe her blood and be smothered. He wanted her to be a virgin and not a virgin, all at once. He wanted to know her. Intimate secrets: Why poetry? Why so sad? Why that grayness in her eyes? Why so alone? Not lonely, just alone – riding her bike across campus or sitting off by herself in the cafeteria – even dancing, she danced alone – and it was the aloneness that filled him with love. He remembered telling her that one evening. How she nodded and looked away. And how, later, when he kissed her, she received the kiss without returning it, her eyes wide open, not afraid, not a virgin's eyes, just flat and uninvolved.

Lieutenant Cross gazed at the tunnel. But he was not there. He was buried with Martha under the white sand at the Jersey shore. They were pressed together, and the pebble in his mouth was her tongue. He was smiling. Vaguely, he was aware of how quiet the day was, the sullen paddies, yet he could not bring himself to worry about matters of

security. He was beyond that. He was just a kid at war, in love. He was twenty-four years old. He couldn't help it.

A few moments later Lee Strunk crawled out of the tunnel. He came up grinning, filthy but alive. Lieutenant Cross nodded and closed his eyes while the others clapped Strunk on the back and made jokes about rising from the dead.

Worms, Rat Kiley said. Right out of the grave. Fuckin' zombie.

The men laughed. They all felt great relief.

Spook city, said Mitchell Sanders.

Lee Strunk made a funny ghost sound, a kind of moaning, yet very happy, and right then, when Strunk made that high happy moaning sound, when he went Ahhooooo, right then Ted Lavender was shot in the head on his way back from peeing. He lay with his mouth open. The teeth were broken. There was a swollen black bruise under his left eye.

The cheekbone was gone. Oh shit, Rat Kiley said, the guy's dead. The guy's dead, he kept saying, which seemed profound – the guy's dead. I mean really.

After the chopper took Lavender away, Lieutenant Jimmy Cross led his men into the village of Than Khe. They burned everything. They shot chickens and dogs, they trashed the village well, they called in artillery and watched the wreckage, then they marched for several hours through the hot afternoon, and then at dusk, while Kiowa explained how Lavender died, Lieutenant Cross found himself trembling.

He tried not to cry. With his entrenching tool, which weighed 5 pounds, he began digging a hole in the earth. He felt shame. He hated himself. He had loved Martha more than his men, and as a consequence Lavender was now dead, and this was something he would have to carry like a stone in his stomach for the rest of the war.

All he could do was dig. He used his entrenching tool like an ax, slashing, feeling both love and hate, and then later, when it was full dark, he sat at the bottom of his foxhole and wept. It went on for a long while. In part, he was grieving for Ted Lavender, but mostly it was for Martha, and for himself, because she belonged to another world, which was not quite real, and because she was a junior at Mount Sebastian College in New Jersey, a poet and a virgin and uninvolved, and because he realized she did not love him and never would.

They carried all the emotional baggage of men who might die. Grief, terror, love, longing – these were intangibles, but the intangibles had their own mass and specific gravity, they had tangible weight. They carried shameful memories. They carried the common secret of cowardice barely restrained, the instinct to run or freeze or hide, and in many respects this was the heaviest burden of all, for it could never be put down, it required perfect balance and perfect posture. They carried their reputations. They carried the soldier's greatest fear, which was the fear of blushing. Men killed, and died, because they were embarrassed not to. It was what had brought them to the war in the first place, nothing positive, no dreams of glory or honor, just to avoid the blush of dishonor. They died so as not to die of embarrassment. They crawled into tunnels and walked point and advanced under fire. Each morning, despite the unknowns, they made their legs move. They endured. They kept humping. They did not submit to the obvious alternative, which was simply to close the eyes and fall. So easy, really. Go limp and tumble to the ground and let the muscles unwind and not speak and not budge until your buddies picked you up and lifted you into the chopper that would roar and dip its nose and carry you off to the world. A mere matter of falling, yet no one ever fell. It was not courage, exactly; the object was not valor. Rather, they were too frightened to be cowards.

By and large they carried these things inside, maintaining the masks of composure. They sneered at sick call. They spoke bitterly about guys who had found release by shooting off their own toes or fingers. Pussies, they'd say. Candy-asses. It was fierce, mocking talk, with only a trace of envy or awe, but even so the image played itself out behind their eyes.

They imagined the muzzle against flesh. So easy: squeeze the trigger and blow away a toe. They imagined it. They imagined the quick, sweet pain, then the evacuation to Japan, then a hospital with warm beds and cute geisha nurses.

On the morning after Ted Lavender died, First Lieutenant Jimmy Cross crouched at the bottom of his foxhole and burned Martha's letters. Then he burned the two photographs. There was a steady rain falling, which made it difficult, but he used heat tabs and Sterno to build a small fire, screening it with his body, holding the photographs over the tight blue

flame with the tips of his fingers.

He realized it was only a gesture. Stupid, he thought. Sentimental, too, but mostly just stupid.

Lavender was dead. You couldn't burn the blame.

Besides, the letters were in his head. And even now, without photographs, Lieutenant Cross could see Martha playing volleyball in her white gym shorts and yellow T-shirt. He could see her moving in the rain.

When the fire died out, Lieutenant Cross pulled his poncho over his shoulders and ate breakfast from a can.

There was no great mystery, he decided.

In those burned letters Martha had never mentioned the war, except to say, Jimmy, take care of yourself. She wasn't involved. She signed the letters Love, but it wasn't love, and all the fine lines and technicalities did not matter. Virginity was no longer an issue. He hated her. Yes, he did. He hated her. Love, too, but it was a hard, hating kind of love.

The morning came up wet and blurry. Everything seemed part of everything else, the fog and Martha and the deepening rain.

He was a soldier, after all.

Half smiling, Lieutenant Jimmy Cross took out his maps. He shook his head hard, as if to clear it, then bent forward and began planning the day's march. In ten minutes, or maybe twenty, he would rouse the men and they would pack up and head west, where the maps showed the country to be green and inviting. They would do what they had always done. The rain might add some weight, but otherwise it would be one more day layered upon all the other days.

He was realistic about it. There was that new hardness in his stomach. He loved her but he hated her.

No more fantasies, he told himself.

Henceforth, when he thought about Martha, it would be only to think that she belonged elsewhere. He would shut down the daydreams. This was not Mount Sebastian, it was another world, where there were no pretty poems or midterm exams, a place where men died because of carelessness and gross stupidity. Kiowa was right. Boom-down, and you were dead, never partly dead.

Briefly, in the rain, Lieutenant Cross saw Martha's gray eyes gazing back at him. He understood.

It was very sad, he thought. The things men carried inside. The things men did or felt they had to do.

He almost nodded at her, but didn't.

Instead he went back to his maps. He was now determined to perform his duties firmly and without negligence. It wouldn't help Lavender, he knew that, but from this point on he would comport himself as an officer. He would dispose of his good-luck pebble. Swallow it, maybe, or use Lee Strunk's slingshot, or just drop it along the trail. On the march he would impose strict field discipline. He would be careful to send out flank security, to prevent straggling or bunching up, to keep his troops moving at the proper pace and at the proper interval. He would insist on clean weapons. He would confiscate the remainder of Lavender's dope. Later in the day, perhaps, he would call the men together and speak to them plainly. He would accept the blame for what had happened to Ted Lavender. He would be a man about it. He would look them in the eyes, keeping his chin level, and he would issue the new SOPs in a calm, impersonal tone of voice, a lieutenant's voice, leaving no room for argument or discussion. Commencing immediately, he'd tell them, they would no longer abandon equipment along the route of march. They would police up their acts. They would get their shit together, and keep it together, and maintain it neatly and in good working order.

He would not tolerate laxity. He would show strength, distancing himself.

Among the men there would be grumbling, of course, and maybe worse, because their days would seem longer and their loads heavier, but Lieutenant Jimmy Cross reminded himself that his obligation was not to be loved but to lead. He would dispense with love; it was not now a factor. And if anyone quarreled or complained, he would simply tighten his lips and arrange his shoulders in the correct command posture. He might give a curt little nod. Or he might not. He might just shrug and say, Carry on, then they would saddle up and form into a column and move out toward the villages west of Than Khe.

LOVE

Many years after the war Jimmy Cross came to visit me at my home in Massachusetts, and for a full day we drank coffee and smoked cigarettes and talked about everything we had seen and done so long ago, all the things we still carried through our lives. Spread out across the kitchen table were maybe a hundred old photographs. There were pictures of Rat Kiley and Kiowa and Mitchell Sanders, all of us, the faces incredibly soft and young. At one point, I remember, we paused over a snapshot of Ted Lavender, and after a while Jimmy rubbed his eyes and said he'd never forgiven himself for Lavender's death. It was something that would never go away, he said quietly, and I nodded and told him I felt the same about certain things. Then for a long time neither of us could think of much to say. The thing to do, we decided, was to forget the coffee and switch to gin, which improved the mood, and not much later we were laughing about some of the craziness that used to go on. The way Henry Dobbins carried his girlfriend's pantyhose around his neck like a comforter. Kiowa's moccasins and hunting hatchet. Rat Kiley's comic books. By midnight we were both a little high, and I decided there was no harm in asking about Martha. I'm not sure how I phrased it – just a general question – but Jimmy Cross looked up in surprise. "You writer types," he said, "you've got long memories." Then he smiled and excused himself and went up to the guest room and came back with a small framed photograph. It was the volleyball shot: Martha bent horizontal to the floor, reaching, the palms of her hands in sharp focus.

"Remember this?" he said.

I nodded and told him I was surprised. I thought he'd burned it.

Jimmy kept smiling. For a while he stared down at the photograph, his eyes very bright, then he shrugged and said, "Well, I did – I burned it. After Lavender died, I couldn't…. This is a new one. Martha gave it to me herself."

They'd run into each other, he said, at a college reunion in 1979. Nothing had changed. He still loved her. For eight or nine hours, he said, they spent most of their time together. There was a banquet, and then a dance, and then afterward they took a walk across the campus and talked about their lives. Martha was a Lutheran missionary now.

A trained nurse, although nursing wasn't the point, and she had done service in Ethiopia and Guatemala and Mexico. She had never married, she said, and probably never would. She didn't know why. But as she said this, her eyes seemed to slide sideways, and it occurred to him that there were things about her he would never know. Her eyes were gray and neutral. Later, when he took her hand, there was no pressure in return, and later still, when he told her he still loved her, she kept walking and didn't answer and then after several minutes looked at her wristwatch and said it was getting late. He walked her back to the dormitory. For a few moments he considered asking her to his room, but instead he laughed and told her how back in college he'd almost done something very brave. It was after seeing *Bonnie and Clyde,* he said, and on this same spot he'd almost picked her up and carried her to his room and tied her to the bed and put his hand on her knee and just held it there all night long. It came close, he told her – he'd almost done it. Martha shut her eyes. She crossed her arms at her chest, as if suddenly cold, rocking slightly, then after a time she looked at him and said she was glad he hadn't tried it. She didn't understand how men could do those things. What things? He asked, and Martha said, The things men do. Then he nodded. It began to form. Oh, he said, those things. At breakfast the next morning she told him she was sorry. She explained that there was nothing she could do about it, and he said he understood, and then she laughed and gave him the picture and told him not to burn this one up.

Jimmy shook his head. "It doesn't matter," he finally said. "I love her."

For the rest of his visit I steered the conversation away from Martha. At the end, though, as we were walking out to his car, I told him that I'd like to write a story about some of this. Jimmy thought it over and then gave me a little smile. "Why not?" he said. "Maybe she'll read it and come begging. There's always hope, right?"

"Right," I said.

He got into his car and rolled down the window. "Make me out to be a good guy, okay? Brave and handsome, all that stuff. Best platoon leader ever." He hesitated for a second. "And do me a favor. Don't mention anything about – "

"No," I said, "I won't."

War is ugly, horrible, evil, and it is reasonable for men to hate all that. But I believe that most men who have been to war would have to admit ... that somewhere inside themselves they loved it too, loved it as much as anything that has happened to them before or since.

WILLIAM BROYLES, JR[76]

JOHN CRAWFORD

No Crying in Baseball

The satellite phone was hot against my cheek. It was barely 10 AM and already the temperature was soaring into the triple digits. On the fourth mechanical ring, a barely audible hello came through.

"Hey darling," I said in my sweetest voice, scarcely able to contain my excitement. I had been away from home for eight months, and no matter how many times I called, I always got shivers when my wife answered the phone.

"Oh hey." I could hear the tension in her voice, and I prepared myself for the worst.

"Is everything OK?" I realized I was holding my breath in anticipation. When all you have time to do is worry about what is going on at home, you start to imagine some terrible things.

"No." Melanie let out a long dramatic sigh and then continued.

"Murphy shit all over the house, ate the cushions on the sofa and a pair of my shoes, and I've only been gone for a couple hours."

I tried unsuccessfully to suppress a smile. She had bought that puppy against my advice, and over a year later it was still a monster.

"I'm sorry hon." I gave her my best sympathetic voice, but I think the facade was detected.

"Fuck, more piss!" My wife blurted out as she stumbled onto another sticky puddle.

"Well, it could be worse, I mean, I'd give anything to be at home cleaning up dog shit."

"What could be grosser than cleaning up a house full of dog shit?" The disgust in Melanie's voice was apparent.

"Well, could be brains, that's pretty damn nasty." I tried to catch the words and pull them back even as they left my mouth, but to no avail. It's hard living with a bunch of soldiers and then trying to talk like a normal person to your family on the phone.

"When did you clean up brains? Tell me about it, I want to know." There was curiosity and naiveté in her voice, but the self-pity was gone. What can it hurt, I thought, so I told her about my day.

We had been the battalion's quick reaction force for three uneventful days, and I was enjoying the time to myself, getting more than a full night's sleep and relaxing.

"Wake up, we gotta go!" Sergeant Brunelle said as he stormed into our room, which was previously the Republican Guard officer's club.

"What's going on?" I groaned through half-closed eyes.

"Pohl's squad got hit, get your shit on." With that Brunelle abruptly turned and left the room, heading back to his own bunk and his gear.

"Shit," was all I could muster, and that about summed it up. It took the squad less than five minutes to get on our gear and get in the Humvees. I looked at my watch. It was 04:45 in the morning.

"You gotta love this job," I joked halfheartedly as we kicked up gravel while leaving the back gate.

Our destination was right around the corner and it only took a minute or so to get there. I clambered out of the vehicle, fighting against my weapon and body armor as gravity and sleepiness held me down. There was already a squad there and in between the hovering soldiers was a smoking tan BMW, the motor rattling in protest. On the rooftops of the dilapidated apartment buildings around us were underwear-clad Iraqi men watching the show.

"Hey Pohl, what's going on?" I asked lazily as I walked up to the crowd. They parted, and I got my answer.

"We were on our way in and this fucker drives by with his lights off. When he sees us he hauls ass." Pohl's voice continued, but I could scarcely hear it as I stared at the carnage.

"So we took off after them and this dick starts shooting at us. So Reeves lit their asses up. Only two shots, can you believe it?" I glanced up and Specialist Reeves, a slight-voiced country boy from South

Georgia who looked more like a mechanic than a soldier. He was still struggling impotently with the Browning Mark II .50 caliber machine gun mounted on top of his Humvee. He had only fired two shots because there was a malfunction, and time hadn't yet permitted him to get the weapon back up.

On the ground were two blood-soaked Iraqi men. Both were on their faces with their hands zip-tied behind their backs. The skinnier one was crying, and with a nudge of his foot someone tried to shut him up.

"There's no crying in baseball." We all giggled a little at that. The other guy was overweight and had a head full of curly hair. He was so drenched in blood and chunks of meat that I asked repeatedly if he was hit.

"I don't think so," was the response. I contemplated reaching down and checking him for wounds, but I didn't have any rubber gloves, and there was no way I was getting that shit all over me. He just stared straight ahead with eyes like saucers. Then I turned to the car.

A .50 caliber round is one hell of a big bullet. Built more for destroying light armored vehicles and aircraft, it is not intended to be used on people. In fact, it is technically against Geneva Conventions to fire a .50 caliber at "dismounts." Reeves may have fired only two shots, but at closer than fifty meters, his accuracy was never in question. The mechanic from Georgia had done his work well. The first round entered at the bumper and went through the trunk. It slammed into the left backseat passenger, the one with the rifle. His hip was transformed instantly into Jell-o. It was impossible to tell where his torso ended and his legs began. They were twisted over each other and bones were pointing in every possible direction. The bullet then continued forward, hitting the driver's hand and cutting it in half before finally passing through the speedometer and embedding itself in the engine block.

The machine gun, bucking against the first explosion, sent the second bullet higher. That one hit the unlucky fellow without the hips on the right side of his head, and a chunk the size of my open hand was missing. The bullet then continued, no longer flying straight but tumbling and impacted in the center of the driver's neck, splitting it wide open in a gash that was easily six inches by and eight inches.

The driver now lay slumped over the seat, his spine hanging out of

the wound, the blood slowing to all but a trickle onto the seat. His left hand still rested on the steering wheel, even in death trying to escape by making one last turn to get their car out of the sector. The gore itself was impressive enough and warranted a moment of notice, but it was what the man in back was doing that had all our hearts in our mouths. He was looking at us, both eyes perfectly focused despite the fact that half his brain was all over the car.

"Just nerves," I thought. His brain cells are going, and he's already dead. But then his eyes shifted, first from me, then to Pohl, then back to me. They settled on me and he began to mumble in Arabic, holding my gaze, staring at me from the abyss. I could see halfway through this man's head and he was looking at me, talking to me in an unknown language. His breath was coming in wheezing gasps, and the hole in his head glistened in the streetlight like fairy dust. The entire car was filled with brain fragments and shards of bone. Had that man gotten up that morning and thought, "I might die today?" What was he thinking now as he realized that his life was over? Was he simply saying the obvious, "Oh fuck, I have a hole the size of a softball in my head and I'm dying."

I couldn't help but wonder if it was something else; if his jumbled words revealed the mysteries of the universe. Slowly his eyes dimmed, and his voice trailed away. The gasps ebbed and his life gave way. When he fell over onto the seat of the car, the rest of his brain became dislodged and slid onto the floor of the car leaving a slug's trail behind it. The whole squad was standing there looking, unable to speak, and then it started.

"Hey Crawford, what do you think the last thing that went through his head was?" Sergeant Howell asked me with half a grin on his face. An overweight medic that had tagged along quoted a line from the movie Boondock Saints: "Hey buddy, where you goin'? Nowhere!"

"Hey man, we gotta turn off the car." I don't know who said it, but I walked over to the driver's side and leaned in the window. I couldn't reach the keys without sticking my head all the way into the already reeking vehicle.

"Hey Sellers, you wanna turn off the car or what?" I called out in an attempt to get out of the inevitable.

"Fuck you, I'm not on brain detail." I looked again at the inside of the car and hesitated. The squat medic with the sense of humor saw the dilemma and arrived to save the day with his latex gloves.

The Iraqi police are never prompt, so after calling them, we sat back and waited, counting the minutes, hoping we would not miss breakfast.

"Hey, you think the cooks got off their lazy asses and even made something?"

"Fuck no, probably coffee and T-rat cake."

It would take over two hours for the Iraqi police to arrive and cleanup. In the meantime we buzzed about impatiently. The night was finished and the sun was peeking its way over the horizon, searching for us. For the time being however we were protected from its probing eye by the shade of nearby buildings. Before long the streets were busy with morning traffic and pedestrians, and half the neighborhood had seen the carnage. As they passed by we motioned them over in small groups to look closer and when in curiosity they turned to us, we would gesture to the bodies.

"No fucking Jerri-cans!" we would say, alluding to the common Iraqi practice of illegally re-selling gasoline out of buckets and jugs.

"Fucking Ali Baba, watch out now." Ali Baba is the generic Arabic term for a thief. After the taunting grew old and it became apparent that we would miss breakfast chow, I sat on the hood of the BMW and ate a country captain chicken MRE while blood pooled underneath the car and trickled downhill.

"Hey Crawford, you got brains on your boot," Pohl said matter-of-factly in between bites of chocolate mint pound cake.

"I'll be damned, I sure do," I answered. Attempting to shake it off proved futile. There was a flake of bone attached, and its sharpened edge was lodged firmly into the rubber sole of my boot. I flicked it off with the handle of my MRE spoon and took another bite of processed chicken in sauce.

There was silence on the other end of the phone, and I didn't know if I should attribute it to the three-second delay that often plagues satellite phones.

"Hon, are you there?" I asked, mournful that I had shared something of myself from this shithole country.

"Oh my God, I didn't know. That sounds terrible." Melanie's voice was full of sympathy and longing, but she was right, she didn't know. No one did and that was what made it worse, and better.

"What are you gonna do when you get back? I mean, are you going to be OK?"

"Oh yeah, I'll be fine, I'm just tired." My voice was full of confidence, and I prayed that I was appeasing her worries. Either way, she wouldn't complain about cleaning up dog shit anymore. I just wanted her to understand, to tell me it was OK. I needed reassurance. Waiting on the line, I shivered unconsciously despite the heat.

Every society rests on the death of men.
Oliver Wendell Holmes[77]

War is not all bad; it may not make
a man of you, but it teaches you that
manhood is not something to scoff.
Tim O'Brien[78]

I was a coward. I went to the war.

TIM O'BRIEN[79]

It may take guts to go, but it takes balls to say no.

KIM JIN-SU[80]

Victor Ayscough

My Vietnam

I remember the room, though I was there for just ten minutes, fifty years ago.

> The army sergeant unlocked the classroom door as late afternoon sun, strained through aluminum blinds, glared at the linoleum floor. Fifty guys, in our teens through twenties, trooped in and headed for desks that filled the space.
>
> We'd been bussed in from army induction centers around Philadelphia. Though some of us had recently graduated college, most had just finished high school. No longer cloaked by student deferments, we shuffled in our skivvies through the Army Induction Center on North Broad Street, exposed to the Vietnam war's draft apparatus.
>
> The sergeant, wine-barrel chested and buzz cut, had apparently been sent by the army's Office of Central Casting and, true to script, barked as we filed in: "Take a pencil from Corporal Doyle. Take a Loyalty Oath from Corporal Klein."

The Vietnam War consumed the mind of every draft-age American male in the 1960s and '70s. Nothing, not college, career, love, marriage, or sex, played a larger role in young men's lives.

Vietnam black-shadowed my two-year run-up to graduation as I took classes from the American Friends Service Committee (AFSC) about alternatives to fighting in Vietnam. Their overarching thesis, repeated at every meeting, was, "You don't have to go if you don't want to."

I did not want to.

The implications of this message were complex. No, I didn't *have* to go; with luck, I could evade the draft. But if luck were not with me, I could finish with a run to Canada, or a five-year stint in jail.

There were many paths to evading the draft. I tried one: sending my draft board a certified letter, asking for an interview with its medical officer regarding my health, an interview that by their own regulations they had to grant. As the AFSC suggested might happen, the board never replied, leaving me with a legal card to play if other evasion tactics failed.

> In the exam room where a doctor was giving cursory physicals, a kid pointed out his flat feet. The M.D. tried unsuccessfully to run a letter opener under the guy's arches, took off his glasses, rubbed his eyes and said, "These are the flattest feet I've ever seen. You're not going to 'Nam."
>
> The kid smiled and turned. As he walked by me, I said, "Boy did you get lucky."
>
> "Lucky, my foot. These dogs pain me every day of my life."
>
> I hoped the doctor would hear a hay fever rasp in his stethoscope when he pressed it to my chest. But allergy season was over, and he ended the physical with, "You're good to go, young man."
>
> "But doctor, I requested an interview with my draft board's medical officer. They never even...."
>
> "Tell it to the judge, kid."

The AFSC said if the army accepted a man's claim to be a sole surviving son, divinity student, or conscientious objector, they could order him to alternative service – work at a V.A. hospital, for instance. I was none of these. With the doctor's curt dismissal of the draft board letter, my last tactic to evade the draft was refusing to sign the army's Loyalty Oath.

"Refusing to sign" as the AFSC called it, would put army intelligence on my trail. The two security officers tasked with investigating me would review my FBI record and talk to friends, teachers, and neighbors. If they determined I was not a security risk, the army would take me into their ranks without my signature on the oath. But in those days,

with so many guys refusing to sign, it took two years before two agents were available for an investigation. Maybe they'd let me go.

Signing the oath affirmed I was not a member of any organization advocating overthrowing the government by force, violence, or other unlawful means. I had no problem with that. But occupying a country on the other side of the globe, napalming it down to the rice paddies while killing tens of thousands of Americans and hundreds of thousands of Vietnamese, was immoral.

I took a desk in the last row of the classroom. The sergeant bellowed, "Listen up, men. Does everyone have a pencil?"

If you had a hand, you had a pencil. We "yes-sirred" him.

"Does everyone have a document that says 'Loyalty Oath' at the top?"

If you had an index finger and an opposing thumb, you had the oath. We "yes-sirred" again.

"Hold the pencil in your right hand."

I thought, *What if you're left-handed?* but knew this was not a good moment to ask; silence hushed the room.

"Now sign your name on the dotted line at the bottom."

The scratching of forty-nine pencils scripting names filled the quiet.

When the room went silent, the sergeant asked, "Has everyone signed the Loyalty Oath?"

A short beat, and then from the back, a lone voice, "No sir."

Forty-nine heads turned around to look at me.

"Will you sign the loyalty oath, mister?"

"No sir, I will not."

A low murmur.

Now in a louder voice, "Underneath the dotted line, write a statement saying you are refusing to sign, and then sign the statement."

The AFSC had warned us of this ruse. You were not to put your name *anywhere* on this piece of paper.

"No sir, I will not."

A few "holy shits" skittered across the room.

"*What is your name, mister?*"

"Ayscough, sir."

He looked at his clipboard. "Eyeskoff?"

Rarely had my name been mispronounced so badly.

"Yes sir!"

"Do you know what I can do to you if you don't sign this paper, Mr. Eyeskoff?"

"You can keep me here for seventy-two hours and then you've got to let me go."

"Is that so?"

"That is the law, sir."

"Gentlemen, hand me your Loyalty Oaths as you exit the room. Dismissed."

I was the last to leave, and held my breath as the sergeant glared at me.

An hour later, my years of draft evasion efforts came to a head. I joined a line of guys at a desk where a lone sergeant sat. As each boy stepped up, he told the officer his name; the sergeant told the kid his draft status.

A status of 1-A meant you were available for military service and would be called up for boot camp soon. Most guys here were 1-A.

4-F, a permanent deferment, made you ineligible for the army. Mr. Flat-feet, limping from a day of standing, had been designated 4-F.

1-Y was a temporary deferment. You could be called to duty only for a national emergency, such as war with China, something most of us believed would never happen. Very few guys were getting 1-Y's.

"What's your name, mister?" the sergeant asked.

"Ayscough, sir."

He looked down at his roster. "Victor Ayscough?" He pronounced my last name perfectly.

"Yes sir."

"You're 1-Y, Ayscough. ... Next."

I stumbled from the desk, dazed, laughing. One of the guys who had been in the classroom approached me. "Hey man, can you help? They gave me a 1-A."

"Call the American Friends Service Committee as soon as you can. And good luck."

I took a bus home, ran a hot tub, raided my dad's liquor cabinet, and poured myself a triple Scotch-rocks, straight up. I downed it in five gagging gulps, eased into the tub and, slipping a rolled towel behind my neck, closed my eyes.

Night was settling as cold water woke me to a thudding headache.

My Vietnam was over.

JONATHAN GOTTSCHALL

What About Women?

There's a famous moment in Homer's *Odyssey* when Odysseus's faithful wife, Penelope – exhausted by two decades of waiting for her husband's return from the Trojan War – finally succumbs to the pressure from her suitors and says she is ready to remarry. She has more than one hundred eager suitors – all strong, healthy, and well-bred. How's a girl to choose? Penelope has her servants set twelve axes in a row and bury the butts in the ground. She announces that she will marry the suitor who can use Odysseus's bow to zing a single arrow through the tiny gap in all twelve axe heads. Penelope sits and watches as the men try futilely to bend and string Odysseus's mighty bow. Their humiliation is magnified when a beggar who's been hanging around the house takes up the bow, strings it with ease, and almost casually fires an arrow through all the axe heads. The beggar then reveals his true identity: it's Odysseus himself who, through this sportlike display of prowess, once again proves he is a man above all others – the perfect man for the perfect woman.

Ritual combat is often seen as a process whereby active, strapping males battle it out among themselves, with the victor "taking" the passive females – who have no choice in the matter. This is ass-backward, or at least one-sided. Remember Penelope: she's the one who sets up the contest for her hand, and she does so in her own best interests. The same goes for other species. It may look like the males have the power and have set up contests for rights to the females, but try to look at things the other way around: the females have the power, and they have set up grueling, dangerous contests to eliminate fakers and reveal

mates of authentic quality. In most species females could, if they chose, refuse the dominant male. An elephant seal cow[81] could flop away from the magnificently fat alpha male and debauch to her heart's content with the losers on the bachelors' beach. Instead, she normally does the opposite: she sprawls out on the sand and bawls in protest if a low-ranking male tries to mount her – which has the effect of summoning all the males within earshot to come and fight over her. Similarly, the doe could trot safely away from the victorious buck, but she usually doesn't. Females in many species directly instigate male mating competition, or at least cooperate with the winners.[82]

Given the high costs of sports, we should expect them to come with at least potentially high rewards. The very word athlete comes from the Greek *athlon,* meaning "prize" or "reward." An athlete is one who competes for a prize. At the Greek Olympics the most common prize was a laurel wreath – a crown of woven branches and leaves. According to Herodotus, the Persians were shocked[83] that Greek athletes competed not for gold or silver but for mere foliage. But clearly the Greeks weren't competing for a handful of leaves. They were competing for the enormous social status symbolized by those leaves. And that status was so valuable partly because of its links to sex.

That athletes have more sexual success is something almost everyone who went to high school or college knows about. Anecdotes about young women flocking to high-level professional athletes are backed up by studies showing that even small-time high school and college jocks do better with the ladies.[84] The same goes for athletes all around the world. Among the Mursi of Ethiopia, young women instigate wild stickfighting contests among young men and lavish their attention[85] on the winners. In the Micronesian state of Truk, the boys get drunk and fight[86] in no small part because they know the girls are watching. Among the Sereer people of Senegal and the Mehinaku of central Brazil, winning wrestlers attract more wives and have more children than non-wrestlers.[87] And in ancient Rome, gladiators were sex symbols[88] despite their lowly social status.

Women's attraction to athletes is, of course, matched by an attraction to athletic physiques.[89] Michelangelo's statue of David is a timeless ideal

of male physical beauty. But David also represents a poignant paradox in the beauty of men. David is a warrior, and Michelangelo portrays him glaring across the battlefield, in the moment before he crushes Goliath's skull with a river-polished stone. The statue is a reminder that the beauty of a man's body correlates almost perfectly with its destructive potential. Everything beautiful about David's body – his broad shoulders, swollen muscles, and agile legs – is a cue of his formidability, his capacity to project physical force. Michelangelo carved David out of marble, lovingly shaping all his contours. Similarly, over eons, our grandmothers and great-grandmothers have, through their loving, carved such features into the genes of men. Women, in their aggregate mate choices, have created men over time, sculpting better providers and protectors. In the modern world, of course, women no longer need men to provide them with meat or to protect their children from bears. But evolution works slowly, and modern women still respond to the cues of physical prowess that moved their great-grandmothers.

This is all noteworthy, because it is so not what men are looking for in their mates. Men generally like women's bodies to be fit and graceful, yes, but they are not looking for the heavy bones or bulging muscles advertising a woman's physical formidability. To the contrary, they are looking for bulging fat deposits, which, though they interfere with a woman's ability to do some types of work, provide good signals of her age and fertility. Men are, in other words, choosing mates based on cues of reproduction (fertility), while women are selecting them based on cues of production (ability to do work). (This is why, when entering the prime years of reproductive competition, pubescent girls naturally plump up with fat, while pubescent boys pump up with muscle.) In other words, as the biological anthropologist David Puts argues, when it comes to the mating game, men seek physical beauties, while women seek physical beasts.[90]

Men typically report higher preferences for younger, more physically attractive women, while women prefer men who are wealthier and of higher status.

SCHELLER, MATORRES, TOMPKINS, LITTLE, DE SOUSA[91]

Whether in men or musk oxen, masculinity is for prevailing in the competition for mates.

JONATHAN GOTTSCHALL[92]

8. At Peace with Men

If these writers have brought you closer to men, if you see us more clearly, are more at peace with us, then *Heart of a Man* has done its work.

The world faces critical issues that affect us all: the rise of pollution, hunger and thirst, and the effects of a global climate change on all life. A strong bond between women and men is central to tackling these problems successfully.

In the love between my brothers and my sisters there is strength.

Humankind is powerful.

HENRI J. M. NOUWEN

The Real Questions

Did I offer peace today?

Did I bring a smile
to someone's face?

Did I say words of healing?

Did I let go of my anger
and resentment?

Did I forgive?

Did I love?

These are the real questions.

The Contributors

JOE E. ARMSTRONG was a retired university professor when he wrote "Hog Killing." His books, *Tales of a Fledgling Homestead* and *Preacher Kids from Arkansas,* were published by Misty Hill Press. His writing has been compared to Eudora Welty's. A gifted back- and front-porch teller, his stories feature family tales from Arkansas, and flying stories from his years as a Navy pilot. Joe passed on May 13, 2010, and is missed by all who knew and loved him.

VICTOR AYSCOUGH lives off the grid on a California rancho with his wife. [His submission was one of two that arrived via snail-mail. –*ed.*] They raise chickens, goats, llamas, strawberries, and Sour Diesel. This is his first time in print.

RICHARD BAUSCH has authored eleven novels and eight story collections. His novel, *The Last Good Time,* was made into a feature-length film. His short stories have appeared in *The New Yorker, Esquire, The Atlantic Monthly, Harper's,* and *Gentleman's Quarterly.* His many awards include a Guggenheim Fellowship, two National Magazine Awards, and the 2004 PEN/Malamud Award. A member of the Fellowship of Southern Writers, Bausch is editor of *The Norton Anthology of Short Fiction.*

JOHN BIESECKER writes from an undisclosed bunker deep in the mountains of Colorado. His stories, both genre and literary, have appeared in print and in various journals across the "internets." He is currently seeking representation for his first novel. When not writing he tries to keep up with his family on the ski slopes. Visit him at JohnBiesecker.com.

CRAIG BROOKE-WEISS has been a New York City street vendor, an unofficial rock-n-roll t-shirt merchant, a K-8 teacher-in-training, and currently, a loving father and husband. He co-founded Fatherlove, a non-profit that works to include fathers and other important men in children's lives. His most important adventure has been as "Daddy" and "Pops" to Levi, who at 27 is on the road, making adventures of his own.

LORD BYRON, AKA George Gordon (1788–1824), was an English poet, peer,

politician, and a leading figure in the Romantic movement. He is regarded as one of the greatest British poets and remains widely read and influential. Among his best-known works are the lengthy narrative poems, *Don Juan* (quoted in this anthology), *Childe Harold's Pilgrimage*, and the short lyric poem, "She Walks in Beauty." [from his Wikipedia entry]

MICHAEL CHABON's *The Amazing Adventures of Kavalier & Clay*, published in 2000, won a Pulitzer Prize in 2001. *The Yiddish Policemen's Union,* published in 2007, won the Hugo, Sidewise, Nebula and Ignotus awards. Other novels include *The Mysteries of Pittsburgh, Wonder Boys, Gentlemen of the Road, Middlemarch,* and *Moonglow.* He has written screenplays, children's books, comics, and the non-fiction book, *Manhood for Amateurs,* from which his contributions to this anthology are excerpted. [from his Wikipedia entry]

MIKE CHERRY was an ironworker and writer. He started working in a wire rolling factory and moved to high steel construction, rising to the job of connector where he worked at the top of construction sites, putting buildings together. *On High Steel* is one of two books I found by an ironworker about his job; the other, *Steel Beams and Iron Men,* is also by Cherry.

STEPHEN CRANE, nineteenth-century American poet, novelist and short story writer, began writing at the age of four and penned his first short story at fourteen. He wrote notable works in the Realist tradition as well as early examples of American Naturalism and Impressionism. He is recognized by modern critics as one of the most innovative writers of his generation, and it has been said that his writing made a deep impression on Ernest Hemingway.

JOHN CRAWFORD, a U.S. veteran of the Iraq War, is renowned for his bestselling memoir, *The Last True Story I'll Ever Tell,* about his tour of duty. In 2003, his unit was deployed to Kuwait and later Iraq during the early stages of the war. Crawford has made appearances on National Public Radio and *The Daily Show.* [from his Wikipedia entry]

JED DIAMOND is a licensed psychotherapist with a Ph.D. in International Health and Master's degree in Social Work. His passion is to help men do three things:

live a fully authentic life; love deeply and well; and make a positive difference in the world. For fifty years he has been a pioneer in the field of gender medicine and men's health. Please visit him at www.MenAlive.com. He'll enjoy hearing from you.

DON DOYLE was a Professor Emeritus at Arizona State University where he taught courses in theatre and storytelling for 30 years. He is a past board member of the National Storytelling Network, and is a full-time professional teller. He narrated the CD, *Platero & I,* a poem by the Andalusian poet, Juan Ramón Jiménez, who won the Nobel Prize in 1956. Frank Koonce played guitar. Don can be reached at ddoyle800@msn.com.

ANDRE DUBUS III is the author of six books, including the *New York Times'* bestsellers *House of Sand and Fog, The Garden of Last Days,* and his memoir, *Townie.* Mr. Dubus has been a finalist for the National Book Award, and has been awarded a Guggenheim Fellowship, The National Magazine Award for Fiction, two Pushcart Prizes, and is a recipient of an American Academy of Arts and Letters Award in Literature.

MICHAEL ESTABROOK is retired. No more useless meetings under florescent lights in stuffy windowless rooms, he is able instead to focus on making better poems when he's not endeavoring to satisfy his wife's legendary Honey-Do List. His latest collection of poems is *Bouncy House,* edited by Larry Fagin (Green Zone Editions, 2016).

JEFF GERE, a professional storyteller, performs constantly. For decades he produced Talk Story Festival, Hawaii's largest storytelling celebration, Story TV, radio shows, camps and conferences. Jeff taught storytelling at University of Hawaii, Manoa (Spring, 2017). He performed at the National Storytelling Festival (2010, Residency 2013) and in Hong Kong, Taiwan, Turkey, Vancouver and the Yukon. Jeff retired from Oahu's Parks Department in 2014, and has since toured to Thailand, Australia, India and Romania. (www.jeffgere.com)

JONATHAN GOTTSCHALL is distinguished fellow in the English department at Washington & Jefferson College. His research has been covered in the *New*

York Times, Scientific American, The New Yorker, The Atlantic, The Chronicle Of Higher Education, Nature, and *NPR.* He authored or edited seven books, including *The Storytelling Animal,* a New York Times editor's choice selection and a finalist for the LA Times Book Prize. His piece, "What About Women" is from his book, *The Professor In the Cage: Why Men Fight and Why We Like to Watch.*

BILL HARLEY is an author, songwriter, playwright, workshop leader, and story-teller known for his work with families. A two-time Grammy Award winner, he speaks to both sides of the generation gap, often at the same time. Author of fifteen books, including the popular *Charlie Bumpers* series, and a long-time commentator on NPR's *All Things Considered,* Harley makes his home in Seekonk, Massachusetts.

PAUL HOSTOVSKY is the author of nine books of poetry, most recently, *Is That What That Is* (FutureCycle Press, 2017). His poems have won a Pushcart Prize, two Best of the Net awards, and have been featured on Poetry Daily, Verse Daily, and NPR's The Writer's Almanac. Website: paulhostovsky.com

SCOTT T. HUTCHISON's work, both poetry and fiction, has appeared in The Southern Review, The Georgia Review and other journals. He is the author of a book of poetry, *Reining In,* published by Black Bird Press. Scott worked six-teen years for Boss Man Ed Stevens at Rockett's Mill Farm in Doswell, Virginia, where his farm baptism took place. He left at age twenty-nine.

RON JONES's stories, "The Acorn People," "The Wave," and "B-Ball" were made into television specials garnering an Emmy, Golden Globe, and Peabody. *Say Ray,* the story of a disabled man abducted to Mexico, was honored as the Amer-ican Book of the Year. His classroom experiment in fascism, *The Wave,* was produced as a feature film *Die Welle,* and a documentary, *Lesson Plan.* The novelized version of *The Wave* has been printed in 23 languages.

EUGENE KARLIN's art has been exhibited at Pennsylvania Academy of the Fine Arts, the Corcoran Gallery, the San Francisco Museum, and New York's Met-ropolitan Museum of Art. Karlin taught at The School of Visual Arts, Pratt

Institute, Cooper Union, and Parsons School of Design. He was a staff artist at *Fortune* magazine in the 1940s, and went on to illustrate for *New Republic, Esquire, Look,* and *Playboy,* and to create book and album art.

JORDAN LEGG is originally from Oshawa, Ontario, and holds a degree in English and Creative Writing from the University of Windsor. He has been published in *Strong Verse, Allegory eZine,* and several anthologies, and has recently received Honorable Mention in the L. Ron Hubbard Writers of the Future Contest. When not writing he enjoys drawing, soccer, reading, and cycling. (Twitter: @TheJordanLegg)

JULIUS LESTER has written 43 books since 1968. He won the Newberry Honor Medal, Lewis Carroll Shelf Award, Boston Globe/Horn Book Award, and Coretta Scott King Award, given to outstanding African American authors of books for young adults that demonstrate an appreciation of universal human values. A University of Massachusetts faculty member for 30 years where he was a professor of Judaic and Near Eastern Studies, he won the Chancellor's Medal, the university's highest honor. Julius passed on January 18, 2018.

RUSS ALLISON LOAR was a musician and songwriter for 12 years, returning to college and earning a degree in journalism. He spent the next 15 years as a newspaper reporter, followed by a stint teaching newswriting at Orange Coast College. He retired from journalism after writing for the Los Angeles Times during his last years. His poetry, prose and photography have been published by numerous websites and literary journals. He lives in Claremont, California.

MICHAEL MORGAN was born in Detroit. He held a variety of jobs in Detroit and received degrees in English and teaching from The University of Michigan and Eastern Michigan University. Expert storyteller Mary Morris recommended him for a scholarship to the Bread Loaf Writers' Conference at Middlebury College, Vermont, where he was mentored by acclaimed novelist, Tim O'Brien. Michael retired from the University of Detroit Mercy where he worked as an educator for twenty-six years.

DON NARKEVIC received an MFA from National University. His recent poetry has appeared in *The Binnacle, Nassau Review,* and *About Place Journal.*

Laundry, a poetry chapbook, was published in 2005 by Main Street Rag. His plays have received readings in Chicago, New York, and Virginia. FutureCycle Press published *Admissions,* a book of poems, in 2013. He lives in Nutter Fort, West Virginia.

HENRI J. M. NOUWEN (1932 - 1936) was a Dutch Catholic priest, professor, writer and theologian. His interests were rooted primarily in psychology, pastoral ministry, spirituality, social justice and community. After nearly two decades of teaching at academic institutions including the University of Notre Dame, Yale Divinity School and Harvard Divinity School, Nouwen went on to work with individuals with intellectual and developmental disabilities at the L'Arche Daybreak community in Richmond Hill, Ontario. [from his Wikipedia entry]

TIM O'BRIEN served as a U.S. Army infantryman in Vietnam. *The New Yorker, Esquire, Harper's, The Atlantic,* and *Playboy* have published his short fiction. O'Brien received the National Magazine Award for "The Things They Carried," which was selected for inclusion in *The Best American Short Stories of the Century,* edited by John Updike. He has received literary awards from the American Academy of Arts and Letters, the Guggenheim Foundation, and the NEA.

JON PEARSON is a writer, speaker, artist, and creative thinking consultant. He was a cartoonist for the Oakland Tribune and a supernumerary for the New York Metropolitan Opera. Jon's works were nominated for Pushcart Prizes in 2014 and 2016. He writes to get to the heart of his thinking at the edge of his mind. Jon can be found with his beautiful wife, Elya, in Los Angeles, and on the web at jonpearsoncreative.com.

JOEL PECKHAM is an essayist, poet, and scholar. His recent publications include the poetry collection, *God's Bicycle,* and a book of essays, *Resisting Elegy: On Grief and Recovery.* He teaches at Marshall University and lives in Huntington, West Virginia, with his wife and son. A shortened version of "Phys-ed" appeared in the December 2016 issue of *The Sun.* (joelpeckham.com)

RUSSELL REECE has received Best of the Net nominations, and awards from the Delaware Press Association and the Faulkner-Wisdom competition. In 2019 he won the Pat Herold Nielsen Poetry Prize. His work recently appeared

in *Blueline, Under the Gum Tree, The 3288 Review* and *Proud to Be: Writing by American Warriors.* In 2015 he was granted fellowships in literature from both The Delaware Division of the Arts and the Virginia Center for the Creative Arts.

Philip Roth was one of the most awarded American writers of his generation. His books have received the National Book Award, the National Book Critics Circle award, and the PEN/Faulkner Award. He received a Pulitzer Prize for his 1997 novel, *American Pastoral. The Human Stain* (2000) was awarded the United Kingdom's WH Smith Literary Award for the best book of the year. In 2001, in Prague, Roth received the inaugural Franz Kafka Prize. He passed away on May 22, 2018. [from his Wikipedia entry]

Richard Schiffman, a Manhattanite, is the author of *What the Dust Doesn't Know,* a collection of poems published by Salmon Poetry in February 2017.

Mike Schneider received the 2012 Editors Award in Poetry from *The Florida Review*, and the 2016 Robert Phillips Prize (selected by Richard Foerster) from *Texas Review Press*, which in 2017 published his second chapbook, *How Many Faces Do You Have?* He has published many poems in literary journals, including *New Ohio Review, Notre Dame Review*, and *Poetry.* He lives in Pittsburgh.

William Shakespeare (1564–1616) was an English poet, playwright, and actor, widely regarded as the greatest writer in the English language and the world's pre-eminent dramatist. Like Bob Dylan, he is often referred to as "The Bard." His extant works, including collaborations, consist of approximately 38 plays, 154 sonnets, two long narrative poems, and a few other verses. [from his Wikipedia entry, with annotations]

John Updike penned more than thirty novels and short-story collections as well as poetry, art and literary criticism, and children's books. He was recognized for his careful craftsmanship, his unique prose style, and his prolific, book-a-year output. His fiction is distinguished by its attention to the lives of average Americans and its preoccupation with sexuality and sensual detail. He is widely considered one of the greatest American writers of his time. [from his Wikipedia entry]

DAVID L. WALKER attended the University of Nebraska Art Department. He served as Scout Dog handler in Vietnam and subsequently traveled in Europe, Africa, South America, and Mexico, where he studied Pre-Columbian Art. He is a studio and plein air painter. As a heavy equipment operator with the Sonoma County Water Agency, he restored endangered species habitats. A cancer survivor, he is now writing his life stories and restoring a classic Corvette.

MARCK T. WILDER moved back to his first home, Los Angeles, after completing his studies in the written arts and literary analysis at The Evergreen State College in Washington State. His current writing projects range from stories and novel chapters to screenplays and rap songs about chess strategies. His short story, "He Was Running On Fumes," was published by *Creative Colloquy* in June of 2016.

BILL AMATNEEK, editor, has been published in *Down Beat, Rolling Stone, Yoga Journal, Storytelling Magazine, Bluegrass Unlimited, Bass World, Musician, Fine Books & Collections,* and anthologized in *Encounters with Bob Dylan: If You See Him Say Hello.* His book, *Acoustic Stories: Pickin' for the Prez and other Unamplified Tales,* was a Foreword Reviews 2013 silver Book of the Year Award Winner in Performing Arts and Music. His 2003 collection, *Acoustic Stories: Playing Bass with Peter, Paul & Mary, Jerry Garcia, and Bill Monroe,* won the BAIPA award for Best Music Book.

Q&A with the Editor (asked by beta-readers & other women)

1. *Why did you choose the pieces you did?*

I had to see something in the male protagonist's behavior that extrapolated to other men; the story had to say something about the man, but also about men. The submission had to say *Yes* to me, and feel good in place.

2. *What kind of pieces did you reject and why?*

I rejected woe-is-men pieces, but very few were submitted. I rejected pieces about men that weren't unique to men. For example, losing a beloved sibling, losing weight, or suffering an illness happens to both men and women.

Some readers say some of these stories could have happened to a woman, and they may be right. Story is in the mind of the beholder. But I think most of these stories are guy-specific or at least told from a male-unique point of view.

I was drawn to stories more than essays because an essay tells; a story shows. I wanted to show who men are. Admittedly some pieces are narrative essay – a personal essay piggybacking on a story – and maybe one is a straight essay brandishing ancient tales. Most of the poems tell stories, and others just struck me, as poems can.

3. *Why didn't you cover other topics like rape, sexual molestation, murder and other sufferings men cause?*

I didn't want to create an anthology of men's transgressions. Moreover, no stories of rape, molestation or murder were submitted.

4. *You have what feels like memoir, which is allegedly non-fiction, and also fiction by Roth and Updike. Doesn't fiction reflect who the author, a man, thinks men are, or wants to portray them as being?*

That's a good question, Dez. On this subject, in *My Life and Times,* Henry Miller wrote, "I struggled in the beginning. I said I was going to write the truth, so help me God. ... I found I couldn't. Nobody can write the absolute truth."

I don't know if individual stories here are Miller's unwritable "absolute truth," factual, autobiographical, semi-autobiographical, fictive, or plain ol' lies. Certainly Updike and Roth's writings can make us believe their avowed fiction is truth.

Storytellers say that "truth" is the heart of the story as the teller feels it. In that sense, these stories are their writers' truths. Maybe they all portray men as the writers want to portray them.

5. You told me this is a book of men's writings, yet you have quotations from women. Why is that?

Some women writers had unique insights into guys. Some of their submissions that completed the phrase "A man is ..." in one sentence were spot on.

Manhood is so close to men we don't see it all. The popped handshake and slap on the back are just the way guys sometimes greet each other. We don't think about it. Norah Vincent's writing in *Self Made Man* showed me how male-unique and male-identifying this greeting is.[93]

My wife calls it "the sting of male bonding."

6. I take it you did a bit of reading during this project. Do you have any books to recommend?

Yes, a few, in alphabetical order:

Book Design and Production, by Pete Masterson

Bookmaking: The Illustrated Guide to Design/Production/Editing, by Marshall Lee

The Boy Crisis: Why Our Boys Are Struggling and What We Can Do About It, by Warren Farrell and John Gray

The Design of Books, by Adrian Wilson

Don Juan, by Lord Byron

The Elements of Typographic Style, by Robert Bringhurst

The Illustrator & the Book in England from 1790 to 1914, by Gordon N. Ray

Letters to my Son: A Father's Wisdom on Manhood, Life, and Love, by Kent Nerburn

Man Made: A Stupid Quest for Masculinity, by Joel Stein

Manhood for Amateurs, by Michael Chabon

The Myth of Male Power, by Warren Farrell

The Odyssey, attributed to Homer

On High Steel: the Education of an Ironworker, by Mike Cherry

The Professor in the Cage, by Jonathan Gottschall

Self-Made Man: My Year Disguised as a Man, by Norah Vincent

The Things They Carried, by Tim O'Brien

7. What was the most difficult task you faced putting this anthology together?

Rejecting submissions that came from friends.

8. What are your plans for the future?

A second edition of *Heart of a Man* is planned, so I'd like to encourage guys to submit their works – stories, personal essays, poems, cartoons, lyrics. The submissions form (if it's there when you read this) is at HeartOfAMan.net.

And if my wife doesn't first have me declared certifiable, Vineyards Press will publish an anthology of women's writings, *Woman's Heart: Women's Stories for Men*. You can use HeartOfAMan.net for sending these submissions in as well.

9. What did you learn doing this project?

I learned how differently women and men see the same word, sentence, paragraph, story, book cover, and book.

I learned that I control the book's contents, but not the writing. All the works here reveal men – I hope – but I don't endorse very word of every work. I don't agree with Byron, for example, when he wrote that women have only one re-source: "To love again, and be again undone." Far from it.

And when William Shakespeare, "The Bard," wrote "men were deceivers ever," did he mean *all* men were deceivers … *always?* Bardolator though I am, I'm not down with your quill there, Will.

Works are here because the reveal men, yes, but also because they fit into the evolving mosaic of story, poem and narrative essay. Or because I liked 'em, or they made good rhythm with the surrounding pieces.

And I learned that I don't control individual reactions to the book or its cover, which as the saying has it, have been *all* over the place. The anthology and its cover are Rorschach tests for the reader, metrics of gender psyche.

10. One of the two people on your cover drawing should be a person of color. And what about diversity? What are the contributors' genders, races and ethnicities?

I've spoken or met maybe eight of the contributors; this has by and large been an electronic project. So I don't know the race, creed, color, ethnicity, religion or gender of the majority of them, and would not want to guess based on name. I do know (or believe I know) their sex: all who arrived in these pages via the calls for submissions signed a contract stating they were male.

The diversity of this anthology is in its themes and voices. If race, gender or ethnicity figure in a story, it's there: an African-American kid struggling through boyhood; a Polish Day celebration; a Polynesian Lei Queen contest. If race, gender and/or ethnicity was not an issue, it wasn't written. Here's an example.

I received an email from a guy whose story is in the anthology, stating he was a cross-dresser. It sounded like it's a major factor in how he's treated. But his story has nothing to do with his cross-dressing. You could read the book carefully and not identify him, because he wasn't writing as a cross-dressing man. He was writing as a man.

Conversely, I used Elias Gebru's words, "A man is a brave lion, a crazy lover, a sensitive believer, and an incredible player," as the anthology's epigraph – no small thing – because of the unexpected but spot-on descriptors he equated with a man, and not because an Ethiopian voice would add to the book's diversity.

My calls for submissions cast what I felt was a wide net. Nine writers' services websites and magazines published them. The gender, race, or ethnicity of the writers or their protagonists, if identified, were not on my mind when I was reading submissions – only the tale the story told. I'd have welcomed more manifestly diversity-diverse submissions; they weren't there.

And Kathie, as to making one of the people in the cover drawing a person of color: My contract with Eugene Karlin's estate stipulates I cannot alter his work. Most importantly, it's beautiful art just as it is.

11. *You said I'm you last beta-reader. Do you have any parting words before the book goes to press?*

One of my readers said the anthology interested her in hearing her husband's stories. She said, "One day I asked him. He couldn't have been more pleased! Listening to his stories, I've come to know and understand him better. I feel closer to him."

So my parting wish for women is this: If there's a man in your life, please ask him to tell you his stories. And guys, if you're so lucky as to have a woman in your life, ask her to tell you hers. Sitting down together, telling our stories and singing our songs to each other – these simple acts have the power to bring us closer and change our world.

Acknowledgments

This book had to progress on many fronts, many of which I had little experience with and less skill. Acknowledging my missteps, I apologize to all whose toes I may have tripped on along the way.

I am indebted to many institutions and people who were key to the evolution of this anthology, above all the men whose contributions are here: thank you for your writing, your patience, and for working with me to bring this document to light. And to the hundreds of men who submitted stories that were not accepted: I salute your works and your efforts. Thank you.

My heart-felt gratitude to Skye Blaine, Gwen Rosewater, Beryl Zimberoff, Desiree Beck, Rachel Lasek, Lyndell Robinson, Ana Rose Gefvert, and Camellia Sinensis for beta-reading the manuscript. I very much appreciate your time, insights, and guidance.

My sincere thanks to Ama Bolton for her patience, poet's pen and ear, British reserve, translations to the Scottish, long-distance friendship, and sound advice. Thank you to Lynne Terry for seeing the long and short of it and for your long friendship. My thanks to Bruce Taylor for his syllabi and book lists, Jonathan Keller of West County Media, and Chris Grim, Matt Kopola, Fox Scarlett, and Carlos De Villasante for their website expertise. I tip my hat to Geoff Leubbert for his falcon eyes, Barbara Nostrand for her cover advice, Becky Parker Geist for her deft BAIPA leadership, Sunil Sharma for his generous time and expertise, and Peter Kahrel and Adi Ravid for their .indd javascripts. Thanks to Bonita Cole, Angela Lloyd, Linda Jay, Steve Litt, Kate Sheridan, Eliot Kenin, Eric Bibb, Peter Rowan, Adriann Saslow, and Herb Frank for their kind and supportive words. A big thank you to David Bullen, string bassist and book design veteran, for his eye-opening book and typesetting insights.

My special gratitude to Katie Watts, my editor, for her eagle eyes and golden ears, purple pen, worldly wisdom, and love of musicals. Thank you, Warren Farrell, for your lifelong advocacy, the hours of your many books, your creativity, leadership, big ears, and evenhanded wisdom.

I'm indebted to Pete Masterson, master book designer, for the two decades of book mentoring he has afforded me, his patience in hearing my questions and the generosity of his responses. His manual, *Book Design and Production,* a beacon for indie publishers, demonstrates his big eyes for codex and type. His generous advice has been central to my book learning. Thank you, Pete.

I am grateful to Seth Evans, webmaster, composer, fellow bass man and Beach Blanket Babylon band alum, for ushering VineyardsPress.com into the Content Management System era. Seth spent many hours shepherding the site's progress, keeping it updated, and futilely trying to educate me about a certain CMS app. Thank you, Brother Seth.

Many thanks to Pete Kessler, Steve Glaizer, Pat O'Connell, Jay Goldberg, Steve Gorn, Gene Tortora, Joel Diamond, Richard Saslow, Larry Wolken, Jerry Zolten, Roger Hartley, John Blakemore, Jeremy Mitchell, John Postma, Dave Walker, Dennis Cole, Kester Smith, Marc Francis, Sean Kullman, Russ Gauthier, and Doug Adamz for their friendship and for having my back.

An effusive tip of the hat to Steve Boga and his Friday afternoon writers' workshop for their support and feedback, without which this book would be a lesser document. Thanks to all for your patience and guidance, and to Santa Rosa Junior College for sponsoring Steve's class.

My gratitude goes to Brian Boldt for saying, "If anyone can do this, Bill, you can," to John Fritschen for showing me that a crowd-funding campaign is about more than raising funds, to Jonathan Kirsch for his wise counsel, and John Wilhelm for directing me to books about men's work.

To the Bay Area Independent Publishers Association (BAIPA), Mathew Rose and the Sebastopol Regional Library, Friends of the Sebastopol Library, bookfinder.com, citationmachine.net, the web/internet, the Mozilla Foundation, The Achenbach Foundation for Graphic Arts, and Wikipedia, my thanks for being there.

For publishing my calls for submissions, my gratitude to *Poets & Writers,* Duotrope.com, North Carolina Writers' Network, TheReviewReview.net, CreativeSonoma.org, Poetry, Crwropps-B, Newpages.com, and Writer's Chronicle.

A loud shout-out to the eleven contributors to *The Men's Issue* of *Storytelling Magazine*: Jeff Gere, Charlie Chin, Tim Tingle, Ron Jones, Jim May, Garth Gilchrist, Michael Parent, Bill Harley, Don Doyle, Jay O'Callahan, and may he rest in peace, Joe E. Armstrong.

The drawings by Eugene Karlin were made possible through the generosity of his daughters, Lorie Karlin and Nina Karlin Jacob. Thank you, Lorie and Nina, for the gift of your father's work.

Most importantly, I am indebted to my wife, Lenona Winter. Thank you, Princess, for your abiding love.

Copyrights & Permissions

Endnotes

1 Dr. Gebru, Ethiopian peace activist, painter, writer, and doctor of the near future, wrote the first one-sentence completion of the phrase, "A man is …" that I received. Reading it still makes me smile.

2 Geary, David. Male, Female: the Evolution of Human Sex Differences. American Psychological Association, 2010. 289

3 A red signal flare used especially for protecting stalled trains and trucks

4 McKay, Kate. "Coming of Age and Male Rites of Passage." The Art of Manliness, 16 Nov. 2017, www.artofmanliness.com/articles/coming-of-age-the-importance-of-male-rites-of-passage/

5 Sex, Art, and American Culture. New York: Vintage, 1992. 53

6 More Matter. New York: Alfred A. Knopf, 1999. 606

7 Mead, Margaret. Male and Female (1949): The Classic Study of the Sexes. 2nd Edition. Quill (HarperCollins) 1998

8 O'Brien, Tim. If I Die in a Combat Zone, Box Me up and Ship Me Home. Broadway Books, 2014, p. 138.

9 Spoken by the character Tom Branson in Downton Abbey. "The Finale." Season 6, episode 9. Directed by Michael Engler. Written by Julian Fellowes. Carnival Films and Masterpiece. First aired 12/25/2015.

10 The Professor in the Cage: Why Men Fight and Why We Like to Watch. New York: Penguin Books, 2016. 173

11 "Invictus" is a short poem by the Victorian era English poet William Ernest Henley. Julius Lester may be referring to one of the poem's most famous lines, "I am the master of my fate, I am the captain of my soul."

12 American Manhood. New York: Basic Books, 1963. 1

13 The Professor in the Cage. New York: Penguin, 2015. 77

14 To Be a Man. Los Angeles: Jeremy P. Tarcher, Inc., 1991. xv

15 In Jack London's story, "The Wife of a King" from his 1900 short story collection, The Son of the Wolf.

16 In "Proverbs of Hell" from The Marriage of Heaven and Hell

17 Jiles Perry "J. P." Richardson Jr., known as The Big Bopper, was an American musician, singer, songwriter, and disc jockey. His best known compositions include "Chantilly Lace" and "White Lightning."

18 Captain of Fire Station 27 of the Los Angeles Fire Department, as quoted by Joel Stein in Man Made: a Stupid Quest for Masculinity. New York: Grand Central Publishing, 2013. 26

19 Ms. Zilberberg, a Melbourne-based writer and editor, sent these words in response to the call to complete the phrase "A man is …" in one sentence.

20 Man Made. New York: Grand Central Publishing, 2012. 278

21 Cashdan, E. "Are Men More Competitive than Women?" The British Journal of Social Psychology, U.S. National Library of Medicine, June 1998, www.ncbi.nlm.nih.gov/pubmed/9639863

22 Cherry, Kendra. "The Oedipal Complex: One of Freud's Most Controversial Ideas." Very well Mind, www.verywellmind.com/what-is-an-oedipal-complex-2795403

23 Pennington, Bill. "Parents Behaving Badly: A Youth Sports Crisis Caught on Video." The New York Times, The New York Times, 18 July 2018, www.nytimes.com/2018/07/18/sports/referee-parents-abuse-videos.html.

24 "Male-Male Competition - Evolutionary Biology - Oxford Bibliographies, 16 Apr. 2019, www.oxfordbibliographies.com/view/document/obo-9780199941728/obo-9780199941728-0042.xml.

25 Belson, Ken. "What Makes Someone a Fan?" The New York Times, The New York Times, 19 Sept. 2019, https://www.nytimes.com/2019/09/19/sports/rich-luker-fan-psychology.html.

26 Faurie, Charlotte, Dominique Pontierb, and Michael Raymond. "Student Athletes Claim to Have More Sexual Partners Than Other Students." Evolution and Human Behavior 25 (2004)

27 Willingham, AJ. "Deaths on College and High School Football Fields Are a Rare – but Reliable – Tragedy." CNN, Cable News Network, 1 Oct. 2018, www.cnn.com/2018/09/21/health/football-deaths-season-injuries-high-school-college-trnd/index.html.

28 https://www.healthline.com/health-news/likelihood-high-school-football-player-gets-injured#3

29 Philostratus was a 3rd-century philosopher.

30 The quote and its attribution to Hemingway are easily found on the web. But where Hemingway said or wrote it, and so *if* he wrote it, is something else. *If* he wrote it, Papa missed the sports of base jumping (not around during his era), Jallikattu (maybe unknown to him), but also bull riding and boxing, all killers, none games.

31 Orwell in "The Sporting Spirit" First published in the Tribune, London, December 1945

32 Self-Made Man: My Year Disguised As a Man. New York: Viking Penguin, 2006. 239

33 Chabon, Michael. Manhood for Amateurs: the Pleasures and Regrets of a Husband, Father, and Son. Harper, 2009.

34 Hann, Michael. "Bruce Springsteen: 'You can change a life in three minutes with the right song.'" The Observer, Guardian News and Media, 30 Oct. 2016, www.theguardian.com/music/2016/oct/30/bruce-springsteen-interview-born-to-run-change-someones-life-right-song-donald-trump.

35 Farrell, Warren. The Myth of Male Power. New York: Simon & Schuster. 1993. 82

36 Home Game. New York: W. W. Norton & Company, 2009. 75

37 Ruhl, Sarah. Eurydice. London: A & C Black Publishers Limited, 2005

38 Streeter, Edward. Father of the Bride. New York: Simon and Schuster, 1949

39 McKay, Kate & Brett. "The History of Male Friendships." The Art of Manliness, January 7, 2020. https://www.artofmanliness.com/articles/the-history-and-nature-of-man-friendships/

40 "How Are Men's Friendships Different From Women's?" Psychology Today, Sussex Publishers, www.psychologytoday.com/us/blog/cutting-edge-leadership/201410/how-are-men-s-friendships-different-women-s.

41 https://www.theatlantic.com/sexes/archive/2013/01/the-challenges-and-rewards-of-male-on-male-friendship/267284/

42 Now known as Ponce de Leon Inlet

43 From a Jeanette Rankin Brigade leaflet, distributed 1/15/1968 in D.C.

44 Self-Made Man: My Year Disguised As a Man. New York: Viking Penguin, 2006. 25

45 "Ironworkers." CNNMoney, Cable News Network, money.cnn.com/gallery/pf/jobs/2013/08/22/dangerous-jobs/5.html

46 Johnson, David. "The Top 10 Most Dangerous Jobs in America." Time, 22 Dec. 2017, time.com/5074471/most-dangerous-jobs/. The most dangerous is logging, with 128 deaths per 100,000 workers. Logging is followed by fishermen, airplane pilots, roofers, trash collectors, and then ironworkers.

47 Cherry, Mike. On High Steel: the Education of an Ironworker. New York: Quadrangle. 1974. 26

48 Weitzman, David. Skywalkers: Mohawk Ironworkers Build the City. New York: Roaring Brook. 2010. 106

49 Tim [no last name given] was quoted in "The Firefighters." Reported by Ben Court, Josh Dean, Sean Flynn, Tom Foster, Devin Friedman, Alex Markels, Michael Rey, and David Willey in Men's Journal, November 2001. 87

50 "Two-blocking" occurs when a crane hoists a load as far as it can go. The cable passes through a block at the boom end. If the cable is in more than one "part" – each part being a run between the blocks – there is also a block at the hook end. The higher a load is lifted, the closer together come the two blocks. When they have come all the way together the load is "two-blocked," hoisted as far as it can go, seriously interfering with safe operation of the crane. By extension, "two-blocking" is carrying anything to its limit. You can see a two-block fail at https://www.youtube.com/watch?v=q-NJuhwSAu8

51 That is, not a member of the Ironworkers Union local where the job is located.

52 Farrell, Warren. The Myth of Male Power. New York: Simon & Schuster. 1993. 107

53 Commercial ocean fishing is still dangerous. It's the 2nd most fatal profession in America. Stebbins, Samuel, et al. "Workplace Fatalities: 25 Most Dangerous Jobs in America." USA Today, Gannett Satellite Information Network, 9 Jan. 2018, www.usatoday.com/story/money/careers/2018/01/09/workplace-fatalities-25-most-dangerous-jobs-america/1002500001/

54 Scott, Sir Walter. The Antiquary, 1816. Volume I, Chapter 11

55 Sexual Personae: Art and Decadence from Nefertiti to Emily Dickinson. London: Yale University Press. 1990. 37

56 Lehrer, Jonah. A Book about Love. Simon & Schuster Paperbacks, 2017. 4

57 Title of a Tolstoy short story also know as "Martin the Cobbler"

58 Blood Wedding and Yerma, New York: Theatre Communications Group, 1994.

59 Kupuna – a Hawaiian word meaning "elder"

60 This quotation is so old I couldn't find it on the web. Either that or I created it.

61 Sexual Personae. New York: Vintage Books, 1991. 30

62 Campbell, Joseph. "Ep. 3: Joseph Campbell and the Power of Myth – 'The First Storytellers'." BillMoyers.com, 23 June 1988, billmoyers.com/content/ep-3-joseph-campbell-and-the-power-of-myth-the-first-storytellers-audio/.

63 J. Michael Lennon, ed. Conversations with Norman Mailer. University Press of Mississippi. 1988

64 I believe I know the name of the American actress who wrote these words but have not been able to corroborate it. So I have left them "anonymous."

65 Girls. "American Bitch." Season 6, Episode 3. Spoken by the character Hannah Horvath. Directed by Richard Shepard. Written by Lena Dunham. HBO, 2/26/17

66 The editor's wife, in our kitchen, 11/11/17

67 Camille Sweeney interviewing Carl Reiner, "Old Masters at the Top of Their Game," nytimes.com/interactive/2014/10/23/magazine/old-masters-at-top-of-their-game.html, 10/23/2014

68 "Timeline of the Life of Harriet Tubman." Harriet Tubman, http://www.harriet-tubman.org/timeline/

69 https://en.wikipedia.org/wiki/Joan_of_Arc#Military_campaigns

70 Credit to Dan Baldwin for "Don't blame war on the warrior." Baldwin, Dan. "Don't Blame War on the Warrior." TheUnion.com, 20 Mar. 2003, https://www.theunion.com/opinion/dont-blame-war-on-the-warrior/.

71 "Tommy" is slang for a soldier in the British Army.

72 Amatneek, Bill. Acoustic Stories: Pickin' for the Prez and Other Unamplified tales. Vineyards Press, 2013. 189

73 Farrell, Warren. The Myth of Male Power. New York: Simon and Schuster. 2000, 124

74 "War." The Moth. Ed. Catherine Burns. New York: Hatchette Books, 2014, 235

75 C. J. Chivers quoting Sam Siatta, Afghanistan veteran, in "The Fighter," nytimes.com/2016/12/28/magazine/afghanistan-soldier-ptsd-the-fighter.html, 12/28/2016

76 "Why Men Love War." Esquire. November, 1984: 54. Print

77 Howe, Mark De Wolfe. Holmes: Pollock Letters. Harvard U. Press. 1961. 36

78 O'Brien, Tim. If I Die in a Combat Zone, Box Me up and Ship Me Home. Broadway Books, 2014, p. 207.

79 O'Brien, Tim. The Things They Carried. New York: Houghton Mifflin, 2009. 58

80 Quoted in Sweet, Matthew. Operation Chaos: the Vietnam Deserters Who Fought the CIA, the Brainwashers, and Themselves. New York: Holt. 2018. 19

81 Cox, Cathleen R., and Burney J. Le Boeuf. "Female Incitation of Male Competition: A Mechanism in Sexual Selection." American Naturalist 111 (1977) 317-35

82 Puts, David. "Beauty and the Beast: Mechanisms of Sexual Selection in Humans." Evolution and Human Behavior 31 (2010) 157-75

83 Kyle, Donald. Sport and Spectacle in the Ancient World. Malden, MA: Blackwell, 2007

84 Examples: Lombardo, Michael. "On the Evolution of Sport." Evolutionary Psychology 10 (2012) 13; Campbell, Ann. A Mind of Her Own: The Evolutionary Psychology of Women. Oxford: Oxford University Press, 2002, 107; Faurie, Charlotte, Dominique Pontierb, and Michael Raymond. "Student Athletes Claim to Have More Sexual Partners Than Other Students." Evolution and Human Behavior 25 (2004)

85 Turton, David. "The Same Only Different: War and Dueling as Boundary Marking Rituals in Mursiland, Southwest Ethiopia." In War and Games, edited by T. Cornell and T.B. Allen, 171-92. San Francisco: Boydell Press, 2002

86 Gilmore, David. Manhood in the Making: Cultural Concepts of Masculinity. New Haven, CT: Yale University Press, 1990, 71

87 Llaurens, V., M. Raymond, and C. Faurie. "Ritual Fights and Male Reproductive Success in a Human Population." Journal of Evolutionary Biology 22 (2009), 22

88 Baker, Allen. The Gladiator: The Secret History of Rome's Warrior Slaves. New York: Da Capo, 2000

89 Frederick, David, and Martie Haselton. "Why is Muscularity Sexy? Tests

of the Fitness Indicator Hypotheses." Personality and Social Psychology Bulletin 33 (2007): 1167-83

90 Puts, David. "Beauty and the Beast: Mechanisms of Sexual Selection in Humans." Evolution and Human Behavior 31 (2010) 157-75

91 Meike Scheller, Francine Matorres, Lucy Tompkins, Anthony C. Little, Alexandra de Sousa. "Beauty is not always in the eye of the beholder: the role of vision in the emergence of mate preferences" https://psyarxiv.com/nt3xj

92 Gottschall, Jonathan. The Professor in the Cage: Why Men Fight and Why We Like to Watch. New York: Penguin Books, 2016, 73

93 Vincent, Norah. Self-Made Man: My Year Disguised as a Man. New York: Penguin Books, 2006

Text & titles are set in Minion Pro

Other typefaces include Bernhard Tango, Parisian & OCR-B

Vineyards
Press
Sebastopol

Made in the USA
San Bernardino, CA
24 July 2020